The Professional Chef's
ART OF GARDE MANGER

The Professional Chef's
ART OF GARDE MANGER

FREDERIC H. SONNENSCHMIDT

JEAN NICOLAS

Jule Wilkinson, Editor

Published by
INSTITUTIONS/VOLUME FEEDING MAGAZINE

Distributed by
Cahners Books, 89 Franklin Street, Boston, Mass. 02110

ISBN 0-8436-0557-X

Library of Congress Catalog Card No. 72-92377

Printed in the United States of America

To Joseph Amendola
Vice President, Culinary Institute of America

ACKNOWLEDGEMENTS

The authors would like to express their appreciation to the following people who helped in the preparation of this book: Franz K. Lemoine, Facilities and Organization Instructor, Culinary Institute of America, for consultation on planning layouts for the garde manger; Wm. Brandt Cutlery Co., Inc.; Rougie and Cie, Calviac, France; Clement A. Gareri, Jr., black and white photographs; John Hugelmeyer, color photographs and black and white photographs, pp. viii, 201, 202, 203.

TABLE OF CONTENTS

INTRODUCTION   vii

WHAT IS THE ART OF GARDE MANGER?   ix

   I: GARDE MANGER AREA PLANNING   1

  II: FOOD DECORATION   12

 III: ASPIC–GELEE–CHAUD FROID   23

 IV: APPETIZERS–HORS D'OEUVRE   35

  V: FOIE GRAS–TRUFFLES–CAVIAR   59

 VI: FORCEMEAT   68

VII: PATE–TERRINE   73

VIII: GALANTINES   91

 IX: MOUSSE   104

  X: MARINADES   110

 XI: ESSENTIAL INGREDIENTS   115

XII: COLD SAUCES–BUTTER/CHEESE MIXTURES   135

XIII: COLD FOOD PRESENTATION   144

XIV: SALADS   148

XV: CHEESES   177

XVI: NON EDIBLE DISPLAYS   182

XVII: BUFFET PRESENTATION–LOW CALORIE BUFFETS   191

INTRODUCTION

When two arts are married, the outcome often (but not always) will be the creation of a third art greater than either one. This, in my opinion, is the case with the art of food decoration and buffet work.

It is incontestable that food preparation and cookery is a great art, but when to the exciting flavor and aroma of the food there is added the art of sculpture and other visual arts, then unsurpassed greatness is achieved. Historically, it is interesting to note that it was Careme himself who gave testimony to this principle and exemplified it with his innovative pieces montees.

As a matter of fact, the modern buffet reverts to the old dining tradition of the age of Careme, with an important difference. Then, the Chef loaded the table with a bewildering variety (as many as a hundred) of spectacularly decorated dishes. But most of the food had turned cold before it could be eaten, and diners could taste only the very few dishes within their immediate reach. The modern buffet provides the spectacle, but each guest can sample anything he wishes, and the hot dishes are hot.

It is important to note that two arts are involved. A merely beautiful presentation with inferior food violates the principle; in fact, is objectionable, because it fails to fulfill the promise it makes. This means that a buffet artist must be first and foremost a fine Chef. By the same token, the supreme practitioners of the art strongly insist that the materials and results of their productions be edible, and this means reducing to an absolute minimum the use of papier mache, styrofoam, and other such materials. To avoid these easy and obvious elements requires superlative creativity in the use of food materials, and also in the artistic skills of ice carving, sugar work, etc.

And, fortunately, in the art of buffets we are not dealing with art for art's sake only—but with a most practical and valuable economic help to the foodservice industry. Not only does a buffet minimize labor and labor costs, but in many instances can increase customer satisfaction. It offers tremendous variety and choice in visual form and reduces much of the indecisiveness when choices must be made from mere words on a menu. It helps sell less expensive items which few guests would order from a menu. And it eliminates the annoyance which often results when an item is crossed off a menu, or worse yet, when a waiter has to tell a guest that they're out of something ordered. If lobster salad was on the table and is all gone, a new appetizing plate of tuna or other fish salad can be substituted without creating ill-will.

The authors of this work have proven both by the economics and art of the magnificent buffets they have produced at the Culinary Institute that they are superbly qualified for the undertaking of an outstanding text.

Jacob Rosenthal
President
Culinary Institute of America

Specialties of the Garde Manger

This Austrian-German Buffet focuses attention on the food presentation that can be accomplished in the garde manger department. Chefs F. H. Sonnenschmidt (co-author of this book), B. Elmer and S. Heywood with students of the Culinary Institute of America created all elements of this display. Butter sculptures—the mountain goat and Lorelei set the theme. Among the dishes offered: top level—Galantine of Veal; Pate of Pheasant; Poached Salmon with Stuffed Eggs and Cucumbers; Saddle of Venison a la Diane. Lower level—Italian meat salad; carrot salad with mustard seed; chicken salad with pineapple; lobster salad, cucumber salad; Roast Sirloin of Beef circled by blue cheese roses on tomato wedges flanked by bread baskets of marinated vegetables. Chafing dishes hold Noisettes of Venison with mushrooms and Spaetzle in brown butter.

WHAT IS THE ART OF GARDE MANGER?

Reputations for fine food in many eating places are dependent on the performance of the garde manger department. In smaller operations, although there may be no formal department, the same food specialties usually created in a garde manger department must be prepared using the techniques that have been developed over centuries by masters of garde manger work. It is these methods and techniques that are presented in this book. However, the garde manger work shown and described here has been updated. Modern methods for garde manger work have been developed that are adapted to today's menu requirements, food products and equipment.

Garde manger tasks were so-called because in French the term garde manger meant storage place; the work that was done in that location also was described by the term, garde manger.

In France, the garde manger area was located next to the kitchen and it was here that foods required for preparation of meals were stored. All preparatory work on meat, poultry, game and other provisions also took place in this area. Since the area was located in a cool, airy spot that usually had some kind of food chilling provisions, cold food specialties were also prepared, decorated and arranged for service there. This is how the work known as garde manger developed.

Since the basis of fine cuisine continues to include the preparation of specialties using aspic, chaud froid, forcemeat, pate, mousse, marinades, sauces and dressings, the art of garde manger work is essential to culinary expertise.

The work done in the garde manger department starts with the preparation of basic ingredients—meat, poultry, fish and seafood, fruits and vegetables. Larding, trussing and the creation of fruit and vegetable decorations are among the skills to be learned.

The creation of display pieces such as a roast turkey is a process involving many steps. The turkey must be properly prepared for roasting; when roasted, the breast must be properly carved out; a mousse must be prepared to fill the cavity; the breast must be sliced and arranged over the mousse. The decorative touches needed must be selected, created and put in place both on the bird and on the platter used in its presentation. All of these tasks require skills and methods learned in the garde manger department.

Garde manger output is also the foundation of such showcase items as canapes, hors d'oeuvre, salads, galantines and all of the cold food presentations that highlight the buffet. Knowledge of the use of the ingredients essential to these presentations is indispensable.

An operation does not have to be large, formal or committed to high food costs to profit from the art of garde manger. Preparation of a sizable number of specialties is not necessary; actually, it only takes one or two unique presentations to gain extra attention for a buffet or a special menu. Because garde manger specialties can be tailored to match menu requirements, the mastery of garde manger skills is an invaluable asset in food preparation for foodservice operations of every size and style.

I: GARDE MANGER AREA PLANNING

Arranging the layout for a garde manger department can be a complex task. Unlike other departments that can depend on a basic menu and a basic workload, the garde manger department is unique in its operation. It is often a complete foodservice facility within a larger foodservice facility. On a daily basis, the garde manger department will (or may) handle its own butchering, its own baking, its own sauce making, its own frying, its own smoking of fish, meat and poultry, all the decorating, perhaps including tallow and ice carvings, plus a complete line of "charcuterie" products (sausages, galantines, pates, terrines).

How does this department relate to the entire operation?

Knowing exactly how this department relates to the whole foodservice facility makes it easier to select the proper layout. The garde manger department can relate to a foodservice operation in three ways:

        1. On a "pick-up" basis
        2. On a "distribution" basis
        3. On a combination of the two

What is meant by "pick-up" basis? distribution basis?

When a garde manger department executes the food orders (from the waiters) on an "a la carte" basis, this is known as *"PICK-UP,"* since the waiters first place their orders, then later pick them up. This system, of necessity, operates in an unpredictable fashion (since the timing for the orders and the number of guests in the party cannot be known in advance).

This method of operation is often found in "a la carte" restaurants. Where pick-up is the system used, the workloads of the garde manger department will be set on the basis of a predetermined number of dishes that are listed on the menu. Because the menu is approximately the same each day, the "mise en place" or arrangement of the space for preparing the dishes can be determined, and the layout can be worked out properly. (See Fig.1)

When a garde manger department executes food orders *in advance,* for a *known quantity,* to be *delivered to a given location at a definite time,* (i. e. for group feeding), this is known as the *"DISTRIBUTION"* basis. This situation is often found in hotels, where the garde manger department always knows about banquets,

LAYOUTS FOR GARDE MANGER DEPARTMENT

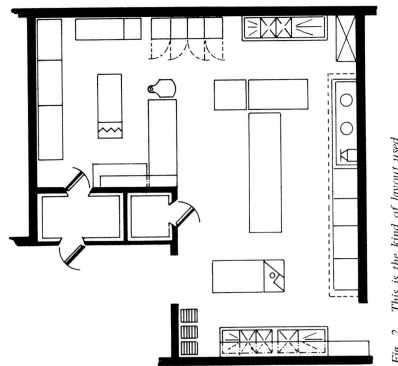

Fig. 2. This is the kind of layout used when the garde manger operates on the distribution system, preparing known quantities of food in advance.

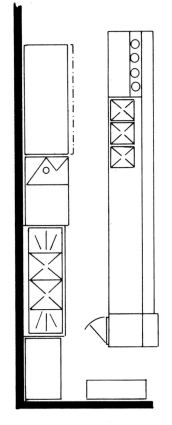

Fig. 1. Layout for garde manger department operating on an a la carte or pick-up basis.

Fig. 3. This is the layout needed when an operation must operate on both the pick-up and distribution system.

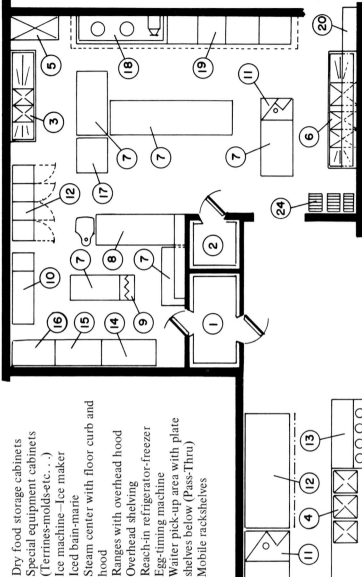

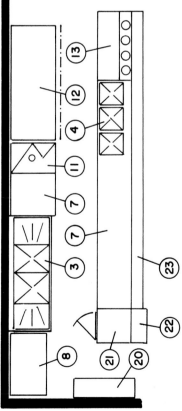

1. Walk-in cooler
2. Walk-in freezer
3. Sinks for foodstuffs
4. Clam and oyster sinks
5. Cooling sink
6. Pot sinks
7. Work benches
8. Chopper-Bench-Mixer
9. Meat saw
10. Electric blender—Work bench
11. Slicer
12. Reach-in refrigerators
13. Salad center incl. dressing and bain-marie
14. Dry food storage cabinets
15. Special equipment cabinets (Terrines-molds-etc. . .)
16. Ice machine—Ice maker
17. Iced bain-marie
18. Steam center with floor curb and hood
19. Ranges with overhead hood
20. Overhead shelving
21. Reach-in refrigerator-freezer
22. Egg-timing machine
23. Waiter pick-up area with plate shelves below (Pass-Thru)
24. Mobile rackshelves

private functions and room service requests in advance. The only drawback is that the workloads will be different each day since function and room service requests will vary as to kind and amounts of food to be prepared; therefore, it is difficult to establish an appropriate "mise en place." The layout for this kind of operation should be planned with basic preparations in mind, rather than for specific dishes. (See Fig. 2, p. 2)

SPECIAL TOOLS AND EQUIPMENT

In every industry today workers depend on special tools. Such tools have long been important in foodservice. For each item made by the chef or his helper, a tool is needed and having the proper tool will not only make it easier to work, but actually is essential to proper preparation. For example, to create the various food decorations, a small paring knife is necessary; for chopping parsley, a French knife; when working with melon, a melon ball cutter. Pictured here is a collection of some of the most important tools. After collecting the necessary tools, the foodservice worker must protect them as he would his hands. The experienced chef follows the rule: "Respect your working tools as you would respect yourself." He knows that the tool that is not properly cared for soon becomes worthless, making work harder rather than easier.

1. French knife (10 in.)
2. French knife (8 in.)
3. Chef's slicer (8 in.)
4. French knife (6 in.)
5. Paring knife, stainless (4½ in.)
6. Paring knife (3½ in.)
7. Paring knife (2½ in.)
8. Zesteur or cester for fruit carving
9. Zesteur or cester for melon carving
10. Zesteur or cester for butter decoration and lemon or orange peeler
11. Parisian scoop (2 sizes)
12. Olivette cutter
13. Tiny Parisian scoop for decorative work
14. Scalpel to cut leeks or carrots
15. Applecutter, can be used for radishes
16. Set of pastry tubes, can be used as round cutters and for truffles
17, 18, 19. Fancy aspic cutters, miniature, medium, large
20. Larding and curved sewing needle
21. Hatelets or decorative silver skewers
22. Column cutters
23. Boning knife
24. Spatula (6 in.)
25. Sandwich spreader with flexible blade
26. Spatula (2½ in.), for pates and small timbales

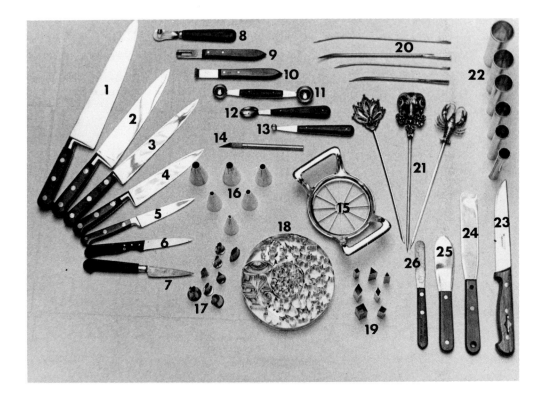

How are "pick-up" and "distribution" combined?

The type of layout needed when pick-up and distribution are both in use in the same operation is shown in Fig. 3, p. 2. It represents a combination of Fig. 1 and Fig. 2. This layout is appropriate when the garde manger department is located *between* an "a la carte" *dining room* and *banquet rooms,* but on the same floor. When the banquet rooms are located on a different floor, the garde manger dept. (Fig. 2) can be located by itself or in conjunction with a separate banquet kitchen on the same floor as the banquet room. When it fills a combined pick-up and distribution function, the garde manger dept. (Fig. 1) can become a part of, or be located close to, the main kitchen on the same floor with the "a la carte"dining room, and may receive some of the bulk preparation from facilities shown in Fig. 2.

Refrigeration–Primary Equipment for Garde-Manger–After finding out how a garde manger dept. relates to the whole operation (pick-up basis, distribution basis or combination of the two), attention can be directed to the equipment needed.

Refrigeration equipment is of prime importance since without refrigeration (refrigerators, freezers, cold bain-marie, refrigerated counter tops, etc.), a garde manger department could not exist, or if it did exist, the output and the type of dishes would have to be very limited, as foods prepared in such a department would be limited in variety and easily contaminated.

The problems of food preparation in the garde manger department are complicated by the fact that in no other department is food manipulated as often as it is there. Frequent manipulation of food stuffs accelerates deterioration, detracts from the appearance of the finished product, as well as the odor and taste, and can lead to contamination.

To prevent these developments, it is not enough for workers to be knowledgeable about keeping hands, tools, and garments immaculately clean; there must also be proper refrigeration equipment and the worker must make proper use of it.

Anyone working on food preparation should have a good basic understanding of what refrigeration is all about and how it works. When this is understood, it will be easy to select the appropriate refrigeration or freezing unit where food is to be held and to know how to use and maintain such a unit.

There is one basic principle of refrigeration that must be understood: cold is not created, but rather, cold is obtained by removing heat. Therefore, all refrigerators, freezers, and air-conditioning units are equipped with machinery designed for heat removal.

Basically, heat is removed from a refrigerator via the three methods of heat transfer: conduction, radiation, and convection. However, because the first two methods (conduction and radiation) occur in a negligible percentage in equipment, it can be stated that the convection method is responsible almost exclusively for removing the heat.

How does heat come into a refrigerator?

There are three ways heat enters a refrigerator:

A. Because a refrigerator has doors, it cannot be completely insulated; therefore, heat keeps seeping through around the doors. Although the amount of heat that gets in is not large, it seeps in steadily.

B. When food is placed in a refrigerator, the food itself introduces a certain amount of heat, especially if the food has been stored at temperatures above 72°F.

C. The frequency of door opening is another source by which heat "walks in" the refrigerator.

The Refrigeration Cycle—Heat is removed from a refrigerator through a series of heat transfers; this is known as the refrigeration cycle. Specifically, there are four elements involved in the process of heat transfer:

   1. The evaporator   3. The compressor
   2. The refrigerant   4. The condensor

The refrigeration cycle goes through the following phases: (See Fig. A)

1. Heat present in a refrigerator is dispersed throughout the air in the unit.

2. As it rises, the air then transfers the added heat to the evaporator, which is made out of tubing surrounded by fins. The fins have many surfaces which collect the heat and then transfer it to the refrigerant flowing in the tubing.

3. The refrigerant carries the heat to the compressor. The refrigerant is a gas, either Freon or Genetron that expands as it collects the heat.

4. The compressor (which is a pump) removes the heat from the refrigerant by compressing it back to its original volume and, in turn, the compressor transfers the heat to a condensor.

5. The condensor collects the heat in its tubing and they again transfer the heat to the numerous surfaces of the fins surrounding the tubing. At that point, a fan blows the heat out of the refrigerator.

6. The now compressed, cold refrigerant returns to the evaporator to collect more heat, and the cycle takes place again and again.

Depending on the type of refrigerator, various engineering methods are used to complete the refrigeration cycle. Some condensors are water-cooled. In this

Fig. A. INTERIOR OF INSULATED ENCLOSURE

1. **Inside Air**

2. **Evaporator**

3. **Refrigerant**

4. **Compressor**

5. **Condensor**

6. **Outside Air**

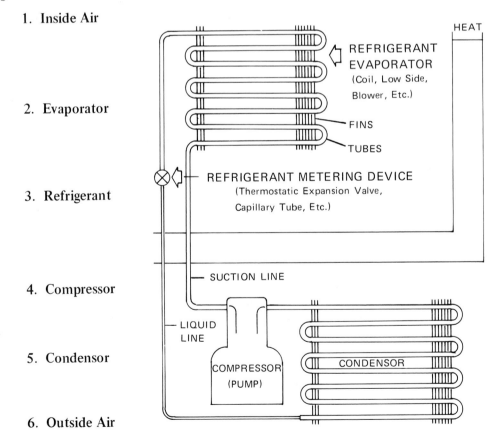

case, heat is transferred to the water which carries the heat along to a drain or, again, back to the evaporator where it evaporates.

What makes a good refrigerator?

A good refrigerator is one that is engineered to keep a:
1. *Constant* appropriate temperature
2. *Constant* relative humidity
3. *Constant* air flow

"Constant appropriate temperature" is achieved through:
1. Insulation
2. Door gasket or lining
3. Door "hardware," mainly the lock and/or hinges

Providing proper humidity in a refrigerator depends on the following process. Like a sponge holding water, air holds water vapor, or moisture; the warmer the air in a refrigerator, the more moisture it will hold with absolute humidity at 100%. However, the cold air in a refrigerator only holds a certain percentage of moisture and most food will respond well to an 80% to 85% relative humidity. When the relative humidity is too low (below 80%), the dry cold air will begin to absorb humidity from the moisture contained in certain foods, causing these foodstuffs to discolor, dry up, and "crack." When the relative humidity is too high (above 80%) the air in the refrigerator will release some of its moisture, and dry foodstuffs will become soggy or shiny or covered with "sweat " (condensation).

Unless a refrigerator is designated to contain only one type of food, it is difficult to control the relative humidity. Most stored foods, if they are of the heterogeneous type (some dry and some moist), will be affected by the relative humidity. This is why some refrigerators are designed to contain a homogeneous type of food (all dry and/or all moist items—for example, dough or meat, respectively). See Fig. B.

Fig. B.   Refrigerator storage space—for pans (left); for bakery products (center); for varied foods (right).

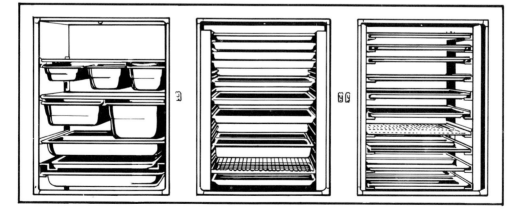

Air flow is important because foodstuffs do not respond well to a "stagnant climate." Natural air movement exists inside a refrigerator but, depending on how the food is being stored, some containers may "block" air movement and prevent other foods from getting proper air circulation. For this reason, modern refrigerators use "forced air" circulation, produced by a fan located in the vicinity of the evaporator. Well designed air circulation is also found in refrigerators equipped with a louvered vertical "shaft" that can distribute the air through all of the shelves, no matter how the food is stored. (See Fig. C)

Because there are so many refrigerator designs on the market, only a few basic designs and their suggested purposes can be listed here:

"WALK-INS" (Fig. D) excellent for storing food in bulk (usually found in main storage areas).

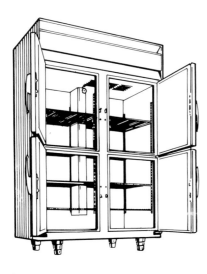

Fig. C.

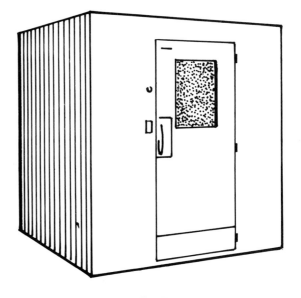

Fig. D.

Because air circulation is necessary for refrigerated foods, ways of moving air are an important part of refrigerator design. Here louvered shaft distributes air to food on all shelves.

"ROLL-INS" (Fig. E) similar to "walk-ins," but equipped with a small ramp at the door to the area to allow hand trucks and mobile shelves to be wheeled in. These are excellent for quantity storage of pre-portioned food (especially for high volume operations).

When used for such storage, there should be three compartments (3 doors), one for dairy, one for meat, one for vegetable; dairy and vegetable products can be combined, as these products usually are kept at the same temperature.

"REACH-INS" WITH FULL LENGTH DOORS (Fig. F) excellent for storage in small operations, or as "hold" refrigerators for foods to be held in temporary storage awaiting further preparation steps.

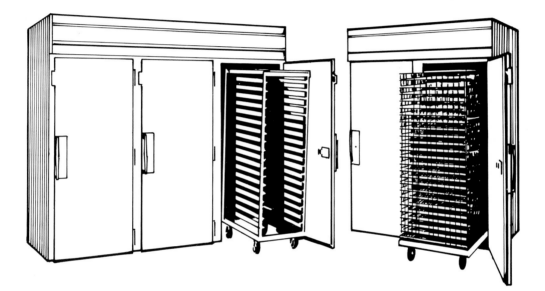

Fig. E (alternate view)

Fig. F

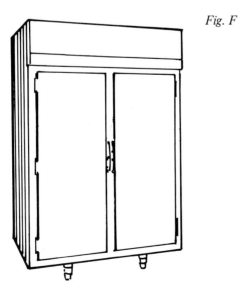

"REACH-INS" WITH HALF LENGTH DOORS (Fig. G) excellent when heterogeneous types of food are used within the same preparation area. Also for heterogeneous portions of prepared foods that have to be located in the immediate vicinity of cooking appliances for processing "to order."

"PASS-THROUGHS" WITH FULL OR HALF LENGTH DOORS excellent when located between preparation and service areas.

"PULL-OUTS" (Fig. H) excellent when refrigerator must have mobility from one area to another. This design prevents spillage while in motion.

All the above mentioned refrigerators are designed with swinging doors (right or left-hinged) or sliding doors. Sliding doors, also available in solid or in a glazed **type** glass door, make it easy to locate a specified food without having to open the doors unnecessarily.

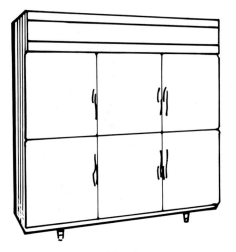

Fig. G

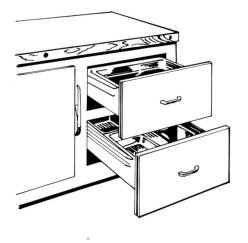

Fig. H

STORING AND THAWING FROZEN FOODS

Foodstuffs	For Freezing	Storage	Defrosting
BAKERY			
Bread	Very good	2-4 months	At room temperature or in 300° oven
Rolls	Very good		Heat in oven (low temperature)
BEEF—Cuts Not			
Listed Below	Very good	Up to 12 months	At room temperature
Bones	Good	6-8 months	Use frozen
Chopped beef	Good	4-6 months	In the refrigerator
Liver	Good	3-6 months	Do not defrost; cook frozen
Stew meat	Good	4-6 months	In the refrigerator
DAIRY PRODUCTS			
Butter	Very good	8-10 months	Refrigerator
Egg without shell	Good	8-10 months	In refrigerator
Egg yolk	Good	8-10 months	In refrigerator
Egg white	Very good	10-12 months	In refrigerator
FISH			
Fat Fish (Mackerel, Herring or Salmon)	Good	1-3 months	Whole frozen fish should be defrosted in cold water
Fillet of Fish (Sole or Haddock)	Very good	3-4 months	Do not defrost, just wash and cook
Lean Fish (Trout or Cod)	Very good	4-6 months	Defrost in cold water
Smoked Fish		1-2 months	In the refrigerator
GAME			
Birds	Very good	8-10 months	Defrost at room temperature
Meat	Very good	Up to 12 months	Put frozen in marinade
HERBS (in an aluminum pouch)			
Fresh	Very good	8-10 months	Use frozen
PATE (Maison)	Good	2-3 months	Refrigerator
PORK—Cuts Not			
Listed Below	Very good	6-8 months (If very fat not over 4 months)	At room temperature
Fatback	Good	4-6 months	At room temperature
Sausages	Good	4-6 months (If strongly seasoned not over 3 months)	At room temperature
POULTRY			
Broilers	Very good	8-10 months	Remove from wrappings
Capon	Very good	8-10 months	Defrost at room temperature
Duck	Good	4-6 months	Defrost at room temperature
Other	Very good	8-10 months	Defrost at room temperature
VEAL	Good	6-8 months	At room temperature
VEGETABLES			
Asparagus	Very good	10-12 months	In boiling water
Button Mushrooms	Good	6-8 months	While cooking
Cabbage (Savoy)	Good	10-12 months	While cooking
Carrots (sliced)	Very good	10-12 months	Do not defrost
Cauliflower	Good	8-10 months	In boiling water
Corn	Very good	10-12 months	While cooking
Cucumber (sliced)	Very good	6-8 months	Defrost in marinade
Green Pepper	Very good	6-8 months	At room temperature
Peas	Excellent	10-12 months	Saute in fat
Spinach	Excellent	10-12 months	Do not defrost (will defrost while cooking)
String Beans	Excellent	10-12 months	In boiling water (while cooking)

II: FOOD DECORATION

Food decoration is the art of shaping and arranging raw or cooked food in pleasing designs, created by putting proper emphasis on the combination of patterns, color, and texture of the design elements in relation to the kind and size of food to be decorated. These decorations should preferably be made up of foodstuffs. Only when a color cannot be found in natural food products is it permissible to resort to artificial food coloring, with one exception. *Blue* is not considered conducive to tantalizing appetites and, therefore, is not recommended.

Patterns and designs often serve to identify the type of dish that may seem "buried" under a thick coating of "chaud-froid" sauce. For example, a piece of fish filet, after being coated, may be decorated with an outline design of the fish from which the filet was cut. Or the true nature of the coated piece may be indicated by a simple fish figure made of assorted ingredients and put in place with various decorating tools.

When the shape of the food to be decorated is readily recognizable to viewers, as in the case of a whole ham, then the pattern or design used might be geometrical or the "artist" may choose a subject such as an animal or human figure. When a theme has been set for an occasion, the food may be decorated with a design appropriate to the theme. If a ham were intended to be displayed on a Dutch or International Buffet Table, for example, the top of a whole ham might be decorated with a pair of wooden shoes carved from turnips.

How many ways are there to decorate food?

Although there are countless ways to decorate food and food platters, the two major approaches outlined below should be understood before considering the types of materials available to the "Garde Manger," or the cook or chef in charge of preparing, decorating, arranging, and displaying cold dishes. These are:
  A. The Classical Approach
  B. The Commercial Approach

The Classical Approach–Marie-Antoine Careme, called Antonin Careme (1784-1833), was responsible for what is known today as the Classical Cuisine, and

Among the many items that can be made from fruits and vegetables to en-hance food arrangements: 1. lemon baskets; 2. cucumber baskets and slices; 3. radish flowers; 4. tomato stars and flowers; 5. onion flowers; 6. carrot slices; 7. turnip flowers; 8. carved mushrooms.

its application to food decoration. Too poor to finance his education towards a career in architecture, he instead chose to apply architectural principles to food decoration. In his day, food decoration and the general appearance of food platters on buffet tables were often gaudy. In fact, these displays often exhibited atrocious taste, as the heavy use of non-edible materials took away from the artistry in the so-called "piece-montees."

Careme felt that the food decoration should be appropriate to the recipe involved and that design elements should be assembled with simplicity and taste. Later, Master Chef Auguste Escoffier (1847-1935) supported Careme's approach by his emphasis on exclusive use of edibles in food decoration. This approach has been abandoned today, except in a few exclusive eating establishments, because labor costs and food costs have become prohibitive, because the taste of today's diners is less sophisticated and because they are not willing to pay the high prices engendered by this type of food preparation.

The Commercial Approach—There continues to be a great challenge to today's chefs to find feasible methods to decorate food and food platters, as well as entire buffet tables, and to train others to follow in their steps. The methods stem from the past, but must be adapted toward economic feasibility to meet today's marketing conditions.

The methods described and pictured in this book meet modern economic requirements although, on occasion, they will be reminiscent of the methods used by the great Careme and Escoffier. The return to the methods of earlier days only occurs in those situations where old-time results cannot be achieved by new technological means.

What are the edible ingredients used in food decoration?

There are 12 *basic* ingredients that can be used efficiently and economically in food decoration:

Fresh raw vegetables	Fresh herbs
Fresh cooked vegetables	"Aspic" sheets
Canned or marinated vegetables	Hard-boiled eggs
Fresh raw fruits	Fish roes
Canned fruits	Baked goods
Candied fruits	Dairy products

How are fresh raw vegetables used in food decoration?

The following are the vegetables chiefly used in food or food platter decoration; however, others. not listed here, can also be used at the garde-manger's discretion, based on his experience and imagination:

Carrots	Leeks	Turnips
Radishes	Tomatoes	Celery
Cucumbers	Red Cabbage	Potatoes

There are three *basic* ways the vegetables listed here can be used:

1. Slicing
2. Carving, for instance into "flowers"
3. Arranging in "bouquet"

Fresh raw vegetables that are to be sliced should be *blanched* and *marinated* first. However, those that are to be used for carving do not have to be either blanched or marinated.

NOTE: Blanching insures adherance of the slices to other foodstuffs, especially aspics, or other coatings, such as chaud-froid sauces.

Slicing—Fresh raw vegetables can either be peeled or left unpeeled before slicing, depending on the effect desired. However, they should always be *thoroughly washed.*

Carving—The beginner who wants to learn how to carve vegetables can start developing his skills by carving flowers, since they are relatively simple and do not require much time to create.

Depending on the artistic talent of the preparer, the time element, and the way the selected vegetables hold up through the final stages of carving, designs of all kinds can be fashioned. Among the possibilities are flowers, shoes, chains, fishnets, and other intricate designs.

Fruit and vegetable decorations to heighten impact of food presentation; reading right from palm tree, made with carrot trunk and top carved from green pepper half; apple bird perched on pineapple pedestal; whole red beets and white mushroom carved to resemble flowers; potato roses made by rolling paper thin raw potato slices around carrot stick before deep frying; pale leek and carrot flowers and a tomato rose framed in parsley.

Carrot flowers lend a colorful note as part of a floral centerpiece or as an accent on a buffet platter. To make flowers, first peel carrot, then slice lengthwise. Flower will require 5 thin pieces, 3 to 5 inches long.

1. Cut lines through carrot slices and shape as shown in diagram. (below)

2. Fold first carrot slice over as shown in diagram (bottom of column) and insert toothpick to hold it together.

3. Fold next carrot slice and place on same toothpick. Repeat with remaining slices, securing each to expanding flower with toothpick. When all slices are in place, flower is ready for finishing touch.

4. As final step, place one round slice of carrot in center of flower to hold it all in place. Place carrot flower in cold water until sides curl up.

5. Two carrot flowers on bed of parsley highlight tray of smoked trout with creamed horseradish.

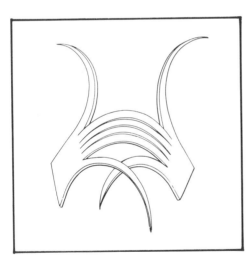

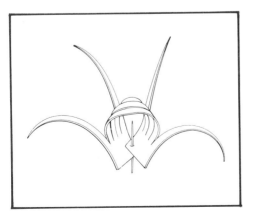

The apple bird, poised for flight on a pine-apple perch, provides a conversation-making accent for any food presentation.

1. To make the apple bird, slice off one-third of an apple to be used later for the neck and head. Removing this much of the apple also provides a flat base for the bird to rest on. Next cut out small wedge from apple and start cutting slices around the wedge. Taco-shaped slices will become larger as more slices are cut. (See picture below.)

2. Leaving a ridge of apple in place, as shown, to provide a foundation for the wings and tail, continue to cut taco-shaped slices from either side of the two rims.

3. When enough slices have been cut away to assemble for the wings and tail, pieces can be laid out in the pattern shown. (right above).

4. Fit slices together, lapping them slightly to form wings and tail as at right.

5. Using one-third of apple set aside in Step No. 1, cut thin piece shaped to form bird's neck and head. Insert two cloves for eyes and place neck and head between wings as shown below right. Perch completed bird on pedestal.

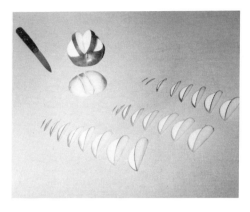

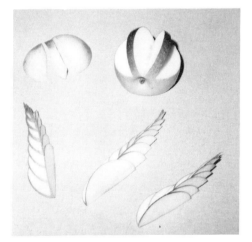

Raw mushrooms to be carved must be firm. Holding the mushroom as shown, insert paring knife and slice off small wedge, slicing from top to bottom. When small wedges have been cut off all around the mushroom, press the tip of the knife into the top of the mushroom to make star.

To make flower, cut root off leek. Next cut 2-3 inch piece from white part of leek. Push toothpick about ½ in. into root end. Holding leek by toothpick, slice 1/8-in. wide strips through to center of leek and down to (top picture) top of toothpick. Continue cutting similar strips all around leek. Push a thin carrot circle down over top of toothpick in center of leek. Then press leek lightly against surface of cutting board so strips spread out (pictured above) to create flower. Hold in cold water.

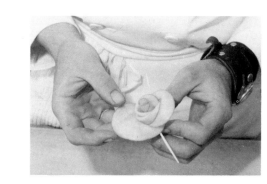

To make potato rose, cut one large unpeeled potato and one small potato into paper thin slices. (Do not hold in water.) Trim a 3-in. carrot to the thickness of a pencil. Roll a small slice of potato around the carrot as in picture at top. Roll additional small slices around carrot, holding them in place with toothpicks as shown above. Use larger slices for the outside leaves, shaping them as shown top right. When flower is fully formed, place it in cold water for 5 min. Deep fry flower, then cool. When cold, remove carrot and toothpicks.

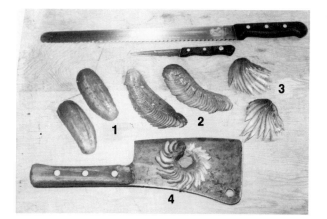

Pickles to be used as buffet garnishes are given a special twist. Tools needed to reproduce the pickle decorations are shown in the illustration. 1. Slice pickle crosswise and press lightly with slicer. 2. Cut stem off whole pickle, then slice vertically. 3. Fan each sliced half out and trim as illustrated. 4. Pickle halves can be fanned separately as shown in step 3 or arrange as follows: press one half until both ends meet and a circle is formed, as shown in arrangement on meat cleaver above.

The tomato rose is an eye-appealing decora-
tion and is simple to make. Peel the skin,with
a little of the pulp (for added firmness),in a

continuing slice from a firm, ripe red tomato.
Roll this slice up into the shape of a rose and
add stems made from the green end of leeks.

Bouquet Arrangement—Fresh raw vegetables such as asparagus, string beans, or any other vegetables that can be cut in julienne, are usually blanched and marinated, then trimmed (each piece cut to an exact size), and assembled in bunches, or bundles. Those that are "loose" (peas, sliced carrots, or other diced vegetables) can be assembled in bunches or bundles by "cradling" them in pastry shells, artichoke bottoms, or other carved foodstuffs. The carving can be kept quite simple or, when more elaborate designs are feasible, baskets or readily identifiable objects such as shoes or fish can be produced.

NOTE: The uses for fresh raw vegetables in food decoration as explained above can be duplicated with fresh cooked vegetables and canned or marinated vegetables.

How are fruits used in food decoration?

Fresh raw fruits can be used in exactly the same way as fresh raw vegetables, except that they need not be blanched and/or marinated. However, they should be thoroughly washed, as they are always used unpeeled, or the peel alone is often used.

Large pieces of fresh raw fruits can be carved and used as containers from which other foodstuffs are served. For example, a watermelon can be carved in the shape of a baby carriage and filled with fruit salad. Or a watermelon could be carved into a fish from which shrimp cocktail would be served.

Canned and candied fruits are mostly used "en Bordure" (i.e. along the edge of a platter or a "container" made by carving out fresh raw fruits or vegetables, as described earlier).

How are fresh herbs used in food decoration?

Generally herbs are used to add to the design, the color, or the texture (relief) of a surface to be decorated. Whole leaves are used mostly, although sometimes the stems can also be used. Fresh herbs work well in the design of trees, flowers, or other floral motifs.

How is aspic used in food decoration?

Although aspic (meat gelatine) is often thought of as a means of covering or wrapping foodstuffs, in food decoration this important material is also used to produce aspic sheets that can either be neutral or produced in a wide range of colors.

To make colored sheets of aspic, the aspic is mixed with natural food coloring (yellow from eggs, orange from pimiento, green from spinach, black from truffles, red from tomato paste, etc.). The colored aspic is then poured into a metal or plastic tray in a thin layer and chilled until it sets into a solid sheet. When aspic is solid, metal cutters of various shapes and designs are used to stamp out decorations. (see basic recipe and illustrations, pgs. 24-26).

How are hard-cooked eggs used in food decorations?

Hard-cooked eggs can be used whole, as wedges, sliced, stuffed, or chopped (yolk and/or white). The following illustrations show many of the ways eggs can be prepared to serve as decorative additions to platters.

To make centerpiece, bake an egg-shaped pastry shell. Fill with Russian salad and top with mayonnaise. Decorate with spears of asparagus and flowers made of stuffed tomatoes. Individual eggs and cherry tomatoes are filled with liver mousse and deviled egg mixture and are garnished with pistachio nuts, bits of radishes and olives.

How is fish roe used in food decoration?

Fish roe is used in food decoration primarily for color. However, the roe can also be used for texture, and in forming designs or patterns of all kinds. Of all the fish roe available, that of salmon (red caviar), sturgeon (black or grey caviar) or lobster (red coral) are usually favored by "Garde-Mangers."

Salmon mousse is piped into hard-cooked egg whites, making an attractive color combination. Stuffed eggs are presented on toasted croutons. Vegetable roses in center of tray are tinted. The star shaped cherry tomato shells hold balls of salmon mousse topped with black caviar.

How are baked goods and dairy products used in food decoration?

Baked goods can be used to contain other foodstuffs: "barquettes" (little boats); "tartelettes" (little tarts), or as an "en bordure" decoration such as "fleurons" (flower shaped or leaf-shaped).

Dairy products are mostly used when the application must be done with the help of a pastry bag, ("piping"). The shape and pattern of the piped product will be determined by the type of metal tube that is set through the small end of the cone-shaped pastry bag. Note varied sizes of these cream cheese roses.

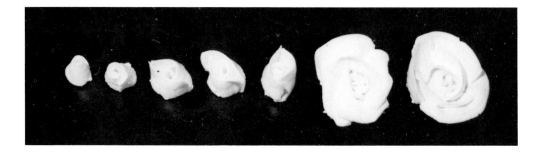

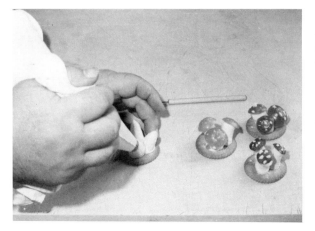

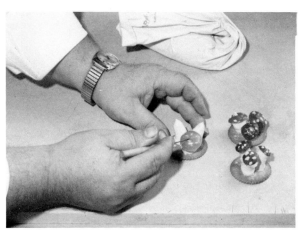

Cream cheese columns are piped from pastry tube onto cracker as first step in making mushroom clumps. Each column is topped with a circle of tomato skin with thin layer of pulp left to keep its shape. Cream cheese dots are placed on tomato as last step.

III: ASPIC-GELEE-
CHAUD FROID

Aspic and gelee play an important part in the preparation of many of the cold dishes created in the garde manger department. The glistening coating or sparkling bases supplied by aspic and gelee highlight the ingredients being presented. Proper preparation and application of aspic and gelee is essential to assure maximum impact.

Aspic and Gelee

In American cuisine there is usually no distinction between aspic and gelee. In continental cuisine, however, a gelee, or jelly, is a gelatinous meat or fish stock. A gelee becomes an aspic gelee or aspic jelly when it is clarified. The word aspic is used to refer to a combination of cold meat, fish, vegetables, eggs, etc. placed in a mold to form a decorative arrangement that is then covered with aspic jelly. When thoroughly chilled, the arrangement is unmolded on a silver platter and surrounded with aspic jelly croutons.

The aspic jelly must always be crystal clear and of a light, golden color. The quantity of gelatin used in the aspic jelly should be well proportioned so that the jelly, when set, is neither too firm nor too light in consistency. The aspic jelly provides special protection for cold dishes. A display of poultry, fish, game or other ingredients when covered with aspic jelly will keep its original flavor and freshness for a longer period.

The making of a fresh aspic jelly is elaborate and in modern kitchens is often considered very time consuming. However, aspic jelly can be bought commercially in powdered form and can be used with acceptable results when time does not allow the preparation of fresh aspic jelly.

How do you prepare aspic jelly?

The preparation of an aspic jelly consists of several steps:

1. A stock must be made using gelatinous products, such as veal bones, calves feet, pork skin, etc.

2. The reduction and clarification of the stock and the addition of aromatic products (vegetables, wines, seasonings) must be accomplished next.

3. Finally, the jelly must be tested to determine the consistency when cold.

WHITE ASPIC JELLY

Yield: 1 gal.

Ingredients

Veal Bones, cut into small pieces	3 lb.
Calves Feet, split in half lengthwise	2
Pork Skin	8 oz.
Veal Shank	1
Beef Chuck	2 lb.
Carrots	3 to 4
Onions, medium	2
Leeks, white portion	2
Celery	2 pcs.
Water	6 qts.
Salt, Pepper, Sachet Bag	

Method

Blanch the bones, calves feet, and pork skin. Rinse well in cold water. Place in a pot and add veal shank and beef. Cover with water and bring to a boil.

Skim boiling liquid, then add all the vegetables and seasonings. Cook for 5 to 6 hours on low fire. Pour stock through a strainer, cool, remove all fat. Reduce stock to 1 gallon

CLARIFICATION FOR 1 GALLON STOCK

Ingredients

Beef, lean ground	1 lb.
Leeks, celery and onion, diced fine	8 oz.
Egg White	2
Cold Stock	1 gal.

Method

Mix other ingredients well, then add one gallon of cold stock. Bring to a boil, stirring occasionally with a wooden spoon.

Simmer for ½ hour and strain through a cheese cloth. Add 1½ cups of Madiera, port or sherry wine. In order to know the consistency of gelatin contained in the gelee, a sample should be refrigerated. If it sets to desired consistency, the aspic jelly is ready to be used. If the jelly is to be used to make aspic molds, it is necessary to add an extra amount of unflavored gelatin that has been dissolved in water or wine.

Variations

The above recipe produces clear aspic with practically no color. A light to dark golden aspic can be obtained by using a brown stock. For this stock, brown the bones, meat and vegetables and proceed in the same manner described for white aspic jelly.

For poultry aspic jelly, substitute chicken or other fowl bones for veal bones and shank. A game aspic jelly can be obtained by using veal bones with game bones.

Whatever the aspic to be produced, it is only necessary to brown the appropriate bones and then follow the same recipe that would be used for white aspic jelly.

ASPIC OR MEAT JELLY (COMMERCIAL)

Yield: 3 qts.

Ingredients

Beef, lean, chopped	12 oz.
Celery, Onions, Leeks, diced fine	1 cup
Parsley Stems	2 to 3
Tarragon Sprigs (fresh or dried)	2
(If fresh or dried chervil is available,	
use instead of tarragon)	
Black Peppercorns	1 tsp.
Salt	1 to 2 tsp.
Egg Whites	5 to 6
Gelatin	3 to 4 oz.
Meat Stock (Chicken, Veal or Beef)	3 qt.

How to Clarify the Aspic

1. Put in a large pot, the beef and mirepoix of celery, onions and leeks, together with parsley, tarragon, peppercorns, salt, egg whites and the gelatin. Mix well together. Add meat stock and fold into the mixture.

2. Heat slowly just to the point of simmering. Agitate the pot gently, either by shaking or by stirring slowly with a wooden spoon, so that the ingredients will be thoroughly mixed with the liquid. Simmer 30-40 min.

3. Remove from fire and let rest for 5-10 min. so the raft can settle to the bottom of the pot.

4. Carefully ladle aspic through a fine sieve or a strainer lined with cheesecloth. At this time adjust the seasoning.

5. Cool in the refrigerator, remove fat and melt aspic before using.

NOTE: If fishstock is used, use herbs and egg whites only for clarification. If a golden color is desired, add 1 cup of fine, diced carrots.

How are aspic croutons prepared?

Pour some of the clarified, chilled liquid aspic into a sheetpan, filling it approx. ½ in. thick. Let it set. This aspic sheet has to be very cold and firm (hard) before it can be used.

NOTE: Make sure there are no air bubbles present in the liquid aspic. For garnitures, cut the hard aspic sheet into large squares, triangles, serrated half-moons, stars, diamonds or plain half-moons. The aspic can also be diced (fine or coarsely) to arrange along borders of display pieces or to use to fill in bare spots on platter.

How do you make aspic color sheets?

For decoration, or as background for various food presentations, aspic color sheets are very effective. The recipe that follows is considered a basic formula and can, therefore, be used for all kinds of color sheets:

Aspic croutons can be cut in many shapes and they can also be diced as in dish at left or chopped into finer sizes as in dish at right.

ORANGE ASPIC SHEETS

Size of Sheet: 14-17 inches

Ingredients

Pimentoes, canned	3½ oz.
Water	¾ cup
Salt	pinch
Unflavored Gelatin	1 oz.

Method

Combine pimento and warm water in blender; puree to a fine paste. Slowly add salt and plain gelatin and mix together well. Remove from blender into a small pot and place in hot waterbath for 2 or 3 minutes to remove the air bubbles. Then pour onto a slightly oiled, half-size sheetpan and cool.

Variations

For other colors, use the above recipe, substituting for the pimentoes as follows:

For red aspic, use 1/2 pimento, 1/2 tomato paste.
For yellow aspic, use boiled egg yolks.
For white aspic, use boiled egg whites.
For green aspic, use blanched or frozen spinach.
For light green aspic, use fresh watercress.
For black aspic, use truffle peelings.
For brown aspic, use a mixture of half glace de viande, half aspic.

NOTE: If the mixture is too thick, add aspic jelly until desired thickness is derived. Wine can also be added.

Why True Blue Is Not Suitable—In working out color formulas for aspic sheets, one color is not used; "true blue" is not considered suitable for edible foods because:

a. Blue is not found in natural products, therefore, artificial color would have to be used. Artificial colors may run into other colors and, therefore, are avoided by professionals.

b. Even if blue were found in natural products, it would not be used because of its adverse psychological effect on diners. (Can you imagine eating blue potato salad?)

c. The only way to get a color approximating blue is to blanch the leaves of red cabbage in water and vinegar but when used the moisture might be absorbed by the product covered which could ruin the effect of the decoration. (This is also true of red beets.)

Fish Aspic Jelly—A fish aspic jelly is obtained by first clarifying a reduced fish fumet (a reduced fish stock) and adding either white or red wine to it, the choice depending on the use to be made of the jelly.

Medallion of Veal. To prepare, cut filet of veal into round slices, 1-2 in. thick and about 1 in. diameter. Season and saute. Cool. When cold, pipe a circle of turkey liver pate (see Pate) around the veal medallion; place a fresh or canned black cherry on top and cover with a coat of clear aspic. A center-piece for the platter of Medallions can be prepared to fit the theme of the buffet. For a polynesian buffet, a tree can be made from carrots and a green pepper. For best results, never touch refrigerated aspic; always use a ladle when dipping aspic out of the container it is stored in.

This bouquet of flowers was created from pieces of egg yolk, pimentoes, radish skins, truffle-colored aspic and leeks.

Pieces of aspic that have been colored with pimento were arranged to make this striking red lobster.

The chaud froid coating highlights colorful decorations made from pieces cut from sheets of colored aspic. Design on left was made from truffle sheet, egg sheet, and pimento sheet. Center: truffle sheet, skin of tomatoes and dill. Right: truffle and egg sheets. Decorated chaud froid items should always be given a coat of clear aspic as a finishing touch. The aspic adds sparkle to the designs.

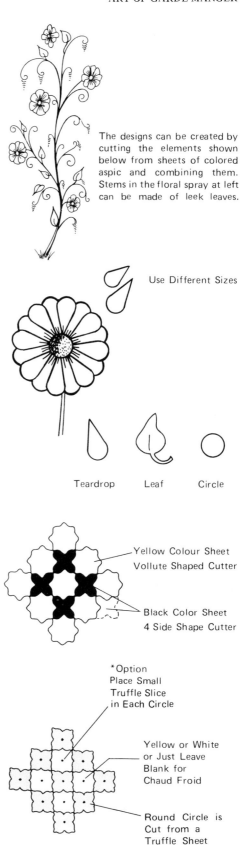

The designs can be created by cutting the elements shown below from sheets of colored aspic and combining them. Stems in the floral spray at left can be made of leek leaves.

Use Different Sizes

Teardrop   Leaf   Circle

Yellow Colour Sheet
Vollute Shaped Cutter

Black Color Sheet
4 Side Shape Cutter

*Option
Place Small
Truffle Slice
in Each Circle

Yellow or White
or Just Leave
Blank for
Chaud Froid

Round Circle is
Cut from a
Truffle Sheet

Chaud Froid

A popular cold sauce used extensively in the garde-manger is the chaud froid sauce. The French word "chaud froid" means "hot-cold," as the sauce is prepared hot, but used cold.

There are several types of chaud froid and their usage is different:

    1.   Classical Chaud Froid
       A. Red Chaud Froid
       B. Green Chaud Froid
    2.   Cream Sauce Chaud Froid
    3.   Mayonnaise Chaud Froid
    4.   Brown Chaud Froid

Classical Chaud Froid—This chaud froid is used to coat meat products, especially poultry, galantines, but mostly pieces of white meat. If well prepared, this chaud froid will enhance the flavor and the presentation of the displays.

CLASSICAL CHAUD FROID SAUCE

Yield: 2 qt.

Ingredients

Veal Stock (see recipe below)	1 qt.
Heavy Cream	1 qt.
Unflavored Gelatin	1/2 to 1 oz.
Salt	1/3 tsp.
Egg Yolks	3
Hot Pepper Sauce	3 drops
VEAL STOCK	
Veal Bones	6 lb.
Carrots	2
Celery	3 stalks
Parsley Stems	4
Wine	1/2 bottle
Salt	½ to 1 oz.
Peppercorns	2 tsps.
Lemon	juice of 2
Garlic Cloves	2

Method

To make veal stock for chaud froid, cut 6 lb. of veal bones into small pieces, blanch and wash in cold water.

Brown bones with carrots, celery, and parsley stems. Deglaze with ½ bottle of white wine. Add salt, peppercorns, juice of two lemons and two cloves of garlic. Place mixture in a stock pot, and cover with water. Simmer for four hours, then strain stock through a cheese cloth.

Reduce the veal stock to 1 qt.

Add 1-1/3 pt. of heavy cream in which 1/2 to 1 oz. of gelatin powder has been diluted. Season with salt and hot pepper sauce. Simmer sauce 5-10 minutes.

Make liaison with the remaining cream and egg yolks. Add to the chaud froid sauce. Strain sauce through a cheese cloth, and cool to the desired consistency.

CHAUD FROID NO. 2

(Due to the shortage of personnel in most kitchens, and in order to save time, the following recipe is a good substitute for the Classical Chaud Froid.)

Yield: 2½ qt.

Ingredients

Butter	4 oz.
Flour	4 oz.
Aspic Jelly	1-1/2 qt.
Heavy Cream	1 cup
Salt	1/3 tsp.

Method

Prepare a roux with butter and flour. Add aspic, mix well and stir until the sauce comes to a boil. Simmer for 15 minutes on low fire.

Add cream and reduce sauce for five minutes on low flame. Season with salt and strain through a cheese cloth.

NOTE: If this chaud froid is used for ham, add ½ cup of sherry wine. When cooling sauce, be sure to stir occasionally to prevent formation of skin.

RED CHAUD FROID–CHAUD FROID TOMATEE (NO.1A)

Yield: 1 qt.

Ingredients

Classical Chaud Froid Sauce	1 quart
Tomato Paste	2 tbsp.
Hungarian Paprika	½ tbsp.
Heavy Cream	1 oz.

Method

Use ready made chaud froid sauce to which tomato paste is added. Mix paprika with cream and add to the sauce.

GREEN CHAUD FROID SAUCE–CHAUD FROID VERTE (NO.1B)

Yield: 1 qt.

Ingredients

Classical Chaud Froid Sauce	1 qt.
Fresh Spinach Leaves	1 oz.
Watercress Leaves	1 oz.
Dill	½ oz.

Method

In a blender, puree spinach, watercress and dill with a little chaud froid and bring to a fast boil. Strain through a cheese cloth, add to remaining chaud froid. It is important to cool this sauce rapidly as it may lose its green color and turn greyish.

CREAM SAUCE CHAUD FROID (NO.2)

Yield: 5 qt.

Ingredients

Flour	8 oz.
Shortening	8 oz.
Milk, boiling	1 gal.
Unflavored Gelatin	1 cup
Salt	1 to 2 oz.

Method

Make a roux with shortening and flour. Add boiling milk and mix until thick and smooth. Cool sauce for 5 minutes and slowly pour in 1 cup of high bloom unflavored gelatin powder.

NOTE: The cream sauce chaud froid is a white suace, generally used on non-edible displays for exhibitions and dummy show pieces for buffets. There are several methods for preparing chaud froid for non-edible displays. Some chefs simply mix light cream with unflavored gelatin. Others use sour cream, cream cheese with water and unflavored gelatin. These methods give excellent results as far as the whiteness of chaud froid is concerned; however, it is better to keep the cost of this type of chaud froid to the minimum by using the above recipe.

Mayonnaise Chaud Froid or Mayonnaise Collee—A mayonnaise chaud froid is made by mixing one part of mayonnaise with one part of cold liquid aspic jelly. Do not whip, as bubbles may form. Mayonnaise chaud froid is usually used to coat fish.

If the mayonnaise is freshly prepared, it is important to use the chaud froid as soon as it has reached the right consistency. A mayonnaise chaud froid containing fresh mayonnaise is apt to break if reheated. A mayonnaise chaud froid containing commercially made mayonnaise can be reheated safely, if necessary.

Brown Chaud Froid—A brown chaud froid consists of:
1/3 Glace de Viande
1/3 Aspic Jelly
1/3 Tomato Sauce

Melt glace de viande with aspic jelly and combine with tomato sauce. Generally, brown chaud froid is flavored with madeira or sherry wine and is used to coat roast meats (beef, pork, turkey, etc.).

How do you use chaud froid sauce?

The method of application of a chaud froid sauce on cold foods plays an important role in the success of a finished food platter. The temperature of the chaud froid will determine the consistency of the sauce. A hot chaud froid is light in consistency but when cooled becomes thicker and will congeal if kept under refrigeration or on ice. The sauce should be placed in a double boiler to melt.

When applying a chaud froid sauce, several steps must be followed in order to be successful:

1. The food to be coated should have a smooth surface and be kept under refrigeration.

2. The item to be coated should be placed on a wire rack with a sheet pan underneath it.

3. When chaud froid is at the right consistency, ladle it over the food item.

The method of application may have to be adjusted depending on the food product:

a. A flat smooth surface, such as a turbot or sole, can easily be coated with a mayonnaise chaud froid just by pouring the chaud froid over the surface. Due to their shapes, ham, turkey, galantine, etc., cannot be coated as easily. To obtain the best results, it is necessary to coat the sides of the item first, then the top.

4. During the process, the chaud froid will have to be reheated in a double boiler, then cooled on ice, to reach the right thickness.

Items to be coated with chaud froid sauce should be smooth and well chilled. Here a ham has been placed on a wire rack with a clean pan under it to catch overflow of coating. Melt chaud froid sauce and set container in an ice-filled pan to cool. Chaud froid must be stirred frequently while it chills to prevent lumps from forming.

Using a ladle, coat object evenly and swiftly, being careful not to let ladle touch surface. Set in refrigerator to set. Repeat this step if another coat seems necessary.

When coating has chilled and set, cover with a coat of clear aspic and the surface will be ready for decorating. Note frill on ham, first step in decorating.

5. The item covered with chaud froid should be refrigerated for a few minutes to allow the coating to congeal, then a second coating can be applied.

6. A chaud froid coating should be smooth and not too thick. Generally, two coatings, sometimes three, are sufficient. If lumpy chaud froid has been used, remove coating and start all over.

7. The excess of sauce which accumulates on the sheet pan can be used again.

There are several advantages to be gained from covering food items with chaud froid sauce:

1. The sauce preserves the food for a longer period of time, providing the whole surface is covered.

2. The smoothness of the chaud froid coating can provide the base for a large variety of decorations.

3. Non-edible products can be used inconspicuously to save the cost of food. For example, a styrofoam ham or turkey can be covered with chaud froid and used as a background display on a buffet table.

Prior to decorating a ham, it should be covered with chaud froid sauce. The chaud froid holds decorations on the ham and also helps preserve the flavor of the meat. After coating the ham, layer thin slices of ham around it, leaving the top of the ham as an oval of white chaud froid.

To create designs such as this Statue of Liberty, first trace the desired design on a sheet of parchment paper with a soft lead pencil. Then press parchment against the cold chaud froid to mark outline of design. To fill in the picture, melt down colored aspic sheets and use liquid to "paint" within the outline. A border of half moon aspic cutouts frames the decoration. Thin slices of ham rolled around pickles are arranged to complete the display.

Pate encroute is sliced, then each slice is coated with clear aspic. Aspic preserves the appearance and flavor of cold foods.

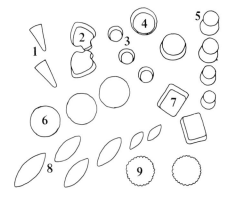

Aspic, timbale and barquette molds come in many shapes and sizes: 1. cornet holder for forming ham and salami rolls; 2. heart shaped aspic mold; 3. small timbale for liver mousse; 4. large aspic mold; 5. timbales for small aspic molds, spinach, eggs, etc.; 6. large aspic mold; 7. rectangular aspic mold; 8. variety of barquette molds; 9. decorative aspic mold.

IV: APPETIZERS-- HORS D'OEUVRE

"Faire manger les sans appetit, faire briller l'esprit de ceux qui en ont en faire trouver a ceux qui en désirent, est le supreme rôle des Hors-d'oeuvre". . .(To those who are not hungry. . .to perk up the spirit of some and to give spirit to others who are without it, this is the major task of the appetizers on a menu.)

Hors d'oeuvre is a French expression and its true definition is: A preparation served outside of the menu proper, at the beginning of a meal before the main course. Therefore, the hors d'oeuvre must be a small tidbit; it should be light, attractive, very delicate and tasty. Hors d'oeuvre is never spelled with an s; there is no plural form of the word in French.

There are four main types of hors d'oeuvre:
- A. Cold hors d'oeuvre
- B. Hot hors d'oeuvre
- C. Zakuski
- D. Canapes (hot and cold)

What is a cold hors d'oeuvre?

The cold hors d'ouvre can be divided into two categories:

1. The ready to serve variety, available in today's market in every conceivable type and form. (Like antipasto, smoked or pickled fish, sausages, etc. . .)

2. Those that require culinary preparation and that, when made properly, have the advantage of being freshly prepared from fresh ingredients with maximum flavor and appeal. This is where fine cuisine can make a very important contribution to eating pleasure.

Cold hors d'oeuvre are also broken into further classifications:

a. Hors d'oeuvre frequently served at luncheons and generally known as *Hors d'Oeuvre a la Française.* This variety is served in small oval, oblong, or square dishes called *raviers.* The basic qualification of an Hors d'oeuvre a la Francaise is that all of it be edible, and included are small salads made from meat, fish, vegetables, eggs, as well as various ham, sausage, or marinated fish dishes.

b. The hors d'oeuvre served before the meal.

The luncheon hors d'oeuvre is part of the meal and has its place in the proper sequence of dishes served at the meal, while the dinner hors d'oeuvre is usually served with cocktails at a time prior to the meal and is not a part of the menu served. It is of vital importance that the chef be given the proper time for service so that all the hors d'oeuvre may be prepared properly.

What are hot hors d'oeuvre?

Hot hors d'oeuvre are generally served at a cocktail party or before a dinner, but seldom if ever are served with a luncheon. Although, there are some hot appetizers that could be considered classical, there are many others that are strictly prototype and serve as a basis for many different preparations. As a matter of fact, every branch of cookery, when reduced to tidbit proportions, is or could be used in the preparation of hot hors d'oeuvre.

For example, from the pastry department we can secure the Paillettes or Allumettes, the Beignets or Frittes, Bouchees, Croustades, Petits Pates, the Rissoles, the Ramequins or the ever classic Quiche Lorraine.

From the saucier and the entremetier, we can get the Attereaux one of the first hot hors d'oeuvre belonging to the old school of cookery. These are delicious when served in small morsels. The Beurrecks, which are of Turkish origin; the Blinis for caviar consumption; the oysters, Casino or Rockefeller; the souffles and, of course, the Cromesquis or Croquettes, and many other commercial preparations help to round out the endless list of hot hors d'oeuvre. While not essential to a meal, they are nevertheless the first contact the guests make with the culinary performance of the operation. The impression made by their preparation and presentation is the basis for the guests' expectations of the dinner.

What are Zakuski?

In the 90's, Zakuski, or in other words, canapes a la Russe, became very popular. These cold hors d'oeuvre of the canape variety are classical, made up of certain specified ingredients; one of these is made of toast covered with smoked fish and finished with a thin gelee or aspic. Their presentation is left to the originality of the chef. Zakuskies are essentially dinner hors d'oeuvre and are larger in size than the average.

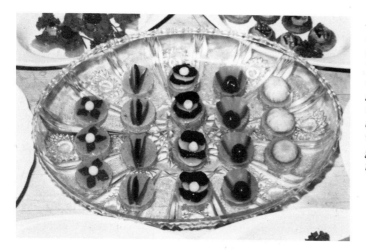

Aspic coated liver medallions are decorated, from left to right with: circle of water chestnut with pimento petals; thin strips of green pepper, pimento and truffle; water chestnut ball and truffles; pineapple bits, whole cherry and slivers of green bean; a whole fluted mushroom.

Massed for maximum color impact, these canapes combine flavors certain to please all tastes. Starting with wedge at upper left: Stuffed Deviled Eggs; Shrimp Canapes surrounded by stuffed green olives; Domino Canapes (swiss cheese slices over truffles on toast triangles); Beluga Caviar Canapes topped with cream cheese; Ham Rolls Stuffed with pickle slices; Stuffed Eggs Mimosa, topped with a caper; Anchovy Canapes, topped with circles of stuffed green olives and ar-
ranged with edging of red pimento strips; Salmon Mousse, with chaud froid and truffle decorations; Fresh Smoked Trout, butter decorations; Pimento Canapes; Cherry Tomatoes filled with Tunafish Mousse; Salmon Caviar Canapes. Colorful circles of canapes in lettuce frame is arranged around mound of stuffed green olives topped with a tomato rose. Tempting triangles are separated by twisted ropes of cream cheese and circled with lettuce to frame display.

How do you define the cold canape?

These tiny, open-face sandwiches are cut into rectangular, round or other shapes, the size and thickness depending on the nature of the ingredients used. Cold canapes are mostly made of toasted bread, crackers or pumpernickel, covered with various butter spreads and topped with various accompaniments. As labor is the important factor in making cold canapes, this type of hors d'oeuvre should be ordered as early as possible. In costing the canape, the price of labor should also be considered. In the past years, canapes, hot or cold, have become very popular and are usually served at cocktail parties or other gatherings to foster the drinking of cocktails.

ARTICHOKE HEARTS A LA GREQUE

Yield: 16
Ingredients

Carrots	3
Shallots	8
Olive Oil	1 cup
Artichoke Hearts, raw	16
Bouquet Garni	1
White Wine	4 cups
Chicken Stock	2 cups
Salt	to taste
Black Peppercorns, crushed	½ to 1 tsp.
Coriander Seeds	12
Lemons	juice of 2

Method

Cut the carrots and shallots into small dice, and saute them in 4 tbsp. olive oil for 15 min. When soft, add the raw artichoke hearts, the bouquet garni, the wine and the stock; season with salt and peppercorns; add coriander and lemon juice. Cover and simmer for about 30 minutes.

When the artichoke hearts are tender, remove from heat; add the rest of the oil and let stand for 2 hours. Remove the artichoke hearts, carrots and shallots; place in a crock. Discard bouquet garni, strain the liquid and reduce to 1½ cups; allow to cool. Pour over artichokes and serve cold.

TOMATOES STUFFED WITH MUSSELS

Yield: 4 servings
Ingredients

Ripe Tomatoes, medium size	4
Salt	pinch
Black Pepper, freshly ground	1/3 tsp.
Mussels, (see recipe on facing page for mussel preparation; omit curry)	1 1/4 lb.
Mayonnaise	3/4 cup
Chervil and Dill, combined	1 tbsp.
Lemon, cut in wedges	1
Parsley sprigs	

Method

Cut tops off tomatoes; scoop out insides; sprinkle cavities with salt and pepper. Prepare mussels, remove from shells; cool them in their liquid. When mussels have cooled, drain them and mix together with mayonnaise. Use mixture to stuff tomatoes, cover with tops; sprinkle tops of stuffed tomatoes with fine chopped herbs; serve with lemon wedges and a sprig of parsley.

MUSHROOMS A LA GREQUE

Yield: 24 oz.

Ingredients

Use recipe for Artichokes a la Greque. Substitute 2 lb. of whole mushrooms for artichokes and reduce cooking time by 15 min.

MUSSEL SALAD A LA BOMBAY

Yield: 3-4 servings

Ingredients

Mussels	1¼ lb.
Shallots, chopped	1½ tbsp.
Dry White Wine	½ cup
Parsley Stalks	2 to 3
Black Pepper, crushed	½ to 1 tsp.
Mild Curry	1 oz.
Mayonnaise	¾ cup

Method

Clean the mussels, put in large kettle together with the shallots, wine, parsley stalks, pepper and ¾ oz. curry. Cover and cook over high heat for 5-10 minutes until shells are open. Remove mussels from shells, strain the liquid, cool and store mussels in stock.

When using mussels for a la Bombay, mix mussels with mayonnaise, remaining curry and a little of the stock. Serve with croutons in a glass dish.

MUSSELS IN MUSTARD SAUCE
(Moules a la Moutarde)

Yield: 4 portions

Ingredients

Mayonnaise	4 oz.
French Mustard	1 oz.
Celery, diced fine	4 oz.
Mussels	8 oz.
Lemon Juice	a few drops
Radish Rose	

Method

Combine mayonnaise, mustard, celery and mussels. Flavor with lemon juice. Serve in a shallow dish, decorated with a radish rose.

AVOCADO SALAD, MEXICAN STYLE

Yield: 4 portions
Ingredients

Lobster, diced	½ cup
King Crabmeat, diced	½ cup
Romaine Lettuce, shredded	1 cup
Capers	4 tsp.
Mayonnaise	4 tbsp.
Lemon	juice of 1
Black Pepper, freshly ground	½ tsp.
Avocados, large	2
Parsley, chopped	3 tsp.
Lobster Coral	2 tsp.

Method
Mix the diced seafood with the shredded romaine and the capers. Bind salad with mayonnaise, lemon juice, and pepper. Adjust seasoning with salt as needed.

Cut the avocados in half lengthwise and remove seeds. (Fill each cavity with salad, and sprinkle with parsley and lobster coral. Garnish with lobster claw. Serve on ice.)

LOBSTER SALAD WITH GRAPEFRUIT

Yield: 4 portions

Ingredients

Supreme Cups	4
Grapefruit, cut into sections	2
Lobster Meat, diced	8 oz.
Lemon	½ tsp.
Worcestershire Sauce	a few drops
Tomato Catsup	½ cup
Chablis (white wine)	4 tbsp.
Croutons	4

Method
Line supreme cups with grapefruit sections. Mix lobster meat with lemon and Worcestershire sauce. Portion lobster into center of supreme cups. Mix catsup with chablis wine and pour over lobster pieces. Decorate with a small heart-shaped crouton dipped in parsley.

Canapes: l to r: Assembled on tray, from left to right— croutons (first row) topped with apricot marmalade, liver pate and truffle dot; (second row) oyster butter, slice of hard cooked egg, smoked oyster and a pimento strip; (third row) parsley butter, cornet of salami and gherkins; (fourth row) mustard butter, ham and radishes; (fifth row) cream cheese and truffle slices; (sixth row) green butter, sardine and truffle dot.

ALASKA KING CRABMEAT HORS D'OEUVRE
(King Crab Salad a la Lucull)

Yield: 4 portions

Ingredients

King Crabmeat, cut in 1 to 2 in. cubes	8 oz.
Sour Cream	1-1/2 oz.
Mayonnaise	1-1/2 oz.
Horseradish, freshly grated	1/2 tbsp.
Cocktail Sauce	3 tbsp.
Paprika (Hungarian)	1/3 tbsp.
Chopped Almonds	1/2 tsp.
Brandy	1/3 oz.
Dill, chopped	1/2 tsp.
Monosodium Glutamate	a pinch
Seedless Green Grapes	3 oz.

Method

Cube crabmeat and squeeze some moisture out. Mix sour cream, mayonnaise, horseradish, cocktail sauce, paprika, chopped almonds, brandy, dill and monosodium glutamate. Add salt if necessary. Add seedless grapes to crabmeat and marinate in sour cream-mayonnaise mixture for 15-20 minutes. Serve on a bed of lettuce.

SHRIMP SALAD

Yield: 4 portions

Ingredients

Shrimp, medium size	8 oz.
Orange Sections, fresh	4 oz.
Lemon	juice of 1/2
Black Pepper, freshly crushed	pinch
Salt	pinch
Mango Chutney	2 tsp.
Orange	juice of 1/2
Fresh Dill, chopped	1/2 tsp.
Horseradish	1-1/2 tsp.
Whipped Cream, unflavored	1/3 cup
Boston Lettuce	4 leaves
Supreme Cups	4
Lemon Sections, to garnish	4
Orange Sections, to garnish	4

Method

Mix shrimp and orange sections together. Add lemon juice, pepper, salt, mango chutney, orange juice, dill, horseradish, then fold whipped cream into center of shrimp-orange section mixture. Line a supreme with lettuce and fill with the shrimp salad. Garnish with lemon and orange sections (1 of each), and a little parsley. Serve cold.

TARTELETTES A LA WALTERSPIEL

Yield: 12 portions

Ingredients

Tartelettes, small	12
Langostinos	12 oz.
Horseradish	1 to 2 oz.
Heavy Cream, whipped	1/2 cup
Salt	1/3 oz.
Sugar	1/3 oz.
Paprika (Hungarian)	2 tsp.
Lemon	1/2 tsp.
Caviar	1/2 oz.

Method

Mix langostinos with horseradish, whipped cream, salt, sugar, and paprika. Season with a few drops of lemon juice. Stuff tartelettes with mixture, and garnish with a little caviar.

NOTE: Mayonnaise may be substituted for heavy cream.

CUCUMBER DANISH STYLE
(Concombre a la Danoise)

Yield: 4 Sherry glasses

Ingredients

Cucumbers, large	2
Smoked Herring, pureed	8 oz.
Eggs, chopped	2
Horseradish, freshly grated	2 oz.
Ripe Olives	4

Method

Peel cucumbers, remove seeds, and cut into small dice. Blanch in salt water and cool in ice water. Marinate with a little vinaigrette sauce.

Mix pureed smoked herring with chopped eggs and horseradish. Put into a sherry glass, alternating a layer of smoked fish puree with a layer of cucumbers. Top with a ripe olive.

Tartelettes a la Walterspiel   *Cucumber Danish Style*

SEAFOOD COCKTAIL

Yield: 4 portions
Ingredients

Tomatoes, large	2
Grapefruit	2
Langostino Tails	20
SAUCE	
Mayonnaise	1/2 cup
Tomato Catsup	3 tbsp.
Tarragon, chopped	1/3 tsp.
White Wine	2 tsp.
Lemon Wedges, to garnish	4

Method
Cut tomatoes into wedges; section grapefruit. Mix tomatoes and grapefruit sections with langostino tails. Combine sauce ingredients. Put first mixture in grapefruit shells and top with sauce. Garnish each serving with a lemon wedge. Serve in a glass dish.

CHICKEN SALAD COCKTAIL

Yield: 4 portions
Ingredients

Chicken, diced	8 oz.
Grapefruit	2
Chopped Ginger	1 tsp.
Curry Powder	1/2 to 1 tsp.
Sour Cream	4 oz.
Tomato Catsup	4 tsp.
Mango Chutney	1 tsp.
Salt	1/2 tsp.
Pepper	1/3 tsp.
Celery, julienne	4 oz.
Vodka	4 tsp.

Method
Section grapefruit. Mix chicken and grapefruit sections together with chopped ginger, curry powder, sour cream, tomato catsup, chutney and seasonings. Fill grapefruit shells with mixture, garnish with julienne of celery, and sprinkle with vodka. Serve olives and salted almonds separately.

STUFFED CUCUMBERS
(Concombres Farcis)

Yield: 3 cucumbers
Ingredients

Salmon, smoked	8 oz.
Butter	8 oz.
English Mustard	1 tsp.
Lemon Juice	a few drops
Cucumbers	2 to 3

Method
Puree salmon and mix with butter, English mustard and lemon juice. Peel cucumber and remove seeds and pulp from center. Fill cavity with salmon mixture. Chill. Cut filled cucumber into 1 to 2 in. slices and serve on Russian pumpernickel bread.

The boars head used as the focal point for this canape display is made from mousse of ham coated with white and brown chaud froid. The nose and mouth are made with ripe olive slices. Eyes are hard cooked egg slices with a circle of stuffed olives in the center. The ears are half circles of toasted dark bread. A row of cherries sets off the head covering made of alternating stripes of chopped egg yolk and chopped egg white separated by pimento strips. Red and black cherries threaded on a skewer provide the colorful topknot.

STUFFED LEEKS
(See picture, p. 146)

Yield: 18 portions
Ingredients

Leeks, large	18
Rice, boiled	1½ cups
Sausage Meat, cooked	½ lb.
White Bread Crumbs	6 oz.
Parsley, Chervil, Dill, chopped	1½ tbsp.
Eggs	1½
Salt	½ oz.
Cayenne Pepper	pinch
Grated Nutmeg	pinch
Oil	5 oz.

Method
Trim leeks by cutting off roots and green ends. Wash leeks thoroughly. Blanch in boiling salted water for 5 to 10 minutes. They should be firm (al dente). Drain them well.

Put rice into a bowl, add sausage meat, bread crumbs, herbs and eggs. Season with salt, cayenne pepper and nutmeg. Mix well.

Core leeks with a vegetable knife and fill the opening with a little of the stuffing. Set the leeks side by side in an oiled shallow casserole dish, sprinkle more oil on top of stuffed leeks and cover with aluminum foil. Cook at 350°F. for 35-40 minutes. Cool and serve.

SHRIMPS A L'INDIENNE
(Tiny Shrimp Salad)

Yield: 4 portions

Ingredients

Tiny Shrimps	8 oz.
Green Peppers, julienne	2 oz.
Lemon Juice	1/2 lemon
Bananas, sliced	3 oz.
SAUCE	
Curry	1/2 tsp.
Butter	1/2 tsp.
White Wine	to moisten
Mayonnaise	1/3 cup
GARNISH	
Lemon Wedges	4
Croutons, dipped in parsley	4
Lettuce Leaves	4

Method

Saute curry slightly in butter, deglaze with a little white wine, cool, and add mayonnaise to mixture. Mix well.

Combine shrimps, bananas, peppers and season with lemon juice. Mix into above sauce. Adjust seasoning.

Serve salad in a small glass shell lined with a lettuce leaf. Garnish with a lemon wedge and crouton dipped in parsley.

MARINATED TROUT

Yield: 6 portions

Ingredients

Trout, fresh or frozen	6
Mushrooms, sliced	8 oz.
Shallots, chopped	6
Parsley Stems	3
Dill Stems	3
Salt	1 oz.
White Wine	½ cup
Lemon	juice of 1
Court Bouillon	2 cups
Lemon Wedges	to garnish
Parsley	to garnish

Method

Wash trout well. Place in buttered shallow casserole. Add mushrooms, shallots, parsley, dill and salt. Cover with wine, lemon juice, and court bouillon. Bring to a boil and simmer 5 minutes per lb. of trout; remove from heat and cool trout in stock.

Fillet or serve whole with part of the marinade. Garnish with lemon wedges and a sprig of parsley.

TOMATO COCKTAIL

Yield: 4 portions
Ingredients

Tomatoes, large	4
Lemon	juice of 1
Oil	4 tbsp.
Salt	½ tsp.
Black Pepper, crushed	½ tsp.
Creamed Horseradish)	
Tomato Catsup)	to garnish
Caviar)	

Method
Peel, remove seeds, and dice tomatoes. Marinate with lemon juice, oil, salt and pepper. Fill a supreme glass and top with a spoonful of tomato catsup and a little creamed horseradish (see cold sauces). Top portion with a sprinkling of caviar.

HORS D'OEUVRE PROVENCAL

Yield: 14 4-oz. portions
Ingredients

Fennel bulbs, fresh	9 to 12
Peeled Tomatoes	1 lb. 2 oz.
Garlic	8 cloves
Olive oil	2 tbsp.
Tarragon, fresh	4 sprigs
Pepper	1/3 tsp.
Salt	1 to 1-1/2 oz.

Method
Bring salted water to boil. Cut fennel in small pieces, lengthwise and cook until tender. Do not overcook.

Chop tomatoes and garlic. Place tomatoes in pot, add oil, and reduce tomatoes until thick. Add garlic, tarragon, salt and pepper. Add fennel, cook briefly to blend flavors, then pour mixture into a dish and allow to cool. Serve cold.

TURBAN OF RICE IN JELLY
(Turban de Riz Compose en Gelee)

Yield: 8 3-oz portions
Ingredients

Rice Pilaff	10 oz.
Green Olives	4 oz.
Smoked Salmon	6 oz.
Mayonnaise Collee	1 cup

Method
Prepare rice pilaff. Chop green olives and smoked salmon fine. Mix with rice pilaff.

Blend in approx. 1 cup of mayonnaise collee (see Chaud Froid, p. 31) freshly made. Line a ring mold with aspic and pack rice mixture into center of mold. Let mold set for 2 to 3 hours.

MOUSSE OF TUNA IN LEMON SHELL
(Citrons a la Creme de Thon)

Yield: 12 lemon halves

Ingredients

Lemons	6
Tuna	1 lb. can
Butter	4 oz.
Dry Mustard	1 level tbsp.
Paprika	1/2 tsp.
Black Pepper, freshly ground	1/3 tsp.
Egg White, beaten to stiff froth	1
Pimento, thin strip	to garnish
Parsley, chopped	to garnish

Method

Cut lemons in half. Remove pulp, being careful not to damage skins. Remove all seeds and save skins. Set pulp and juice aside.

Drain tuna and grind fine in chopper or blender; add butter, mustard, paprika, and pepper. Mix well to obtain a very smooth batter. Mix in one-third of the lemon pulp. Add egg white to lighten the mixture. Heap mixture in lemon shells. Garnish filled shells with: thin strip of pimento, sprinkle of paprika, chopped parsley. Refrigerate for one hour.

PICKLED BEETS

Yield: 3½ lb.

Ingredients

Fresh Beets, cooked	3 lb.
Onion, finely sliced	1
Beet Juice	1 cup
White Vinegar	1½ cup
Sugar	1¼ cup
Cinnamon Stick	1
Thyme	½ tsp.
Salad Oil	¼ cup
Ground White Pepper	¼ tsp.
Salt	½ tsp.

Method

Bring all ingredients except beets to boil, turn heat down and simmer mixture for 5 min. Cool. Add sliced beets, mix well and refrigerate.

Canapes and Zakouski

Anchovy Canape—Butter a canape with anchovy butter; lay strips of anchovies on top, leaving a space in the center to be filled with chopped egg yolks mixed with parsley.

Shrimp Canape—Butter a canape with shrimp butter, arrange shrimp tails on top, finish with a sprinkling of fines herbes.

Caviar Canape—Butter a canape with caviar butter; place a layer of caviar on top, border with chopped yolks and whites of eggs, a sprinkling of chives on top.

Caviar Cigarettes—Spread caviar on a very thin slice of bread; roll to form a cigarette.

Canape Rigoletto—Butter a canape with cayenne butter; sprinkle with a mixture of finely chopped whites and yolks of eggs, ham, tongue, fines herbes and truffles.

Canape a la Danoise—Butter a rye canape with horseradish butter; arrange slices of smoked salmon, caviar and fillets of marinated herring on top of canapé.

Canape of Langostinos—Butter a canape with langostino butter; arrange slices of langostino tails on top; decorate with langostino butter.

Canape of Tongue—Butter a canape with mustard butter; arrange slices of tongue on top and decorate with mustard butter.

Canape of Ham—Follow same procedure as for tongue (see above) replacing the tongue with ham.

Canape of Lobster—Butter a canape with lobster butter; arrange slices of lobster on top; border with chopped eggs.

Canape of Eggs—Butter a canape with mayonnaise; sprinkle top with chopped whites of eggs; border with chopped yolks.

Canape of Eggs a la Greque—Butter a canape with mustard butter; place a hard-cooked egg half on top; cover with mayonnaise; border with chopped eggs sprinkle fines herbes on top.

Canape of Game—Butter a canape with cayenne butter or a game cheese; arrange small mounds of chopped game meat on top; border with fines herbes and chopped capers.

Canape of Fish—Butter a canape with herring roe butter; arrange slices of cooked fish on top of butter; cover with mayonnaise and border with chopped capers and fines herbes.

Canape Cancalaise—Butter a canape with tunafish butter; top with a poached mussel; border with ravigote butter.

Canape of Smoked Salmon—Butter a canape with horseradish butter; place a slice of smoked salmon on top; border with chopped chervil and chives.

Canape of Sardine—Butter a canape with sardine butter; arrange a sardine filet on top; decorate with anchovy butter.

Canape of Lobster Eggs—Butter a canape with lobster cheese, top with a sprinkling of lobster coral; decorate with lobster butter.

Domino Canape—Butter domino-shaped canapes with truffle butter; cover with thin slices of gruyere cheese of the same shape. Cut holes in the cheese to simulate spots on dominoes and fill holes with pieces of truffle.

Canape Rejane—Butter a canape with langouste butter; top with a mound of chopped eggs and mayonnaise. Cover with a light mayonnaise and border with chopped langouste coral. (NOTE: When langouste or lobster coral cannot be obtained, substitute grated egg yolks that have been tinted during cooking.)

Canape of Goujons a la Russe—Poach some cleaned goujons in a court bouillon

*Breast of Chicken Bombay–Place a slice of chicken breast in a
tablespoon, then fill cavity with chicken mousse that has been
seasoned with curry. Top with a second slice of chicken breast.
Coat with curry-flavored chaud froid and decorate as desired,
here radish skin flowers with leek stems are used. Half orange
slices decorated alternately with stuffed olive slices and carrot
balls provide a colorful border that repeats the orange of the
carrot flower in the center of the tray.*

of white wine; cool. Place on canapes and cover with gelatin-mayonnaise and
sprinkle lightly with chopped parsley.

Breast of Chicken Bombay (picture above)–Slice of chicken breast is placed in
tablespoon; cavity is filled with mousse of chicken with curry added, then topped
with a second slice of chicken breast. The combination is covered with curried
chaud froid sauce and garnished with radish and leek flowers.

Canape of Sole a la Brasset–Butter round canapes with herring roe butter;
place a small paupiette of sole on top and cover with a light mayonnaise. Decorate
the sides with chopped coral and put a bit of chopped truffle on top.

Canape a la Nicoise–Butter round canapes with anchovy butter; place three
small stuffed green olives on the canapes; put a fourth olive on top of the three.
Fill in between olives with anchovy butter and decorate as desired.

Canape Paulette–Butter round canapes with anchovy butter; sprinkle one-half
of canape with chopped egg whites and the other half with chopped egg yolks;
separate halves with a row of shrimps.

Small Brioche of Foie Gras–Place a small piece of truffle in the center of a
ball of foie gras, wrap unsweetened brioche dough around foie gras, shaping it like
a small loaf of bread. Bake and cool before serving.

Profiterolles–Bake a pate of choux into tiny round shells. These may be garnished with any kind of puree of meat, fish or cheese.

Canape Vie Ville–Cover a canape with tarragon butter, then top with a slice
of ham; decorate with tarragon leaves.

Canape a la D'Arkangel–Cover one-half of a small tartlet with caviar, the remaining half with puree of smoked salmon. Separate halves with a fillet of anchovy.
NOTE: Most canapes should be spread with either a butter or cheese flavored to
complement the main ingredient to be placed on the canape. A coating of aspic
may be substituted for the butter. A large variety of canape ingredients are available on the market in cans or jars. These may be used either as hors d'oeuvre or as
garnish for canapes.

Fish and Shellfish

Anchovies, Moscovite—On a large circle of cooked potato, place marinated anchovies to form a crown. Place caviar in the center of the crown. Garnish top of caviar with chopped egg white.

Boutargue (Mullet Eggs)—These are available salted and smoked, to be served like caviar. They are highly appetizing.

Salted Codfish a l'Indienne—Soak 2 lb. codfish overnight; cut in scallop-size pieces; roll in flour and fry quickly in hot oil. Saute 2 tbsp. of finely chopped onions in olive oil til golden; sprinkle with curry powder and simmer for one minute. Add 1 cup of dry white wine, juice of 1 lemon, 3 crushed garlic cloves and boil for 5 min. Place codfish pieces in this marinade, bring to a boil, cover and let cool. Serve cooled pieces with some of the marinade. Yield: 12 portions.

Langostine a l'Admiral—Remove meat from cooked langostino carefully so the form of the shell remains intact. Join shells together to form a barquette. Fill barquettes with a ragout made from langostino meat mixed with an anchovy mayonnaise.

Crayfish a la Moscovite—Remove the tail shell from cooked crayfish and serve tails with anchovy mayonnaise. Top with a sprinkling of chopped parsley.

Frog Legs a la Bearnaise—Saute frog legs in olive oil; add diced tomatoes, white wine, lemon juice and herbs; use plenty of salt and pepper; simmer for 5 min.; Serve with some of the liquor they were cooked in and sprinkle with fines herbes.

Goujons a la Russe—Poach some cleaned goujons in white wine and lemon juice. (Remove goujons and reduce cooking liquor by ½). Arrange goujons on a small plate, top with mayonnaise thinned with some of the reduced cooking liquor. Use cucumber salad to complete the plate.

Lobster a la Boulognaise—Cut cooked lobster meat into small pieces, add an equal quantity of celery and finely chopped beets. Mix these ingredients with mayonnaise; season well with finely chopped chervil, tarragon and cayenne. Arrange lobster mixture on lettuce leaves and sprinkle with finely chopped lobster coral.

Herring a la Dieppoise—Poach cleaned, fresh fillets of herring in a marinade of white wine, vinegar, carrots and onions a la russe, and herbs. Serve with some of the marinade.

Herring a la Livonienne—Remove fillets and reserve heads and tails of 12 salted or smoked herrings. Remove skin and dice fillets. Place in bowl with equal quantity of diced boiled potatoes and fresh apples. Season with the following dressing: ½ tsp. salt; pinch of freshly ground white pepper; 1 tsp. each, coarsely chopped parsley, chervil, fennel and tarragon; 6 tbsp. olive oil and 3 tbsp. of red wine vinegar. Mix all ingredients well. On a service platter, mold this preparation into shapes resembling herring; place reserved heads and tails at each extremity, thus simulating the original fish; serve.

Herring a la Lucas—Salad of diced marinated herring in a Sauce Gribiche. Season highly.

Herring a la Russe—Arrange filets of smoked herring on a ravier; border with sliced cold potatoes. Season with a fennel vinaigrette.

Trout a la Saint Menehould with Champagne—Place cleaned trout in a pan; cook slowly for six minutes in a liquor made by sauteeing sliced carrots, onions, garlic in butter seasoned with freshly ground pepper, grated nutmeg, herb mixture and salt and then pouring a bottle of champagne over mixture. Cook for one hour, remove herring and strain liquor. Serve some liquor with fish. (Herring and salmon may be cooked in similar fashion.)

Mackerel in Marinade—Take 12 very fresh mackerel (about ½-lb. size); remove the fillets and place them in a saute pan; season with salt, freshly ground pepper. Sprinkle finely sliced onion, pinch of thyme, 3 parsley sprigs, 1 bayleaf and the juice of 2 lemons over fish. Add sufficient dry white wine to cover and bring to a boil; cover and let simmer for five minutes. Remove from heat and allow to cool; place in refrigerator until jellied.

Marinated Mackerel a la Suedoise—Small mackerel prepared like Herring a la Dieppoise.

Mullets a l'Orientale—Prepare the same as Mullets au Saffron (see below), eliminating the saffron.

Mullets au Saffron—Cook mullets in oil, chopped onions, diced tomatoes, white wine, fish stock, herb mixture and saffron. Serve mullets in liquor with sprinkling of chopped parsley.

Mussels—Poach and clean some mussels; mix with mayonnaise flavored with lemon juice and thinned with poaching liquor reduced by two-thirds. Sprinkle fines herbes on top.

Mussels a l'Antiboise—Garnish a mussel shell with a puree of sardines; place a poached mussel on the puree, a chervil leaf over the mussel and glaze all with aspic.

Mussels a l'Indienne—Prepare mussels in a curry sauce. Arrange within a turban of boiled rice.

Oysters—All types

Pickled Oysters—Parboil 48 oysters in their own liquor; as soon as liquor boils, drain oysters and reserve liquor. Boil 1 pt. vinegar with ½ tsp. cloves, whole white pepper, whole allspice and a pinch of mace for a few minutes, then add the oyster liquor, bring to a boil, strain and pour over oysters. Let oysters marinate in refrigerator for 12 hours.

Slices of Pickerel a la Georgianne—Clean and completely bone a pickerel. Stuff with a highly seasoned forcemeat; wrap as a galantine and cook in a court bouillon made with white wine. When fish is done, cool and cut into slices. On each slice, place a small portion of Russian salad, then place a small slice of lobster on top of the salad. Glaze with aspic.

Salmon, Canadian Style—Cut 2 lb. fresh salmon in large dice, fry briskly in hot oil; season with salt and paprika. Place in a saute pan; add 1 lb. of small fresh okra and the salmon with white wine and the juice of 2 lemons; let simmer for a few minutes, season to taste and cool covered. Sprinkle finely chopped green peppers over servings.

Horns of Salmon a la Imperiale—Make horns of smoked salmon and garnish with caviar butter.

Barquettes of Fillet of Dover Sole Caprice—Fill small barquettes with cucumber salad, seasoned with cream and lemon juice. Arrange small paupiettes of sole stuffed with a puree of truffles over salad, glaze all with aspic.

Paupiettes of Fillet of Dover Sole—Stuff paupiettes (roulades) with puree of red pimentos, poach, cool and cut into rings. Garnish dish with a salad of cucumbers; arrange rings on salad.

Tortillons of Dover Sole a la Diable—Tie slender bands of sole into a knot. Cook in a little oil; then add white wine, lemon juice, a few grains of coriander seed, garlic and a little Worcestershire sauce, crushed thyme and bayleaves. Cool sole; serve with liquor.

Smelts a la Caucasienne—Clean smelts; dry, flour and brown in very hot oil. Place in vinaigrette.

The striking hors d'oeuvre display, lower left,
is made from poached Filet of Dover Sole
coated with chaud froid and decorated with
truffle dots to represent dominoes. Tray at
right above holds cornets of ham stuffed with
cream cheese and ham mousse with a dark
garnish for contrast.

Marinated Smelts (known in French cookery as "Escabeche")—Fry 48 thoroughly dried and floured smelts in hot oil. When done, place in a deep dish and set aside. In the same hot oil, fry 1 large onion and 1 carrot (cut into very thin round slices) with 8 unpeeled cloves of garlic. When slightly brown, drain the oil, then moisten with 1 tbsp. vinegar, the juice of 1 lemon, 1 qt. dry white wine, add freshly ground white pepper, one bay leaf, a pinch of thyme, 3 parsley sprigs, 3 small pimentos and salt to taste. Simmer for 15 min. When ready, cool and pour over smelts. Marinate for 24 hours. Serve smelts with strained marinade.

Shrimp—All forms

Shrimp with Saffron a l'Orientale—Shrimp may be used with or without their shells in this dish. However, leaving the shell on is recommended. Parboil 48 small shrimp, then place them in a saute pan with enough dry white wine to cover; add 1 tsp. olive oil, salt to taste, 3 ripe tomatoes peeled and finely diced, 3 parsley sprigs, 2 fennel leaves, pinch of thyme, 1 bay leaf, 3 cloves of garlic, a few peppercorns and coriander seed and 1 tsp. of saffron. Simmer for 12 min. and allow shrimp to cool in this liquor. Remove shrimp, arrange on a platter and strain liquor over them. Serve chilled.

Sturgeon a la Bariatinski—Cook fillet of sturgeon in a highly seasoned marinade; cool in this marinade. Make an aspic with some of the liquor. Mix a little of this aspic, while still warm, over ice. Coat the bottom of a dish with this aspic. When aspic has set, arrange slices of sturgeon and smoked salmon over it.

Tunafish a la Antiboise—Make a salad of potatoes and tunafish, garnish with slices of tomatoes, quartered eggs, pitted olives and serve with a mayonnaise dressing.

Vegetables

    Artichoke a la Egyptienne—Prepare small artichokes leaving the stem attached, cook in combination of oil, white wine, lemon juice, coriander seed, salt and pepper to which brunoise (carrots, celery, onions) has been added. Frozen artichokes (hearts) may be substituted for fresh.

    Artichokes a la Parisienne—Remove center from small cooked artichokes and fill with diced vegetable salad blended with mayonnaise.

    Artichoke Bottoms—Cooked artichoke bottoms may be garnished in many ways (puree of foie gras, peas, etc.).

    Cardons a l'Italienne—Marinate cardons (oyster plants) and beets in vinaigrette dressing. Arrange slices of cardons with slices of beets.

    Celery a la Grecque—See Artichokes, p. 38 hors d'oeuvre.

    Cucumbers a la Danoise —Carve barquettes out of cucumber, blanch and drain. Put herring filets and egg yolks through a fine sieve; add chopped chives, mustard, olive oil, salt and pepper to taste. Fill barquettes with mixture; decorate with shredded horseradish.

    Filets of Cucumber a la Savoyarde—Cut cucumbers in 1-in. lengths, slice chunks into ribbons, roll up again and cut rolls to form long julienne strips. Season with oil, vinegar, salt and pepper. May be seasoned with sour cream and lemon juice.

    Knob Celery Ravigotte—Julienne knob celery, parboil; chill and combine with a mixture of French dressing, mayonnaise and French mustard.

    Knob Celery a la Viennoise—Season blanched knob celery with oil, vinegar, salt, and pepper, chervil, tarragon and blend with a light mayonnaise. Decorate with anchovy filets and chopped egg yolks.

    Marinated Carrots—Peel small carrots; cook in water, white wine, vinegar, herbs, garlic, olive oil, salt and pepper. Serve chilled in cooking liquor.

    Tomato Antiboise—Cut 1½ in. diam. openings at the top of 12 medium-sized, ripe tomatoes. Using a small spoon, remove all seeds. Marinate tomatoes for 1 hour in French dressing. Remove tomatoes from marinade; dry on absorbent paper. Fill tomatoes with following mixture: 1 cup tunafish, 2 hard-cooked eggs, diced, 1 tbsp. capers, a little finely chopped parsley, chervil and tarragon. Blend with mayonnaise to which mashed anchovy has been added. Refrigerate for one hour and serve.

Salads

The following salads may be used for hors d'oeuvre:

        Tomato and Egg Salad
        Tomato and Potato Salad
        Potato and Chervil Salad
        Potato and Filet of Herring Salad
        Potato and Shrimp Salad
        Shrimp and Egg Salad
        Shrimp and Tomato Salad

Knob Celery Salad
Knob Celery and Truffle Salad
Knob Celery and Chervel Salad
Radish and Mint Vinegar Salad
Radish and Pickled Cherry Salad
Boiled Beef Salad
Cucumber Salad
Beet and Chopped Fennel Salad
Beet and Potato Salad
Mussels, Tomato and Beef Salad
Oyster and Garlic Crouton Salad
Sea Food Salad
Red Cabbage Salad
White Cabbage Salad
Lentil, White Bean, Kidney, (all dried legumes) Salads
Egg Plant Salad
Egg Plant, Tomato and Pimento Salad

Barquettes

Barquettes are small boats made of pie crust dough. They may be featured as follows:

Bagration—Chicken puree, chicken breast, truffles and aspic.

Beauharnois—Chicken and truffles, covered with mayonnaise mixed with puree of tarragon and gelatine and decorated with truffles and aspic.

Cancalaise—Mousse of fish and oysters in aspic.

Marivant—Small dice of shrimps and mushrooms with mayonnaise collee; decorate with hard-cooked egg and aspic.

Normande—Filet of sole, mussels and truffles. Coat with chaud froid, fill with lobster or shrimp and aspic.

Various fillings can be served in barquettes:

Anchovy Salpicons	Vegetables
Smoked Eel	Mussels
Compound Butter for Hors d'oeuvre	Olives
Caviar	Eggs
Cucumber	Sausages
Shrimp	Tuna
Lobster	Tomatoes
Foie Gras	Truffles
Herring	

The following may be used to decorate barquettes:

Capers	Parsley
Gherkins	Chervil
Chopped Aspic	Tarragon
Eggs	Lettuce

Egg Dishes for Hors d'Oeuvre

Hard Cooked Eggs, Spanish Style (see below)

Hard Cooked Eggs, Spanish Style (Oeufs a l'Espagnole) (Picture above)–
Make deviled stuffed eggs, place on marinated tomato slices. Refrigerate ½ hour
before serving. Julienne celery and red peppers and marinate in salt, oil and vinegar.
Arrange tomato slices with eggs in circle on platter; top with marinated celery and
red pepper strips. Garnish with stuffed green olives. Julienne of truffles may also
be added.

Boiled Eggs Moskow Style *(Oeufs a la Moscovite)*–Prepare light mousse of
lobster. Cut into circles and top with half an egg decorated with a small slice of
lobster and a small amount of caviar. Arrange these around a mountain of whipped cream mixed with caviar. Buttered toast is the perfect accompaniment.

Boiled Eggs Danish Style *(Oeufs durs a la Danoise)*–Cut hard-cooked eggs
lengthwise into halves. Remove egg yolks and stuff cavity with diced lobster salad
blended with mayonnaise and egg yolks. Serve on lettuce leaf with parsley and
radish rose.

Hard-Cooked Eggs Stuffed with Seafood *(Oeufs aux fruits de mer)*–Cut hard-
cooked eggs in half. Stuff with combination of finely diced smoked eel, anchovies,
and a few tiny shrimps mixed together with mayonnaise and lemon juice. Garnish
with chopped lobster coral and coat lightly with aspic.

Hard-Cooked Eggs Stuffed with Pheasant *(Oeufs durs a la Justice)*–Cut hard-
cooked eggs in half lengthwise. Pipe a light mousse of pheasant mixed with a small
amount of diced truffles onto the egg. Refrigerate for 15-20 minutes, then coat
with brown aspic and garnish with slice of truffle. Serve on buttered toast.

Russian Eggs *(Oeufs a la Russe)*–Hard-cooked eggs halves are topped with
tartar sauce and decorated with a small amount of caviar.

Hard-Cooked Egg, Norwegian Style *(Oeufs a la Norvegienne)*—Cut hard-cooked eggs in half lengthwise. Pipe a small amount of creamed horseradish (blend of whipped cream, grated horseradish, sugar, salt) over egg. Garnish with tiny shrimps and chopped, boiled lobster coral. Serve on lettuce leaf with radish rose and parsley.

Hard-Cooked Egg, Vegetable Salad *(Oeufs a la Jardiniere)*—Cut hard-cooked eggs in half. Remove yolks and strain through a fine sieve. Mix yolks with mayonnaise and finely diced, mixed vegetables. Fill whites with mixture. Garnish with diced chives.

Eggs Pikant *(Oeufs Piquantes)*—Cut hard-cooked eggs lengthwise. Remove yolks and puree them with anchovies, then whip in a small amount of butter. Pipe yolk mixture into whites. Decorate with slice of radish or small sour gherkins or a bit of anchovy or smoked lox.

Soft Eggs Served in Tomatoes *(Oeufs Mollets aux Tomates)*—A soft-boiled egg (4-5 min.) is placed in a marinated half tomato. Blanched vegetables cut into fine julienne are arranged over the top. A flower made of a mixture of egg yolk, tomato ketchup, and butter is piped on. A few bits of caviar represent center of flower. Serve with Sauce Tyrolienne.

Soft Boiled Eggs, Farmer's Style *(Oeufs Mollets a la Paysanne)*—Place soft boiled eggs on an oval shaped toasted crouton of white bread. Arrange a mound of diced turkey or chicken, cauliflower roses, sliced black olives, fennel which has been marinated in oil, salt, pepper and lemon juice, around eggs. Sprinkle with chopped fresh parsley.

Soft Boiled Egg Nicoise *(Oeufs a la Nicoise)*—Blanch tomatoes 30 seconds and peel. Cut in half, remove seeds. Marinate in combination of oil, vinegar, salt; top tomato half with soft boiled egg and arrange on platter with asparagus and string bean salad. Just before serving, top with Sauce Vincent and garnish with a truffle slice.

Soft Eggs on Croutons *(Oeufs Sur Crouton)*—Cut egg size croutons from white bread and toast. Set soft egg on top of crouton and arrange croutons with eggs around a salad of mussels. Dredge mussels in flour, saute in oil, then marinate for 24 hours in oil and vinegar. Add to marinated mussels, tiny shrimp, small cauliflower roses, chopped chives, parsley, dill and mustard. Let stand for 1 hour.

Poached Eggs, Sicilian Style *(Oeufs Poches a la Sicilienne)*—Blanch medium size tomatoes, remove skin, cut in half, remove seeds. Marinate with unflavored vinegar, salt, pepper and oil. Shortly before serving, strain tomatoes and stuff with a poached egg. Top egg with braised julienne of carrots, celery, mushrooms (button) and truffles (optional), coat with aspic and serve on a glass platter with watercress and mayonnaise

Poached Eggs, Washington *(Oeufs Poches a la Washington)*—Place poached egg in cornets made of ham. Decorate as desired with truffles and tarragon leaves. Cover lightly with aspic and arrange on platter or plate with timbales of ham mousse.

Poached Eggs, Gourmet Style *(Oeufs Poches a la Lucullus)*—Fill small tartlets with lobster mousse; top with poached eggs. Coat with Sauce Chantilly and garnish with truffle bits.

EGGS IN COCOTTES

With the hurried pace set for today's kitchen brigade and the shortage of labor, this method of preparing egg dishes is very welcome since it is not only fast but produces an item that is easy to serve. The appetizer can be made up ahead of time in any quantity. It is especially desirable for fast turnover restaurants.

In most cases, we fill the cocotte (small china mold) with any one of several different mousses, then top the filled cocotte with either a boiled or a poached egg. It can be decorated with truffles, olives, tongue, tarragon leaves or leeks, then the whole coated with aspic. If salad is used as an underlining for cocottes, the eggs should be coated with mayonnaise. To serve, arrange on a doily on a covered platter.

Eggs Hungarian Style *(Oeufs a la Hongroise)*–Mix cooked calves brains, finely pureed, with a little sour cream, prepared mustard, chopped herbs (chervil, parsley, tarragon), salt and paprika to make thick sauce. Insert hard cooked egg in cocotte and top with above sauce.

Frog Eggs (preparation steps pictured left to right) 1. Cut wedge out below center of egg to form mouth. 2. Slice two thin round slices of ripe olive for the eyes and put a dot of egg yolk in the center for the pupil. Dip ripe olive "eyes" in clear aspic and position on egg. 3. Cut two more slices of a ripe olive for the feet. 4. Set a triangle-shaped tongue of pimento into the mouth. 5. Roll a salami slice to form the sombrero and use a toothpick to keep sombrero in position.

Penguin Eggs (preparation steps pictured from right to left)   1. Cut about ½ in. off one end of hard boiled egg so it will stand upright. 2. Take a ripe olive and cut a small slit for the nose and insert a carrot sliver. Make eyes from small, thin pieces of carrot and position on olive. Stick a toothpick into the bottom of the olive and press it into the egg to hold head in place. 3. Cut two 1-in. strips of ripe olive for the arms; dip in clear aspic and set on egg. 4. Slice a ripe olive in half and position as shown for the feet. 5. Cut small circular pieces of olive skin to make the buttons; dip in clear aspic and position on egg. 6. A rolled slice of salami turns into a sombrero when placed on the penguin's head. A toothpick on the back of the sombrero holds it in place.

Eggs Spatini—Mix French cut green beans, cooked al dente, with spicy mayonnaise. Place in china ramekins and top with a poached egg that has been coated with mayonnaise and pistachio nuts.

Eggs German Style—Puree filet of smoked herring with butter; pipe into small ramekins. Top each with a poached egg and coat with lobster sauce.

Eggs Margaret—Make a tasty salad from raw, sliced button mushrooms and truffles, marinated in oil, lemon, salt. Fill cocotte with salad and top with poached egg. Top with mayonnaise and a sprinkling of chopped herbs, (dill and basil) and a slice of truffle.

Eggs with Asparagus Tips—Put poached egg in a cocotte; coat with Sauce Andalouse and garnish with tips of asparagus.

Tea Eggs—Boil eggs for 5-6 min., then cool and break the shell. Submerge shelled eggs in a strong tea solution, flavored with ginger and anise. Marinate for 1-2 hours, crack shells and serve.

PICKLED EGGS

Yield: 10 portions

Ingredients

Dry Mustard	1½ tsp.
Cornstarch	1½ tsp.
White Vinegar	1 pt.
Sugar	1½ to 2 tsp.
Tumeric	½ tsp.
Eggs, hard-cooked	10

Method

1. Dilute dry mustard and cornstarch in a little water.
2. Add vinegar and spices.
3. Boil 10 minutes.
4. Add shelled eggs and refrigerate

Arrangement of decorated poached salmon slices circle center ring of hard-cooked eggs stuffed with whipped cream flavored with horseradish. Color contrast is provided by row of cucumber chunks filled with mousse of salmon. Eggs and cucumbers are topped with langostino tails.

V: FOIE GRAS--
TRUFFLES--CAVIAR

Foie Gras

Nothing is new under the sun—Egyptian maps show slaves force feeding geese. In 52 B. C., Metellus Pius Scipio, Pompey's father-in-law, used to cram geese with figs to obtain fat livers which were used in various recipes. Romans also knew of foie gras which they used to eat hot with raisins.

Nowadays, it is chiefly the cities of Strasbourg and Toulouse that are known for their foie gras. French geese from the regions of Alsace and the southwest of France—after intensive force feeding which generally continues for about four weeks during the winter, become plump and their livers enlarge considerably. The livers, soft pink in color, weigh between 1 and 3 lb. A plain goose liver thus becomes a foie gras, or fat liver. The birds are fed to the limit of their capacities, but their health is watched and treatment is temporarily suspended if they exhibit signs of illness.

The first pate de foie gras was made in France, in Perigueux by a pastry chef whose name was Courtois. In 1780, a French chef by the name of Clause was the first to commercialize foie gras in Strasbourg. The pates of foie gras were prepared in various ways—in terrines, en croutes—and the taste varied considerably.

At the time, black diamonds, or truffles (described in detail on p. 62) were unknown in the region of Alsace. Francois Doyen, the chef for the Magistrate of Bordeaux, introduced truffles to Clause in 1789. As a result, the foie gras of Strasbourg reached the peak of perfection in gastronomy. All foie gras was then sold under the name "Pate de Foie Gras de Strasbourg aux Truffes du Perigord."

Since that time the manufacturing of foie gras has grown to such an extent that several factories in Strasbourg and in the southwest region of France are now exporting their delicacies all over the world.

How is foie gras prepared?

The fattened goose livers are sorted in the factories by color, size and consistency . Ten years of experience is required before a sorter can predict the quality of the finished product. A cooked foie gras may turn into a fatty, tough piece of liver with no interest for connoisseurs. Therefore, professionals are essential to insure that the best livers are selected.

The livers are cleaned by removing all sinews. They are seasoned with a special spice mixture, stuffed with truffles, then poached in madeira or cognac.

Some livers are baked in the oven. Every manufacturer has his particular method of preparation and cooking, although the results do not differ noticeably from one method to another.

Varieties of Foie Gras–Foie gras is sold fresh, in cans, or in terrines. Fresh foie gras, called Foie Gras au Naturel, will keep well or can be preserved for two to four weeks, depending upon the product, under refrigeration. Fresh foie gras has a noticeable flavor advantage over canned foie gras. The cooking method for fresh foie gras assures maximum flavor which when combined with the flavor of truffles produces a unique delicacy.

Manufacturers sell fresh foie gras under various names: Foie Gras Frais; Bloc de Foie Gras Truffe; Supreme de Foie Gras en Gelee; Melons de Foie Gras; Aspics de Foie Gras.

Legally, all of the above foie gras must contain a minimum of 75% goose liver unmixed with other ingredients, and a minimum of 5% truffles.

Foie Gras in Cans or in Terrines–Canned foie gras or terrines of foie gras may be preserved for a much longer period than the fresh foie gras. The terrines of foie gras truffe come in various sizes holding from 2 oz. to over 1 lb. of foie gras with truffles.

The earthenware jars are elaborately decorated. A good foie gras when freshly opened should be covered with a thin layer of yellowish fat. This is rendered from the liver during cooking and should have an appetizing odor.

Canned foie gras is known by several names, which are determined by the size and shape of the can: Parfait Bloc de Foie Gras Truffe; Baby Bloc de Foie Gras Truffe; Bloc de Foie Gras Truffe; Terrine de Foie Gras Truffe. Canned foie gras should meet the same standards as fresh foie gras.

Canned foie gras products are also manufactured using trimmings and cut pieces of goose livers, mixed with goose fat and pork meat. These are called puree, mousse or creme de foie gras and should contain a minimum of 50% foie gras mixed with the other ingredients.

It should be clearly understood that the product described as a "pate de foie" should not be confused with foie gras. Indeed, any French pate de foie contains 80 to 90% of pork liver with less than 1% truffles and a small amount of goose fat.

Foie gras is served as an hors d'oeuvre to begin a meal in chilled slices, decorated with a madiera aspic and accompanied by toast. It may also be served after the main course, before the cheeses or desserts; in this case, a red bordeaux, a burgundy or a champagne brut would be most appropriate as wines to serve with it. If foie gras is to be served as an hors d'oeuvre, a dry white wine such as an Alsace is acceptable.

Foie gras also finds it uses in hot cuisine, especially in sauces, and in various culinary preparations, such as Tournedos Rossini, Beef Wellington, etc.

Perhaps it has best been described by C. Gerard who said "The goose is a kind of living hothouse in which grows the supreme fruit of gastronomy."

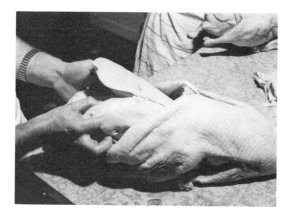

Livers from carefully fattened geese are used in the preparation of foie gras. After liver is removed, it is cleaned and all sinews are removed before it is seasoned, stuffed with truffles and poached or baked. Fresh foie gras is weighed and packed; it will keep from two to four weeks when properly refrigerated. Terrine below left is an attractive serving dish that can be refilled with contents of can.

Truffles

The black bits found in various food preparations, although called Black Diamonds, or Children of the Gods by some knowledgeable professionals, are generally known as truffles. The truffle is a fungus fruit that matures underground; however, not all underground fungi are truffles.

In the days of the Roman Empire, truffles were gathered with much effort, and eaten with much pleasure in western Europe, southern portions of the British Isles, all around the Mediterranean and through the Middle East.

Pythagoras, Theophrastus, Pliny and Orelius recorded their appreciation of truffles which they considered vegetables. Large quantities were brought to Rome from Libya and Spain. This historical fact illustrates the limitation of the scientific knowledge of that age for the far superior black truffles, now known to be abundant in Italy and France, seem not to have been much used.

Classical cooking, after providing hundreds of years of good eating, disappeared with the rest of Greek and Roman civilization; truffles also disappeared, at least from literature, and were reintroduced in Spain in the 14th Century. Since then, they have rarely been neglected.

From 1729 to 1851, the Tulasne brothers of Paris, and two Italians, Pietro Micheli and Vittorio Pico, produced magnificent studies that have been the foundation of all later scientific works on truffles.

Before 1729 the nature of truffles was unknown; they were considered to be products of the earth, since they were found under decayed leaves, branches of trees and bushes. Even through the 19th Century, truffles remained an enigma.

The real story of the growth of truffles is a strange one. The truffle, as commonly observed, is the fruit of a widely spreading system of colorless, microscopic branching threads that penetrate the soil for distances measurable in yards. These threads known as ad hyphae touch the furthest tips of the roots of trees or shrubs.

From the interaction of root and hyphae there is formed a compound structure, part plant and part fungus. However, this fungus cannot further develop without nutrient or vitamins.

When the hyphae have absorbed enough raw material from the soil and the plant they are attached to, they proceed to develop fruit, just as does an apple tree or a grape vine. The fruit which develops from a knot of hyphae is the truffle.

Before men gathered truffles, there were foxes, pigs, squirrels and deer that were very fond of the fungus. Nowadays, two animals are trained to assist men in gathering truffles. In France, hogs locate the truffle by scent; Italians have trained dogs.

What do truffles look like?

Truffles vary in color from a smooth white surface to a dark chestnut brown or black. The rind is usually a compact, resistant layer composed of thick-walled tissue. They are usually round, although some species resemble fresh ginger in shape. The interior of the truffle has elaborate folds or chambers.

The flavor of truffles also varies considerably. One highly prized variety has a touch of garlic in its flavor; those best known to cooks and generally available seem to combine in one rich particle the savor of a filbert and a properly matured cheese. The odor of this is indescribable, at least in prose.

Many kinds of truffles are known: over 30 species are found on the European

Black truffles, native to Perigord, France, are dark brown or black. Here they are being inspected before processing.

This machine brushes the dirt from the truffles gently as the first step in their preparation.

Some truffles are sold fresh in France but most of the crop is canned.

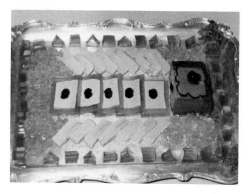

Truffles add sharp black accent to platter of pate arranged on aspic slices; chopped and cubed aspic completes arrangement of Pate Facon du Chef.

continent and 58 species in North America. Many of these specimens are so rare that they are preserved in museums.

In France, the region of Perigord, situated less than 50 miles from the Bordeaux region is well known for its crop of truffles. Perigueux is the capital of the Perigord. In culinary art, Sauce Perigueux naturally contains truffles. The heart of Italy, especially the region of Umbria, produces practically the entire output of Italian black and white truffles. White truffles are not very much in demand in Europe for they are of a lesser quality than black truffles.

Geographically, the truffle regions are relatively close to wine regions. A good year for wines will probably result in a poor year for truffles and vice versa. The year 1968 is a perfect example: A rainy summer gave excellent crops of truffles but the quality of the 1968 wine vintage is considered to be fair to poor.

The value of the truffle has always been in their ineffable odor and flavor. The consumption of truffles in the United States today is negligible. However, the U. S. Dept. of Agriculture is carrying out some experiments on black truffles and they may one day be commercially grown on American soil.

From a dietetic point of view, truffles are comparable to oysters. The composition of a truffle is: 72% water, 8-10% proteins, 4% fat, 13-15% carbohydrates and 2-5% mineral substances.

As described in Chapter V, truffles and truffle sheets are used for decorating a large variety of cold dishes.

Pate of Pheasant, sliced and covered with clear aspic for extra sparkle, is arranged with whole pears poached in white wine and garnished with mint leaves. Skewer on portion of uncut Pate adds height.

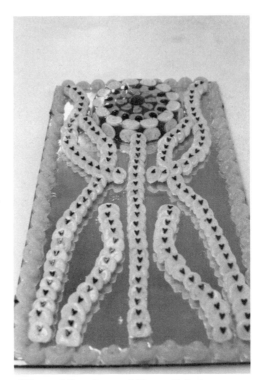

Slices of Paupiette of Dover Sole in serpentine arrangement focus attention on aspic mold containing additional slices. Roulades from which slices were cut are made by filling sole fillets with salmon mousse. Truffles are used to heighten impact of display.

Caviar

Though the word "caviar" brings the Cossack, and therefore Russia, to mind, it does not appear in the Russian language; there it is known as *"Ikra."*

Caviar is derived from the Turkish word *"Khavyah."* The precious roe was brought to Italy by the knights of the Holy Army. In Italy it was named *"Caviala,"* and became quite famous in the Court of Pope Julius II, in 1300 A. D.

From Italy, caviar was introduced to all European countries. Shakespeare mentioned it in "Hamlet," saying "T'was Caviare to the General!" Savarin's Dictionaire de Commerce, written around 1711, makes clear that it was not despised at the highest tables of France.

What is caviar?

What is this novelty that has such irresistible appeal to gourmets all over the world? It is the salted roe of a species of fish called sturgeon. Caviar can also be roe of salmon or other species. Sturgeon are caught in the Caspian or Black Sea as well as in some other locations.

Until industry and pollution came along, the sturgeon was found in rivers running into the Atlantic and Baltic, the Rhine and in North American lakes. Today all caviar comes from Russia, Iran and Rumania.

Most fish containing roe are caught at breeding time. When they leave the deep ocean waters, like salmon, they seek shallow riverbeds in order to spawn. The roe at this time is unsuitable for consumption because it is oily and unpalatable. When caught, during this period, fish are placed in submerged floating cages and, unable to find food, use up the reserve of fat that is stored in the roe, thus making the roe less oily. When roe is right for salting, the fish will be killed.

Of the varieties of sturgeon producing caviar, the Beluga is the largest, sometimes reaching 2500 pounds and producing up to 130 lb. of roe. The next size is the Ocictrova or Osetra, weighing around 400 lb., producing 40 lb. of roe. The smallest of the sturgeon family is the Sevruga which weighs 60 lb. and from which only 8 lb. of roe can be harvested.

The size of the roe, even from the same species, does not denote quality. The roe is taken from the fish, carefully sieved, all tissues and membranes are removed, and it is then steeped in a salt solution. The strength of the solution is carefully controlled as the extent of salting determines the quality of the caviar.

The amount of salt used depends on the grade of the sturgeon roe to be prepared, the weather, the condition of the roe, and the market for which it is destined. Only after the salt has been added to the Sturgeon roe does it become caviar, therefore, there is no such thing as unsalted caviar. For the U. S. market, only salt is used as a preservative; in European countries, salt and borax may be used. Caviar prepared with salt and borax tastes sweeter.

First quality caviar is known as Malosol. This word does not denote a type of caviar, as it means "little salt," and it is used in conjunction with the word Beluga, Osetra or Sevruga.

The best caviar is prepared from sturgeon caught between March and April, when the water is cool and the fish roe are firm and fresh. Fall fishing does not produce such fine quality caviar because the weather is hotter and this causes the roe to lose its firmness.

Caviar prepared in Russia or Iran and qualifying for the Malosol grade, is packed in puds weighing 41 lbs. and sent to the consumer in refrigerated containers. Non-refrigerated caviar, i.e. processed caviar, has a shelf life of about 3 months and usually comes vacuum-packed in 1 oz. to 5 oz. glass jars. After 3 months, white specks may appear; the spots are fat and crystallized salt and are absolutely harmless although not always eye-appealing.

Caviar made by one special process is known as Paiusnaya, or "pressed" caviar. After cleaning the eggs (roe) in the usual way, the caviar is packed in linen bags and hung to drain like cottage cheese. This destroys the natural shape of the roe, as they are pressed together. The caviar is then packed in puds holding 50-100 lb.

It has a much saltier taste than Malosol caviar and it looks very much like a solid mass. It is a great favorite in Russia and among connoisseurs is greatly prized.

The color of all caviar ranges between grey and black. Color is no indication of quality, although some eggs are more eye appealing than others. There are other products sold under the label of caviar, Keta (Red Caviar), made from salmon roe, and labelled as such, and the Lumpfish caviar, or whitefish caviar, which looks like caviar, but in fact is not. Lumpfish caviar is prepared, not from sturgeon, but from a fish producing yellow or green roe that is later dyed with charcoal.

All fresh caviar keeps best at a temperature between 28°F. and 32°F. Caviar should never be frozen or held below 28°F. as it will change into a soupy substance.

Caviar that has been exposed to the air should be eaten within a few days, as air will cause it to deteriorate rapidly. Any container that has been opened should be covered and kept under refrigeration.

Malosol caviar should always be served with toast and unsalted butter. A lesser quality can be served with lemon, toast and butter. Salty caviar should be served with a garnish of finely chopped white onion, chopped egg white, chopped egg yolk, lemon, toast and butter. Sometimes, caviar can be served with "blinis," (little pancakes made of fermented batter of buckwheat) and topped with sour cream. A mixture of whipped cream and caviar can also be made to be served in conjunction with blinis. Caviar should always be served on ice, as room temperature can alter its taste very rapidly.

THERE IS NO SUBSTITUTE FOR GENUINE CAVIAR!!!!!!

(Some of the above information was supplied through the courtesy of the Romanoff Caviar Company).

Caviar even when served simply requires these accompaniments: lemon, butter, chopped, hard cooked
egg white and toast points. Here to
provide the elegance caviar deserves,
butter balls are especially shaped,
lemon halves are cut with jagged
edges and garnished with parsley
and chopped egg is served in wine
glass.

An ice carving provides an attention-getting base for a
caviar set-up. Chopped onion, chopped egg white, toast
points, lemon wedges and chopped egg yolks are suggested accompaniments for caviar.

VI: FORCEMEAT

A basic element in the preparation of many specialties, farce or forcemeat, made of various seasoned ground foods, is widely used in garde manger preparation. Forcemeat or farce is the base for the preparation of pates, terrines, galantines and ballotines. Farces are also used to stuff or garnish meat, eggs, fish, poultry, game, vegetables. They are utilized in the preparation of French specialties such as quenelles and mousses.

Fish farces used in cooking are usually combined with panadas (see description below). The amount of panada added to a farce is equal to one-half of the weight of the farce. Most farces prepared with meat, poultry or game are bound together with eggs or egg whites. Farces used for pates and galantines are seasoned with a special spice mixture described in Chapter VII.

Panadas—A panada is a binding agent made of flour, bread or other starch products. Fish quenelle forcemeats contain panadas, and other fine forcemeats, especially chicken or veal, contain a panada as a substitute for eggs. In some cases, both a panada and eggs may be called for.

Several versions of panadas are used:

PANADA NO. 1 - FLOUR PANADA
Boil 1 cup of milk with 2 tbsp. butter. Add 2½ oz. flour.
Mix well with a wooden spoon until mixture is dry.
This panada should be incorporated in the forcemeat when completely cold.

Flour panada is used for: Pike quenelle forcemeat
Salmon quenelle forcemeat
Sole quenelle forcemeat
Veal and chicken forcemeat

PANADA NO. 2 - BREAD PANADA
Soak 8 oz. of white pullman bread without crusts in
10 oz. of milk. Mix well until bread is soaked.

Season with salt, pepper and nutmeg. Work mixture on fire until dry.

This panada is used cold in fish forcemeat or in veal and poultry forcemeat.

PANADA NO. 3 - POTATO PANADA

Combine 8 oz. of sliced boiled potatoes with 10 oz. milk. Season with salt, pepper and nutmeg. Cook on low fire for 15 to 20 mins.

Mix well to obtain a smooth paste. This panada is added to forcemeat when warm. It is used with white meat and fish forcemeats, i.e. capon, haddock.

The above three panadas are still used as binding agents for forcemeats. The modern chefs are adopting the flour panada more than any other. It brings lightness and body to the forcemeats in which it is used.

FISH QUENELLE FORCEMEAT FOR FISH PATE OR QUENELLES

Yield: 2 lbs.

Ingredients

Raw Fish	14 oz.
Panada No. 1 or No. 2	5 oz.
Egg Whites	3 to 4
Heavy Cream	1½ cups
Salt, White Pepper, Nutmeg	

Method

Remove skin and bones from fish. Mince remaining fish very fine. In a large bowl, placed over a bowl of ice, pound cold panada into minced fish. Add egg white and heavy cream. Season with salt, pepper, nutmeg.

FORCEMEAT USED IN GARDE MANGER

1. Game or Poultry Forcemeat for Galantines, Pates, Terrines.

Yield: 2½ lb.

Ingredients

Pheasant Meat, Chicken, or Duck Meat, etc.	8 oz.
Lean Veal	3½ oz.
Lean Pork	3½ oz.
Fresh Pork Fat	15 oz.
Eggs	2
Brandy	½ cup
Salt	2 tsp.
Pate Spices	1 tsp.

Method

Dice all meat and pork fat. Put through a meat grinder, two or three times. Add remaining ingredients. Mix well and keep cold until ready to use.

2. Pork or Sausage forcemeat used for galantines.

Combine equal quantities of pork and fresh pork fat. Grind very fine, using a meat grinder.

VEAL OR POULTRY QUENELLE FORCEMEAT

Yield: 12 oz.

Ingredients

Raw Veal or Poultry Meat	6 oz.
Salt	1/2 tsp.
Pate Seasoning	1/3 tsp.
Panada No. 2	3 oz.
Melted Butter	1 oz.
Egg	1
Egg Yolk	1
Heavy Cream	1 tbsp.

Method

Remove sinews and fat from meat. Dice meat, then put through grinder several times, using the finest blade. Season with salt and pate seasonings.

Mix with cold panada until smooth, stirring constantly with a wooden spoon. Add the melted butter, egg, egg yolk, and cream.

Test a small piece of forcemeat by poaching in boiling water. If too soft, add an extra egg.

This forcemeat is shaped into quenelles (dumplings) and they are generally poached. Quenelles are served hot or cold with an appropriate sauce.

Truffles or pistachio nuts may be added to the forcemeat to enhance the flavor and add color to the quenelles.

GRATIN FORCEMEAT NO. 1

Gratin Forcemeat is cooked forcemeat, which is usually added to a raw forcemeat. A Gratin Forcemeat contains veal, pork or chicken liver and various vegetables which are all cooked and ground to give an additional flavor to the final combination.

Yield: 1 lb.

Ingredients

Fresh Pork Fat, diced	8 oz.
Veal, diced	8 oz.
Chicken or Veal Liver	8 oz.
Shallots, chopped	1 oz.
Truffles	1 oz.
Mushroom Trimmings	1 oz.
Thyme	1/3 tsp.
Bayleaf	1 to 2
Salt	1 oz.
Pepper	1/2 oz.
Pate Spice	1/2 tsp.
Cognac	1/2 oz.
Madeira	1/2 oz.
Demiglaze	1/2 oz.
Egg Yolks	2
Butter	1 oz.

Method

Saute diced fresh pork fat. Remove from saute pan. In remaining fat, saute the veal and liver, add shallots, spices, seasonings and herbs. Remove all ingredients from pan.

Deglaze pan with cognac and madeira; add demi glaze. Combine all ingredients and allow to cool. When cool, pass through the fine blade of a meat grinder. Mix in 2 egg yolks and a few pieces of fresh butter. Then run through a blender.

GAME GRATIN FORCEMEAT

Ingredients

Fresh Pork Fat	1/3
Game Liver	1/3
Game Meat	1/3

Method

Follow preceding recipe for Gratin Forcemeat.

GRATIN FORCEMEAT NO. 2 FOR CROUTONS OR BARQUETTES

Yield: 1 lb. 10 oz.

Ingredients

Fresh Pork Fat, chopped	8 oz.
Chicken Livers	1 lb.
Shallots, finely chopped	2
Mushroom Trimmings, chopped	1/2 cup
Salt	1/2 to 1 oz.
Pepper	1/3 tsp.
Pate Spices	1/2 tsp.
Thyme	1/3 tsp.
Bay Leaf	1

Method

Melt fresh pork fat in saute pan and saute the chicken livers in hot fat. Do not cook livers well done; remove from pan when medium rare. In the same pan, saute shallots and mushrooms, add seasoning, and spices. Combine all ingredients. Cool and blend in a blender. Then work mixture through a wire sieve, if available. Refrigerate and cover with parchment paper.

LIVER DUMPLING FORCEMEAT

Yield: 3 lb. 4 oz.

Ingredients

Pork, Calf or Chicken Liver	17-2/3 oz.
Lean Pork	17-2/3 oz.
White Bread, without crusts, moistened in milk	7 oz.
Eggs, whole	2 to 3
Leek, white part	1
Shallots, chopped	3-1/2 oz.
Dry Marjoram	1/2 tsp.
Fresh Chives, chopped	2 tsp.
Parsley	1 tsp.
Salt	1 to 2
Pepper	1/2 tsp.

Method

Mince liver, meat, white bread. Saute leeks and shallots. Season, mix together, add eggs. Poach in chicken stock.

MOUSSELINE FORCEMEAT (FARCE)

Yield: 3 lb.

Ingredients

Lean Veal	2 lb.
Egg Whites	2 to 3
Salt	1/2 to 1 oz.
Pepper	1/2 oz.
Heavy Cream	3/4 pt.

Method

Grind thoroughly chilled meat. Combine in food chopper with egg whites and seasonings. Add cream.

NOTE: Keep cold at all times.

Gratin forcemeat used to fill breast cavity in this Capon Roti was covered with white chaud froid and decorated with tomato roses placed on celery leaves. Carrot flowers add color to presentation.

VII: PATES-TERRINES

To many devotees of fine food, the pate sets the standard for foods to come. As defined by the French, a pate is prepared by enclosing a filling of meat, fish, vegetables, or fruit in a pastry case that has a bottom and a top. However, basically, the word "pate" should apply only to meat or fish preparations enclosed in a dough and baked in the oven. In addition, the term is also used to describe any preparation put into an earthenware dish that has been lined with thin layers of fresh pork fat and is then baked in the oven. The correct name for this type of dish is terrine, although common usage has applied the term "pate" to these preparations which are always served cold.

Pates

A large variety of ingredients and garnishes are used in pates; the most common are liver, truffles, various forcemeats and seasonings. The use of goose liver brings a particular flavor to pates. Chicken livers may be substituted and should be soaked in milk for 24 hours. (For more details on the use of goose liver, see Chapter V on Foie Gras.)

Europe has not only the advantage of having fresh goose liver, but also fresh aromatic truffles which play a major part in preparing pates and terrines. However, canned truffles can be used when fresh truffles are not available.

How to Work with Livers—It is essential to handle livers with care. Remove gall bladder, all veins, blood clots, if any, and surrounding skin. Then wash livers in cold water and soak in milk for 24 hours, after which they should be thoroughly drained, seasoned and kept refrigerated.

How to Work with Truffles—Whether fresh or canned, truffles should be thoroughly washed and stored in lightly salted water. Before using, peel and slice, dice or cut into julienne, then marinate in sherry or port wine.

How should forcemeat or farce be prepared for pates and terrines?

Forcemeat or farce is a ground meat mixture that can be seasoned either highly or subtly. Generally it is composed of the following combination:

4 parts of fresh pork fat
3 parts of lean pork or veal
1 part of goose or chicken liver

The seasonings vary according to the recipe.

The forcemeat is prepared by grinding all of the above-mentioned ingredients through the fine plate of a meat grinder or a food chopper. It should be mixed well and precautions should be taken to keep all ingredients cold. (35-40°F.) One whole egg or ¼ oz. of commercial egg albumen per pound of forcemeat is added as a binding agent.

How to Blend the Seasonings—Before adding the seasonings to the forcemeat, the herbs and spices should be combined in a blender until pulverized, then put through a wire sieve and kept in a tightly covered container to preserve the aroma. Only dried spices and herbs should be used.

Here are two spice and herb combinations that can be blended into a forcemeat:

SEASONINGS FOR FORCEMEAT

1) As listed by master chef August Escoffier:

Bay Leaf	1-1/4 oz.
Thyme	3/4 oz.
Coriander	3/4 oz.
Cinnamon	1 oz.
Nutmeg	1-1/2 oz.
Cloves	1 oz.
Ginger	3/4 oz.
Mace	3/4 oz.
Black Pepper	1-1/4 oz.
Cayenne Pepper	1/4 oz.
White Pepper	1-1/4 oz.

2) As listed by the authors:

Cloves	1/2 oz.
Ginger	1/2 oz.
Nutmeg	1/2 oz.
Paprika	1/2 oz.
Basil	1/3 oz.
Black Pepper	1/3 oz.
White Pepper	1/3 oz.
Bay Leaf	1/6 oz.
Thyme	1/2 oz.
Marjoram	1/6 oz.

NOTE: 1/6 oz. of pate spice is used per pound of forcemeat.

DOUGH FOR PATES

Yield: 10 lb.

Ingredients

Bread Flour	5 lb.
Butter	28 oz.
Salt	1 tsp.
Olive Oil	8 oz.
Egg Yolks	12
Ice Cold Water	1 qt.

Method

Combine flour, butter and salt. Mix together. Add remaining ingredients and mix well until a smooth paste is formed. The dough should then rest for 5 hours.

Preparation of Pate en Croute

1. Select a hinged mold, either round, oval, or rectangular (the type of mold will depend on the nature of the pate); oil mold carefully.

2. Take 3/4 of the dough and roll it out with a rolling pin to about 1/8 in. in thickness.

3. Cut dough into 4 pieces. (See illustration) Use 1½ lb. of dough per mold.

4. Press dough all around the walls and into the bottom of the mold. The dough should overlap the edge of the mold about ½ inch and this overlapping dough will later be used to seal the lid.

5. Line the bottom and walls of the mold with thin slices of fat back or slices of bacon, then cover evenly with a thin layer of an appropriate forcemeat.

6. Place the ingredients in the mold as indicated in the recipe. The ingredients put in the center are usually an arrangement of various meats (veal, pork, poultry, etc.) and truffles that have been marinated in brandy and will provide a decorative center for the finished pate. The decorative center or garnish should be placed in the center of the mold and sealed with a small quantity of forcemeat. Fill the mold with the remaining forcemeat and cover with a thin slice of fresh pork fat.

7. Roll out remaining dough and cut into the same shape as the top of the mold. Moisten the edge of the dough with an egg wash and seal on to the top of the mold. Trim neatly with a knife.

8. Decorate the top of the mold with fancy shapes cut from the dough trimmings. Brush with egg wash. In the center of the mold, make a circular hole called a chimney, to allow steam to escape while the pate is baking. A piece of parchment paper rolled into a tube should be placed in the chimney.

How to Bake a Pate—The baking method, unless otherwise indicated in a specific recipe, is the same for all pates. To bake a pate:

1. Preheat oven to 400°–425°F. Bake pate for 10 to 15 minutes, or until dough is golden brown.

2. Reduce temperature to 325°–350°F., then bake pate until well done.

3. To test the doneness of the pate, insert a tester through the chimney all the way into the pate; leave it there briefly; if the tester comes out dry and evenly warm, the pate is ready.

4. Take pate out of the oven and allow to cool for one hour before refrigerating. When thoroughly chilled, fill the cavity of the pate with aspic.

TURKEY LIVER PATE

Yield: 12 portions
Ingredients

Turkey Livers	2 lb.
Onion, medium	½
Butter	1 to 2 oz.
Heavy Cream	7 oz.
White Pepper	1 tsp.
Allspice	½ tsp
Ginger	½ tsp.
Brandy	1 oz.
Salt	½ to 1 oz.
Whole Eggs	3
Flour	4 oz.
Fresh Pork Fat to line mold	7 to 8 oz.

Method
Prepare the livers as directed in the section "How to work with livers," p. 73.

Dice onion fine and saute in butter. Combine livers with onions, heavy cream, spices, brandy and salt. Mix to a fine paste in an electric blender. Add eggs and flour and mix all ingredients.

Pour liquid forcemeat into a mold lined with slices of fresh pork fat. Cover with thin slices of fresh pork fat and then with aluminum foil. Puncture a hole in foil and bake pate in a waterbath for one hour at 400°F.

CHICKEN LIVER PATE

Yield: 12-14 portions
Ingredients
FORCEMEAT

Fresh Pork Fat	16 oz.
Chicken Livers, prepared as described, p. 73	4 oz.
Lean Pork	12 oz.
Salt	1/2 to 1 oz.
Pate Spice	1/3 tsp.
GARNISH	
Chicken Liver, prepared as described, p. 73	10 oz.
Truffles (optional)	2 oz.
Salt	pinch
Egg White	1/2 oz.

Method
Cut all meats into cubes, add salt and pate spice and cool. Grind mixture through fine blade of food chopper (see "How to Make a Forcemeat" p. 73) and mix well.

Drain livers well, insert pieces of truffle and pork fat in livers and season with salt.

Prepare pate mold (see "How to Make a Pate," p. 75); line prepared mold to about ½ in. thickness with forcemeat; fill center with layers of liver; between each layer of liver spread a little egg albumen. Finish pate as described on preceding page and bake 1-1½ hours in 325°F. oven.

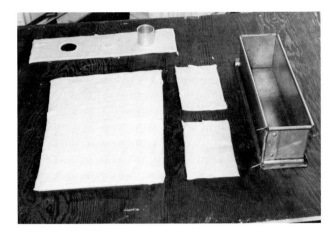

HOW TO PREPARE
A PATE EN CROUTE

1. *Select a hinged mold, either round, oval or rectangular, depending on type of pate, and oil it carefully. Roll out pate dough and cut four pieces as shown here.*

2. *Fold large piece of dough as shown at left in picture, place in the mold, allowing about 1 in. of dough to overlap on each side.*

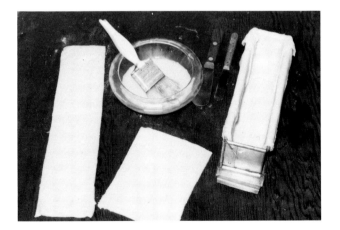

3. *Brush dough with egg wash and fold one of the square pieces of dough over end of mold; allow about 1-1½ in. of dough to overlap and press overlapping layers of dough together to seal. Repeat procedure for the opposite end of the pate mold.*

(cont.)

HOW TO PREPARE A PATE (cont.):

4. *Cover bottom and sides of dough-lined mold with appropriate forcemeat, leaving room in the center for the ingredients that will serve as garnish.*

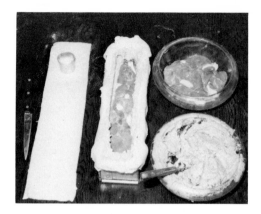

5. *Place prepared garnish (dotted with truffles, if desired) in the center and cover with remaining forcemeat. Here pieces of liver provide the centerpiece for the pate.*

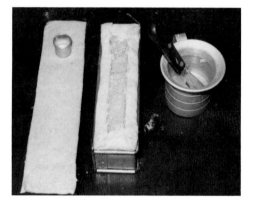

6. *Fold extra dough in over the forcemeat and wash with egg wash. Note round cutter on dough set aside to top pate. It will be used to cut holes for escaping steam.*

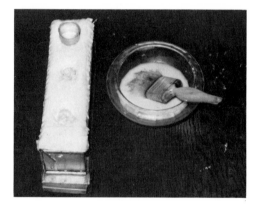

7. *Cover with remaining piece of dough and press down on all sides to seal. Cut holes in dough cover to permit steam to escape. Brush top of dough with egg wash.*

HOW TO SLICE A PATE EN CROUTE

1. To slice pate en croute, arrange a mise en place, using a pan of water and a carving knife.

2. To start slicing, slide knife forward as shown.

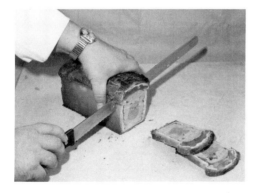

3. Continue slicing, bringing end of knife nearest you down slightly.

4. Cut straight down the rest of the way through the loaf, sawing gently back and forth to complete slices.

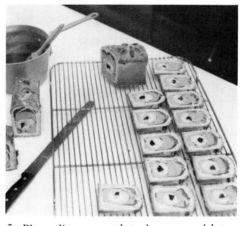

5. Place slices on rack to be arranged later. Decorate an unsliced piece of pate en croute as focal point of presentation.

PATE OF CHICKEN
(See picture below left)

For this recipe follow the directions in section "How to Prepare a Pate," p. 75 using the following ingredients:

Yield: 12-14 portions

Ingredients

FORCEMEAT

Chicken Meat	1 lb.
Fresh Pork Fat	1 lb.
Egg Albumen	½ oz.
Salt	½ to 1 oz.
Pepper	½ tsp.

GARNISH

The garnish consists of a small dice of:

Chicken Breast	1 oz.
Chicken Livers	1 oz.
Truffles (optional)	1 oz.
Smoked Beef Tongue	1 oz.
Fresh Pork Fat	1 oz.
Pistachio Nuts	1 oz.

Pate of Chicken—Pate is centered with a truffle slice in breast of chicken surrounded by smoked tongue. Stuffed tomatoes, carrot and potato roses complete the arrangement.

Pate of Veal and Ham is shown here garnished with wedges cut from orange rind filled with orange gelatin. Recipe for Ham and Veal Pate appears top of facing page.

HAM AND VEAL PATE
(See picture facing page)

Yield: 12-14 portions
Ingredients
FORCEMEAT

	Lean Veal	7½ oz.
	Lean Pork	7½ oz.
	Fresh Pork Fat	15 oz.
	Salt	½ to 1 oz.
	Pepper	½ tsp.
GARNISH		
	Veal	4 oz.
	Fresh Pork Fat	4 oz.
	Ham	4 oz.

Method
Prepare forcemeat from the above mentioned ingredients as directed in: 'How to Make a Forcemeat."

Cut meats for garnish into ½ in. square bars and saute lightly; season with salt and pepper.

Prepare pate as described on page 75.

Fill with forcemeat and layers of garnish, finishing with a layer of forcemeat.

HAM PATE

Yield: 12-14 portions
Ingredients
FORCEMEAT

	Fresh Pork Fat	1 lb.
	Fresh Lean Pork	1 lb.
	Salt	1 to 1½ oz.
	English Mustard	1 tsp.
	Pepper	½ tsp.
GARNISH		
	Canned Ham, cut into large rectangles	4 oz.
	Truffles, cut into large julienne	1 oz.

Method
Follow the procedure indicated under section titled: "How to Prepare a Pate," using above ingredients.

Rooster Baked in Crust a la Gabriela Kriens—Jockey cap garnishes used with this platter are prepared as follows:
1. Marinate small artichoke bottoms and top them with liver pate or egg mixture. 2. Cut a hard cooked egg in half, then cut each half into 4 quarters. Blanch a tomato, cut in half and cut each half into 4 sections. 3. Place two egg and 2 tomato sections alternately around mound of liver pate. 4. Press a small ripe olive into center at top of cap. (See recipe below.)

ROOSTER A LA GABRIELA KRIENS
(The Recipe of a Country Lady)

Yield: 20 portions

Ingredients

Rooster or Chicken, 2-3 lb.	1
Salt	½ tsp.
Forcemeat (use forcemeat from page 73, Chicken Liver Pate)	
Chicken Liver, larded with fresh pork fat and soaked in madeira wine for 15-20 min.	8 oz.
Egg Albumen	¼ oz.
Pate Dough (see page 75)	2 to 2½ lbs.
Madeira Aspic	to fill

Method

Debone the rooster as for a galantine (p. 94) but leave the lower leg bone untouched. Sprinkle salt over bird. Then spread forcemeat ½ in. thick all over the meat and place the prepared livers in the center of the bird. Sprinkle 1/4 oz. of egg albumen over the livers, then fold the rooster together and place cut side down on a piece of pastry that has been rolled to about 1/3 in. thickness. Wrap dough around bird, decorate, cut one chimney. Coat wrapped rooster with eggwash. Bake like a pate; cool and fill with madeira aspic.

GAME PATE
PATE OF PHEASANT   (See picture, p. 85)

Yield: 3 lb. 4 oz. or 17 portions

Ingredients

Smoked Beef Tongue, cut into bars	5 oz.
Truffles, cut into julienne	2 oz.
Madeire Wine, to marinate	
Breasts of Pheasant, medium size	4
Pheasant Meat	10½ oz.
Lean Veal	3½ oz.
Lean Pork	3½ oz.
Gratin Forcemeat (see recipe below)	11½ oz.

Method of Preparation for Pate:

Marinate tongue and truffles in madeira wine.

Bard the pheasant breasts and saute lightly. Finely grind pheasant meat, veal and pork; add seasonings and mix with gratin forcemeat (recipe below).

Line mold with dough, following steps indicated under section titled: "How to Prepare a Pate" p. 75. Fill mold using half of the forcemeat, place the pheasant breasts, pieces of tongue and truffles in a line along the center of the mold; add remaining forcemeat. Seal dough lid over mold. Make foil chimney. Bake for 1½ hours.

When cool, fill with aspic through the chimney

GRATIN FORCEMEAT NO. 3

Yield: 1 lb. 5 oz.

Ingredients

Fresh Pork Fat	5-1/2 oz.
Veal, diced	5-1/2 oz.
Chicken or Pheasant Livers	5-1/2 oz.
Shallots, chopped	1 tsp.
Thyme	1 pinch
Bay Leaf	1
Pate Spice	1/3 tsp.
Salt	1/2 oz.
Pepper	pinch
Brandy	1 oz.
Madeira Wine	1 oz.
Demi Glaze	2 oz.
Egg Yolks	2

Method

Saute the fresh pork fat, remove from pan and set aside. Saute veal and livers over high heat until brown. Remove fat. Add fresh pork fat, shallots, and seasonings. Deglaze pan with brandy and madeira. Add demi glaze and reduce.

Allow the mixture to cool, then grind twice through the meat grinder. Fold eggs into the mixture. Refrigerate

PATE DE GIBIER SIMPLE
(Simple Game Pate)

Yield: 10-12 portions

Ingredients

Hare or Venison	2 lb.
Fresh Pork Fat	1 lb.
Egg Yolks	2
Stock, reduced, rich game	1 tbsp.
Truffles, chopped	1 to 2
Parmesan Cheese, grated	1 to 1-1/2 oz.
Salt	1/2 to 1 oz.
Pepper	1/3 to 1/2 tsp.
Pate Spice	heavy pinch
Aspic Croutons	10 to 12

Method

Trim hare or venison, remove skin and bones. Dice pork fat and grind into a paste. Mix all ingredients well, adding egg yolks and game stock while mixing.

Fold in the truffles and parmesan cheese and marinate 5-10 minutes.

Line a mold with fat back or bacon. Fill with forcemeat and bake in a water-bath for 1 hour at 400°F. Cool and serve with aspic croutons.

PATE OF HARE

Yield: 16-18 portions

Ingredients

Hare	1
Lean Veal	10½ oz.
Lean Pork	10½ oz.
Fresh Pork Fat	21 oz.
Salt	1 to 2 oz.
Pate Spice	½ oz.
GARNISH	
Fresh Pork Fat, cut into strips	5 oz.
Ham, cut into strips	4 oz.
Brandy	1 oz.

Method

Bone the hare. Remove skin and bones from the saddle and legs. Save saddle and filet for later use as a garnish. Grind leg meat, veal, pork and fresh pork fat through the fine blade. Work mixture into a fine paste and season to taste.

Lard the saddle meat and filet with thin strips of fresh pork fat; saute lightly. Marinate garnishes in brandy.

Line mold with dough and slices of fresh pork fat. Place half of the forcemeat in mold. Arrange all garnishes in center and then add the remaining forcemeat Set dough lid into place. Make chimney. Bake for 1½ hours. When cold, fill with aspic, flavored with cognac.

Pate of Pheasant (see recipe, facing page)—Flavorful center in this pate is an arrangement of pheasant breasts, pieces of tongue and truffles. Colorful tomato wedges, mushrooms and parsley spark platter

Saddle of Venison en croute (left, see pate en croute, p. 75)—Center filling consists of chicken livers with truffles, surrounded by fillet of venison, then a layer of pork fat all encased in pate dough. Slices are arranged around an uncut section of the pate en croute and platter is garnished with apples poached in white wine and topped with apricot-glazed pineapple.

Three-dimensional diamond designs made of egg, tomato and truffle-colored aspic sheets highlight slices of turkey liver pate. Apple circles poached in white wine and topped with a black cherry and an almond slice offer color and flavor contrast.

Saddle of Reindeer en croute (see directions for pate en croute)—To prepare, first debone saddle of reindeer. Butterfly fillets and roll around pate of liver. Next, roll into parchment paper and tie to hold in position. Brown roll for 8-12 min. Cool. Then roll pate dough around it and bake.

Fish Pates—Fish pates are made in the same fashion as any of the meat pates although the forcemeat, called quenelle forcemeat, contains different ingredients. The most appropriate fish to be used is pike or salmon. Lemon or Boston sole are good substitutes.

QUENELLE FORCEMEAT FOR FISH

RECIPE NO. 1
Yield: 2 lb.
Ingredients

Panada (recipe below)	5 oz.
Raw Fish	14 oz.
Egg Whites	3 to 4
Heavy Cream	1½ cups
Salt	½ to 1 oz.
White Pepper	½ tsp.
Nutmeg	pinch
PANADA	
Milk	1 cup
Flour	2½ oz.
Butter	2 tbsp.

Method

Remove skin and bones from fish. Mince very fine. In a large bowl over ice, blend minced fish and cold panada. Add egg whites, heavy cream and seasonings. Prepare panada by heating milk and butter; add flour; mix well and cool.

RECIPE NO. 2
Yield: 7 portions
Ingredients

Raw Fish	8 oz.
Salt	1/2 oz.
Pepper	1/3 tsp.
Panada (see recipe No. 1)	5 oz.
Butter, melted	1 oz.
Egg	1
Egg Yolk	1
Heavy Cream	1 tbsp.

Method

Remove skin and bones from fish. Dice and put through a grinder several times, using the finest blade. Season with salt and pepper. Mix with cold panada until smooth. Add melted butter, egg, egg yolk and cream.

Test a small piece of forcemeat by poaching in boiling water. If it does not hold its shape, add an extra egg.

PATE OF SALMON NO. 1

Yield: 10 portions

Ingredients

Salmon Quenelle Forcemeat	1 lb.
Salt	1/3 oz.
Nutmeg	pinch
Salmon Fillet, cut into strips and marinated in white wine	8 oz.
White Truffle Paste	2 oz.
Black Truffles, diced	1 oz.

Method

Follow the procedure for "How to Prepare a Pate." Alternate layers of forcemeat, seasoned with salt and nutmeg, with layers of salmon fillet and truffles. Fill mold only ¾ full, as pate will increase in volume while cooking. Cover with dough. Decorate, cut chimney and bake at 350°F. for 1 hour.

PATE OF SALMON NO. 2

Use the same ingredients as Recipe No. 1.

Slice salmon fillet into thin slices and stuff with the forcemeat to form long roulades. Alternate layers of forcemeat and roulades in pate mold. Set dough lid into place. Bake 40-50 minutes at 350°F.

PATE OF FILLET OF SOLE

Yield: 14 portions

Ingredients

Small Fillets of Sole (grey or lemon sole)	2 lb.
Quenelle Forcemeat	1½ lb.
Black Truffles, diced	1 oz.
Pistachio Nuts	2 oz.
Salt	1/2 oz.
White Pepper	1/3 oz.
Egg Albumen	1 oz.

Method

Open fillet of sole out flat, spread prepared forcemeat over surface and roll up. Allow to rest 10-15 minutes.

Place in a mold lined with dough, alternating forcemeat, fish roulades and garnishes. Make chimney.

Bake for 45 minutes. Cool and fill mold through chimney with aspic, (either veal or fish).

Terrines

Terrines contain the same ingredients as pates. The only difference is that they are cooked in a fireproof earthenware or china dish also called a terrine and are always served cold. Pictured on page 90 are some of the dishes most frequently used in preparing terrines. Both the dish and the contents are called terrines. (See terrine ready for service, facing page.)

How do you prepare a terrine?

The same kinds of ground meats are used as in liver pate. Directions for preparing one kind of terrine follow; there are other varieties.

1. Line terrine evenly with forcemeat.

2. Arrange prepared chicken livers in center of mold and dot with truffles.

3. Shape remaining forcemeat into a dome and cover with slices of bacon or thinly sliced fresh pork fat.

4. Cover terrine with lid and bake in a waterbath. A terrine containing 2 lb. of forcemeat will take 1 to 1½ hours to bake at 400°F.

5. When the terrine is cooked, allow to cool for 10 minutes. Then fill with a mixture of ½ chicken fat and ½ pork fat. Refrigerate. A terrine prepared in this manner may be stored up to 5 weeks. If desired, butter can be substituted for chicken fat and lard.

6. When terrine is ready to be served, take out of the dish. Remove all fat; put back into the dish and cover with a thin layer of gelee or aspic. Serve in terrine.

**HOW TO PREPARE
A TERRINE**

All of the items needed to prepare a terrine are assembled in this mise en place. Shown from top to bottom, left to right: dish for terrine, liver, forcemeat, fresh pork fat, spices, Madeira wine, salt, water for rinsing spatula.

First put layer of forcemeat around inside of terrine.

Next, place chicken livers in center of forcemeat.

FAMILY STYLE TERRINE

(These terrines may be made of veal, chicken, rabbit or game.)

Yield: 8-9 portions

Ingredients

Chicken Meat, diced	12 oz.
Lean Veal, diced	12 oz.
Fresh Pork Fat, diced	10 oz.
Salt and Pepper	½ oz.
Pate Spices	pinch
Onion, finely chopped	1
Parsley	1 oz.
Chervil	1 oz.
Madeira or White Wine	1 oz.

Method

Saute meat until browned but do not cook completely. Combine meat with spices, herbs and seasonings.

Pour into terrine, add wine. Cover and allow to rest 2-3 hours. Bake terrine in waterbath for 1-1½ hours. When cold, cover with aspic.

Then cover chicken livers with forcemeat mounding it in center.

Arrange slices of fresh pork fat to cover all of forcemeat. Terrine is now ready to bake.

When terrine has chilled, take out of dish and remove all fat; put back in dish and cover with thin layer of aspic.

Terrine Family Style is ready for service when garnished with tiny mushrooms, tomato rose and tarragon leaves. (See recipe above)

RILLETTES
(This is a French regional specialty from Tours)

Yield: 4 lb.
Ingredients

Pork Shoulder	5 lb.
Pate Spices	1 tsp.
Salt	1 tsp.
Black Pepper, ground	½ tsp.
Bay Leaves	2

Method

Bone pork shoulder and separate fat from meat. Cut the fat and meat into large julienne. Season with spice blend, pepper and bay leaf.

Cook in heavy pot over a very low heat for 4 hours or until meat falls apart.

Strain fat and reserve. Crush meat into coarse fibers with fork. Press into an earthenware dish and pour strained fat over the meat. Let cool.

When cold, cover with foil. This dish may be kept for several months.

CHICKEN LIVER PARFAIT

Yield:10-12 portions
Ingredients

Chicken Livers, soaked in milk	1-1/2 lb.
Port Wine	1/2 oz.
Pate Spice	1/3 tsp.
Salt	1/2 oz.
Fresh Pork Fat, to line mold	6 to 7 oz.
Egg Albumen	1/2 oz.

Method

Marinate livers in port wine, pate spice and salt for 20 min. Drain livers well and put in terrine lined with slices of fresh pork fat. Sprinkle a little egg albumen between each layer of livers. Cover livers with chicken fat and cover the terrine either with a lid of dough or aluminum foil. Bake in terrine in a water bath for 1½-2 hours at 400°F. Cool overnight. Then remove all fat and press the liver back into the terrine. Garnish with truffle slices and cover with madeira gelee.

Dishes that hold terrines are also called terrines and come in a variety of shapes.

VIII: GALANTINES

Galantines, which are always served cold either as an entree or an a la carte item or attractively displayed on buffet tables, are made of boneless poultry or meat and stuffed with forcemeat, then shaped symmetrically and cooked in a rich stock.

The word "galantine" comes from the old French word "galine," meaning chicken. There was a time when galantines were made only of poultry; today, galantines are prepared using a variety of meats or fish, such as salmon, eel, suckling pig, etc. . .

How does a Ballotine differ from a Galantine?

In a list of French culinary terms, the word "ballotine" might possibly be confused with "galantine," since a ballotine is prepared with boneless meat, poultry or fish, stuffed, rolled and shaped into a "ballot." However, most ballotines are baked or braised and served as hot entrees; for example, Ballotine of Chicken, Ballotine of Veal or Lamb Shoulder. What distinguishes the Ballotine from the Galantine is whether the item is served hot (ballotine) or cold (galantine).

BASIC RECIPE FOR GALANTINE

(This recipe can be adjusted to provide whatever amount of galantine is required.)

A basic recipe for most galantines requires a forcemeat consisting of:

Lean Veal	1 part
Lean Pork	1 part
Fresh Pork Fat	2 parts
Eggs, for each lb. of forcemeat,	1
Seasonings and Brandy	

The garnish for a galantine may consist of several of the following ingredients: truffles, pistachio nuts, diced pork fat, beef or veal tongue, liver, fillet of breast of capon and cooked ham. The black of the truffles, the green of the pistachio nuts, and the white of the fresh pork fat are the most colorful ingredients used in a galantine.

Butter sea horse presides over display of sliced Galantine of Red Snapper. Contrasting with Galantine are zucchini slices topped with cherry tomatoes stuffed with cream cheese. Zucchini slices are blanched and marinated. Egg wedges topped with slices of stuffed olive repeat yellow of butter sculpture.

To make Galantine of Eel pictured here: skin eel; butterfly; fill with fish forcemeat (recipe, p. 69); follow directions for galantine preparation. When cooked and chilled, slice. Here, slices of galantine are set off with stuffed eggs and tomatoes. Display has centerpiece holding caviar.

Suckling Pig's head made from roast pork, pre-sliced for easy service, is filled with forcemeat. Aspic sheet cut-outs were used to decorate head.

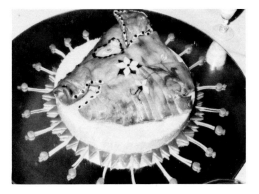

Bone in this fresh ham was replaced with forcemeat (see recipe for Galantine of Suckling Pig) and meat tied in piece of cheesecloth. When cool, cheesecloth was removed and ham was coated with brown aspic. Asparagus spears and slices of forcemeat stuffed ham are fanned out for buffet service. Tomatoes are filled with mousse of ham.

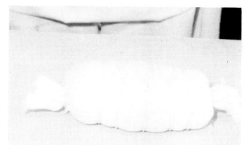

These are the preparation steps required for *Galantine of Chicken:*

Remove skin from chicken carefully.

Place rectangle of skin on cheesecloth; cover skin with forcemeat. Fold skin over filling then use cheesecloth to roll tightly into an oblong shape.

Use string to tie roll at both ends and in middle to hold it in shape during cooking. Poach in a strong chicken stock (made from bones of the carcass) about 20 min. per lb. Cool in stock. When cold, remove galantine from cloth and decorate.

For presentation, slice galantine and arrange slices as shown below. Along one side of slices, place stuffed tomatoes on circles of liver pate. Use carved pickled mushrooms and a coconut carved into a face with a piece of decorated Galantine to complete tray.

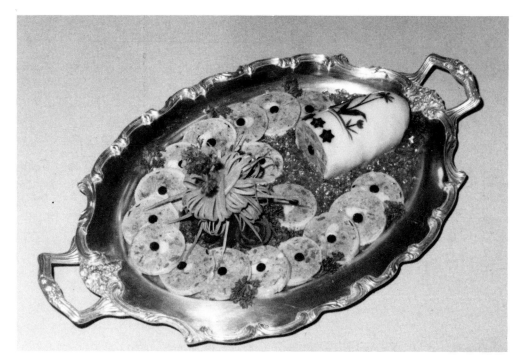

GALANTINE DE VOLAILLE
(See picture above)

Yield: 7 lb. 3 oz.

Ingredients

Capon	4-5 lb.
Brandy	3 tbsp.
Fresh Lean Pork	4 oz.
Fresh Lean Veal	4 oz.
Fresh Pork Fat	8 oz.
Eggs	2
Salt, per lb. of forcemeat	1 to 2 oz.
Pate Spice, per lb. of forcemeat	¼ tsp.
GARNISH	
Ham, finely diced	4 oz.
Beef Tongue, cooked, diced fine	4 oz.
Truffles, finely diced	5 oz. (optional)
Pistachio Nuts	1 oz.

Method

Cut wings of capon at first joint and chop knuckles off drumsticks. Slit skin along backbone. Carefully bone capon. Remove all meat from carcass, making sure meat is free of sinews and fat. Marinate in brandy.

Combine veal, pork and pork fat. Put through the fine plate of the grinder three times. Add whole eggs, salt and pate spice. Combine forcemeat with garnishes and mix well.

Prepare a rich chicken stock using bones of the carcass, strain. Place skin side down on a linen cloth. Spread the forcemeat, to which the brandy used for marinating has been added, all over the capon.

Shape the skin by rolling into a large sausage. Wrap tightly in cheesecloth

To prepare Roast Pheasant with Mushrooms and Galantine of Pheasant—the first step is to roast the pheasant. Cool. When cold, remove breast and fill cavity with liver mousse. Decorate with slices of poached mushrooms and truffles as shown in the picture. Garnish with galantine of pheasant (recipe follows) and colorful arrangement of blanched tomato slices holding asparagus spears.

and tie both ends. Also tie roll loosely with string three times through the middle to hold in shape.

Simmer the galantine in the strained chicken stock for 1½ hours. When cooked, remove stock from heat and cool completely and decorate as desired.

GALANTINE OF PHEASANT

Yield: 12-14 portions

Ingredients

Pheasant	1
Fresh Pork Fat	7 oz.
Lean Pork	7 oz.
Pheasant Meat, lean	5½ oz.
Pheasant Livers	6½ oz.
Eggs	2
Heavy Cream	7 oz.
Flour	1 oz.
Pate Spices	1/3 tsp.
Salt	½ to 1 oz.
GARNISH	
Veal Tongue, diced	1
Small Gherkins, diced	3
Truffles, diced	2 oz.
Mushrooms, whole and sauteed	3½ oz.

Method

Prepare pheasant the same as capon in Galantine de Volaille, facing page.

Cube pork, pheasant, and livers; put through a food chopper to make into a fine paste. Combine forcemeat with the eggs, heavy cream, flour and seasonings; mix well. Add garnish to the prepared forcemeat.

Follow steps outlined in "How to Prepare a Galantine."

Serve galantine with a Cumberland Sauce containing fresh seedless grapes.

GALANTINE OF SUCKLING PIG

Yield: 20-25 portions

Ingredients

Suckling Pig, small size	1
Lean Pork	32 oz.
Fresh Pork Fat	32 oz.
Whole Eggs	6
Salt	2 to 3 oz.
Pate Spices	1 tsp.
English Mustard	2 tsp.
Brandy	1/2 to 1 oz.
Madeira Wine	1/2 to 1 oz.
Pistachio Nuts	3 to 4 oz.

Method

Completely bone suckling pig.

Cube lean pork and fresh pork fat. Put through a meat grinder; add eggs, seasonings, brandy and madeira. Put through food chopper to make fine paste; then mix pistachio nuts into forcemeat. Fill suckling pig with the forcemeat; roll into a piece of cheese cloth; tie at both ends and in the middle Poach in stock.

When cooked, cool. Remove cheese-cloth and coat with a brown chaud froid made of glace de viande.

GALANTINE OF BREAST OF VEAL
(See picture, p. 102)

Yield: 18-20 portions

Ingredients

Veal Breast, small	1
Lean Pork	1 lb.
Fresh Pork Fat	1 lb.
Eggs	2
OR	
Egg Albumen	1 oz.
Salt	½ tsp.
Pate Spices	1 to 1½ tsp.
GARNISH	
Fresh Pork Fat, diced	1 oz.
Beef Tongue, diced	2 oz.
Pistachio Nuts	1½ oz.
White Truffles, if available	1 oz.
Black Truffles	1 oz.

Method

Bone breast of veal. Remove all sinews and fat.

Prepare a forcemeat, using lean pork and fresh pork fat. Add egg albumen. Mix well, season.

Fill the cavity of the breast of veal with the forcemeat, placing garnishes in center. Sew cavity, using butchers twine and a trussing needle. Next, wrap tightly in cheesecloth, tie at both ends and in the middle. Prepare a stock from the veal bones. Poach the galantine 20 minutes per lb. in the stock. When cold, decorate and glaze with brown aspic. This galantine can also be roasted.

DUCK GALANTINE
(See picture above)

Yield: 12 to 14 portions
Ingredients

Duck	3 to 4 lb.
Brandy	1 oz.
Lean Pork	6 oz.
Chicken Meat	6 oz.
Liver Gratin Forcemeat (see page 70)	12 oz.
Tomato Paste	1 tbsp.
Chicken Livers, diced	3 to 4 oz.
Salt	to adjust forcemeat
Pepper	1/3 tsp.
Pate Spices	1/3 tsp.

Method

Skin and bone duck, following directions for capon in recipe for "Galantine de Volaille," p. 94. Marinate breast of duck in brandy.

Finely grind diced pork, chicken meat and remaining lean meat from duck. Add to prepared gratin forcemeat. Combine with tomato paste, diced livers, spices and mix well. Spread prepared forcemeat over the duck skin and roll in cheesecloth. Poach in a strong stock, 20 min. per lb.

When cooked, slice and decorate as desired.

GALANTINE OF VEAL IN ASPIC

Yield: 10 to 12 portions

Ingredients

Pork Caul	1
Lean Veal	1 lb. 12 oz.
Pullman Ham	6 oz.
Fresh Pork Fat	8 oz.
Smoked Beef Tongue	6 oz.
Egg	1
Pistachio Nuts	¾ oz.
Truffles	4 oz. (optional)
Brandy	1 oz.
Madeira	1 oz.
Lean Pork	12 oz.
Veal or Pork Liver	6 oz.
Salt	1-1/2 to 2 tsp.
Pate Seasoning	1/3 to 1/2 tsp.
Butter	1 oz.
ASPIC	
Carrots	3 oz.
Onions	3 oz.
Celery	1 oz.
Leeks	1 oz.
Beef Chuck	1 lb.
Veal Shank	1
Calf's Foot	1
Veal Bones	2 lb.
Sachet Bag	1
Butter	1/2 oz.
Salt	1/3 tsp.
Madeira	3 oz.

Method

Soak pork caul in cold water. Cut the following ingredients into ¼ in. cubes; 12 oz. veal, all ham, 5 oz. pork fat, and all of the beef tongue. Mix the ingredients with egg, add the pistachio nuts and diced truffles. Pour brandy and 1 oz. of the madeira into this mixture. Mix all the ingredients and cover. Keep under refrigeration.

Coarsely grind up the remaining veal, pork fat, pork and liver. Add salt and seasonings, then regrind the mixture until fine. Combine forcemeat and diced ingredients and mix well so that all of the ingredients are evenly distributed.

Remove pork caul from water, drain and spread on table. Spread all ingredients on the pork caul and shape like a sausage; wrap in caul. Spread a piece of cheese cloth on table, brush with melted butter and wrap the galantine in the

Galantine of Veal in Aspic (recipe on facing page)

cheese cloth. Tie both ends of galantine with fine twine and tie three times loosely between the ends of the galantine to hold shape intact.

Make a mirepoix of carrots, onion, celery, leeks and arrange in the bottom of a brazier. Lay the galantine on this bed and add beef chuck, veal shank, calf's foot, veal bones and sachet bag. Add ½ oz. of butter and saute all ingredients until transparent, about 10 min. Cover with lukewarm water to ½ in. above the galantine. Add a pinch of salt and slowly bring to a boil. Skim, cover tightly and turn down to a simmer. Cook for one hour, then turn galantine over and cook another hour.

Remove galantine from brazier and place on a dish. Remove cheesecloth; re-wrap galantine in clean cheesecloth, rolling tightly to avoid air holes. Place 5 to 6 lb. weight on top of galantine and refrigerate for at least 12 hours.

Strain the stock, reduce to 1 qt. Cool and then remove all fat and proceed to clarify it, as follows: Lightly beat up one egg white and pour into the stock. Mix with a wooden spoon. Bring to a boil, stirring constantly; simmer for 20 min. Strain through cheesecloth and cool. Add madeira wine.

Unwrap galantine, slice one half and place on a silver platter coated with a layer of aspic. Coat remaining galantine with aspic, allow to set. Surround the base of the galantine with chopped aspic. (See picture above of galantine arranged for service.)

Striking platter frames Galantine of Salmon with chopped clear aspic, stuffed halves of hard cooked eggs and salmon slices topped with pickled green beans bound with ribbons of pimento. Salmon head and decorated unsliced portion of Galantine are placed at one end of platter, followed by Galantine slices with tomato rose and parsley sprigs at tail.

GALANTINE OF SALMON

Yield: 20 portions

Ingredients

Salmon	5 to 6 lb.
White Bread, crusts removed	10 slices
Egg Whites	8
Heavy Cream	2 cups
Salt	3 tbsp.
White Pepper	1 tbsp.
Nutmeg	to taste.

GARNISH

Combine 1½ oz. pistachio nuts, one 14 oz. can of pimentoes, blanched, peeled, and cut in large dice and white truffle paste (adds very delicate flavor to galantines). Prepare strips of salmon marinated in white wine or strips of smoked salmon.

Method

Remove head and tail of salmon. Bone out salmon without damaging skin. Remove meat, keeping meat and skin intact. Chill meat thoroughly. Prepare stock from fish bones.

Mince meat very fine, put through a wire sieve to remove muscles and bones. Return to refrigerator. Soak bread in heavy cream and egg whites, mix well.

Combine fish, bread, salt, pepper, and nutmeg. Place in chopper. Mix until forcemeat is smooth. Remove forcemeat from chopper and add pimentoes and pistachio nuts. It is very important that the mixture be kept cold at all times.

Poach a teaspoonful of mixture in boiling water; taste it and adjust the seasoning if necessary.

Spread cheesecloth on table and place the salmon skin on top. Spread fish mixture over half the skin. Stuff slices of smoked salmon with some forcemeat and roll up to resemble roulades. Arrange them down the center of the galantine lengthwise. Place remaining fish mixture on top. Fold the skin around the forcemeat. Roll it up in cheesecloth, tie both ends and tie loosely 3 or 4 times between the ends.

Poach in cloth in stock, 20 min. per lb. Turn over when half the cooking time has elapsed.

GALANTINE OF CAPON ROYALE

Yield: 8 lb. 8 oz.

Ingredients

Capon, 5-6 lb.	1
Veal Tongue	9 oz.
Pullman Ham	9 oz.
Brandy	2 oz.
White Wine	1 qt.
Oil	1 tbsp.
Pate Spices	1 tbsp.
Pork	1 lb.
Fresh Pork Fat	1 lb.
Chicken Livers	4 oz.
Salt	1 to 2 oz.
Pepper	½ tsp.
Madeira	½ cup
Veal Caul	1
or	
Pork Cauls	2
Puree of Foie Gras	6 oz.
Large Truffles, wrapped in thinly sliced fresh pork fat	2
STOCK INGREDIENTS	
Bay Leaf	1
White Pepper	1 tsp.
Thyme	pinch
Parsley Stems	3 to 4
Shallots	4
Butter	2 tbsp.
Capon Bones	
Calf's Foot	1
Veal Shank	1
Onions, diced	1 cup
Celery, diced	1 cup
Parsley, chopped	1 tsp.
Tarragon, fresh, chopped	1 tsp.
Scallions	

Method

Dice breast of capon, veal tongue and ham into ½ in. cubes and marinate 3 days in ½ cup of brandy and ½ cup of white wine and 1 tbsp. oil to which pate seasoning has been added. Mix ingredients each day.

Finely grind the pork and pork fat, the remaining chicken meat and chicken livers. Add salt and pepper, add rest of brandy and madeira wine. Refrigerate 3 days.

Spread a piece of cheesecloth on a table. Lay veal caul on the cheesecloth and spread with a layer of forcemeat and an arrangement of garnish. Continue the same operation til all ingredients are used, finishing with a layer of forcemeat. Place the puree of foie gras and truffles, wrapped in a thin sheet of fresh pork fat, in the center. Join both ends of the veal caul and wrap in cheese cloth. Tie both ends tightly.

To cook

Place butter in brazier with chicken bones, calf's foot, veal shank, onions, celery, bay leaf, white pepper, thyme, parsley stems and shallots. Add truffle juice and rest of white wine and the marinade.

Place the galantine in a brazier, cover with lid. Cook in oven at 350°F. for 2½ hours.

When galantine is cooked, remove from brazier, reshape and keep under refrigeration.

Remove fat and meat. Add parsley, tarragon, scallions during clarification.

Place galantine in an appropriate aspic mold. Decorate with figures cut from truffle sheet and fill with fresh aspic. Refrigerate for several hours. Unmold galantine, slice one half. Decorate other half, place with slices on silver platter and surround with fresh chopped aspic.

How to Decorate a Galantine—Coat the galantine with a white chaud froid (see Chapter III, "How to Apply Chaud Froid.")

Decorate the galantine with figures cut from colorful aspic sheets or flowers carved from vegetables, then cover with a crystal clear, cold aspic.

Galantine of Breast of Veal (recipe, p. 96) is fanned out in carefully placed half slices and garnished with tomatoes styled 3 ways: cherry tomatoes and whole tomatoes stuffed with tomato mousse plus a cluster of tomato roses to crown the portion of unsliced galantine. Note wedges cut from whole tomatoes.

CHICKEN GALANTINE A LA ROSENTHAL
(See picture above)

Yield: 10-12 portions

Ingredients

Chicken	5-1/2 oz.
Lean Pork or Veal	5-1/2 oz.
Fresh Pork Fat	13 oz.
Egg Albumen	1/2 oz.
Salt	1/2 to 1 oz.
Pepper	1/3 tsp.
English Mustard	1/2 tsp.
GARNISH	
Beef Tongue	1 oz.
Chicken Liver	1 oz.
Dried Wild Mushrooms, or fresh	1 oz.
Red Pepper, diced	1 oz.
Whole Chicken	2 lbs.
Tarragon)	
Parsley)	
Thyme)	1 tsp.
Chervil)	
Dill)	
Shallots, chopped	1/2 oz.

Method

Cube chicken, pork and fresh pork fat and run through a food chopper (see "How to Prepare Forcemeat"). Add seasonings, egg albumen and the garnish items. Bone a spring chicken, carefully removing all bones. Sprinkle tarragon, parsley, thyme, chervil, dill and shallots over chicken. Place prepared chicken on cheesecloth and spread forcemeat evenly over it; roll and tie. Poach 20 min. per pound. Cool and decorate with chaud froid. Serve with cucumber salad made with dill and sliced raw mushrooms that have been marinated in sour cream.

IX: MOUSSE

The cold mousse is a delicacy that is sure to delight the eye and the palate of patrons. In the garde manger department, the definition of a mousse is: a mixture of cooked ingredients, pureed and held together with unflavored gelatin, veloute sauce or aspic jelly, then mixed with cream and flavored with wine. As a garde manger preparation, the mousse is always served cold, attractively molded.

Other preparations are also called mousses but they are served hot. A fish quenelle forcemeat (see Chap. VI, Forcemeat) can be baked in a mold and served hot with a fish sauce and is called a mousse. Some other hot fish mousses are: Mousse of Dover Sole Joinville, Mousse of Salmon Americaine. Other delicacies also listed as mousse are served as desserts. Examples of these are: Chocolate Mousse; Peach Mousse; Strawberry Mousse.

Whether served cold, hot, or as a dessert, the mousse is a light and delicate preparation containing heavy cream. In this chapter, the preparation of the cold

Molds for mousse come in a variety of shapes that fit many patterns of food presentation.

mousse will be explained since this preparation is part of the work of the garde-manger.

How is a cold mousse prepared?

In the garde-manger department, a mousse is made with cooked meat, fish or poultry. The method of preparation is similar for all recipes: the ingredients are pureed, mixed with a binding agent containing gelatin, then heavy cream and seasonings are blended in. If well prepared, any mousse can be an impressive dish, either for service on a luncheon menu or on a cold buffet table.

The following recipes are for various mousse preparations, using either freshly cooked ingredients or leftovers.

HAM MOUSSE, STRASBOURG STYLE
(Mousse de Jambon Strasbourgeoise)

Yield: 2 1/2 lb.

Ingredients

Pullman Ham, or leftover baked ham	1 lb.
Unflavored Gelatin	1 oz.
Water	½ cup
Liver Pate	4 oz.
Veloute Sauce	1½ cup
Mayonnaise	½ cup
Heavy Cream	½ cup
Salt	1 tsp.
White Pepper	¼ tsp.

Method

Grind ham and liver pate through fine blade. Combine gelatin with water and add to ham mixture. Mix in veloute sauce with mayonnaise. Whip heavy cream and carefully fold in ham mixture. Add a touch of beet juice to intensify pink ham color. Season with salt and pepper and pour into a mold.

MOUSSE OF ROQUEFORT

Yield: 1 lb. 1 oz.

Ingredients

Roquefort Cheese	8 oz.
Cream Cheese	4 oz.
Mayonnaise	¼ cup
Heavy Cream	2 oz.
Walnuts, chopped fine	1 oz.
Salt	½ tsp.
White Pepper	pinch
Worcestershire Sauce	dash

Method

Place Roquefort and cream cheese in a chopper and blend until the mixture is creamy. Remove from blender, then add mayonnaise, heavy cream and walnuts Season with salt, pepper and Worcestershire sauce. Chill mousse before serving.

CHICKEN LIVER MOUSSE

Yield: 58 oz.

Ingredients

Chicken Livers	2 lb.
Bacon	3 oz.
Onions	12 oz.
Celery	3 oz.
Bay Leaf, small	1
Brandy	3 oz.
Hard Cooked Eggs	3
Heavy Cream	½ cup
Worcestershire Sauce	dash
Ripe Olives, diced	1 oz.
Butter or Chicken Fat	6 oz.
Salt	1 tbsp.

Method

Clean livers; devein. Peel onion and celery and dice fine. Cut bacon into small strips and saute in saute pan. Combine onion and celery and cook until transparent. Add livers and bay leaf and cook for a few minutes until dry. Pour in brandy and mix well. Reduce. Remove bay leaf. Put mixture through a meat grinder, then into chopper. Transfer to a bowl. Add chopped hard-cooked eggs, heavy cream, Worcestershire sauce, ripe olives and butter or chicken fat. Season with salt.

AVOCADO MOUSSE

Yield: 16-18 oz.

Ingredients

Avocado, large (12-16 oz.)	1
Salt	½ tsp.
Lemon	juice of 1 + 2 tsp.
Water	½ cup
Unflavored Gelatin	1-1/2 tsp.
Mayonnaise	¼ cup
Heavy Whipped Cream	¼ cup

Method

Cut avocado in half. Remove pit and puree the pulp in a blender. Season with salt and lemon juice.

Dissolve gelatin in water and heat mixture. Add to puree of avocado.

Remove mixture from blender. Mix in mayonnaise and whipped cream. Pour mousse in appropriate mold. Place in refrigerator to gel. Unmold on a bed of shredded lettuce.

Platter of Poached Salmon—Filet salmon and poach 3 min. per lb. Cool. When salmon is cold, cut into slices; place one spear of white asparagus on each slice. To complete arrangement, angle strips of pimento over asparagus. Alternate salmon slices with blanched cucumber ovals filled with salmon mousse (use recipe for fish mousse below). Top with strips of truffle. Fill center with a colorful decoration made from parsley sprigs and radish roses.

FISH MOUSSE

Yield: 2 lb.

Ingredients

Salmon, Sole, Halibut, Pike, or similar fish, cooked	1 lb.
Unflavored Gelatin	1-1/2 tbsp.
Liquid Fish Aspic	½ cup
Salt	1 tsp.
Pepper	1 pinch
Worcestershire Sauce	1 dash
Dill, chopped	1 tsp.
Mayonnaise	½ cup
Dry White Wine	¼ cup
Heavy Cream, whipped	½ cup

Method

Carefully remove all bones and skin from fish. Dissolve gelatin in aspic. Put fish into chopper, adding the aspic gradually. Add seasonings and blend the mixture to a paste consistency.

Transfer the fish mixture to a stainless steel bowl. Add mayonnaise and wine. Mix well with a wooden spoon, then cool on ice.

When mixture has partially congealed, fold in whipped cream.

Fish mousse can be poured into aspic molds and served on buffets. The mousse can also be used as a filling to stuff various items used to accompany the mousse, such as barquettes, vol au vent, cucumbers, tomatoes, mushroom caps and artichoke bottoms.

An interesting variation can be prepared by mixing several kinds of fish mousse in combinations, as follows:

½ trout mousse and ½ sole mousse.

1/3 salmon mousse, 1/3 sole mousse or 1/3 crabmeat mousse.

MOUSSE OF CHICKEN

Yield: 2¾ lb.

Ingredients

Shallots, minced	3 tbsp.
Butter	1 tbsp.
Strong Chicken Stock	2 cups
Gelatin, softened in ¼ cup white wine	2 tbsp.
Cooked Chicken Meat	2 cups
Liver Pate	½ cup
Brandy	3 tbsp.
Salt	1 tbsp.
Pepper	½ tsp.
Whipped Cream	¾ cup

Method

Lightly saute shallots in butter. Add chicken stock and gelatin mixture and simmer for 1 minute.

Combine poultry meat and liver pate. Place in chopper or blender, then add the above liquid ingredients and the brandy. Season with salt and pepper.

Remove mixture from chopper or blender. Place on ice and when it starts to gel, gently incorporate the whipped cream. The same recipe can be used substituting ham, other poultry or game for the chicken meat.

Chicken mousse or other similar meat mousses can be molded in small ramekins or small aspic molds and used as a garnish on a meat platter. The mousse can also be used as stuffing for ham, salami or bologna roulades.

A mousse can also be displayed as a piece montee. For that kind of service, the mousse is portioned into a larger mold and decorated. Sometimes, large molds of various sizes are used and built up in tiers. In addition, mousse can also be used to fill cavities in whole hams, poultry and fish and to level and smooth uneven areas on ham, poultry, etc.

Because Mousse of Chicken is not a colorful dish, it gains in appeal from distinctive decoration. Here the mold is circled with sliced stuffed olives that frame an arrangement of green asparagus spears laced with pimento strips and tomato roses placed on a spray of celery leaves.

This cornucopia holds simulated fruit made from mousse. The cornucopia gains contrast from strips cut from a truffle sheet. The mousse was molded in a banana mold and colored with egg yolk to make the banana at right. Green grapes in bunch are made of circles cut from watercress sheets. Pimento skin covers the apple with its clove stem and plums are made of mousse covered with red fruit skin. Tomato slices outline the cornucopia with 3 half-slices of orange in place at the top.

X: MARINADES

A marinade—a seasoned liquid either cooked or uncooked, is used to season the food steeped in it and thus to improve its flavor. A marinade can also soften the fibers of certain meats as well as make it possible to hold fish and meat for a longer period of time.

How long can meat be kept in a marinade?

The length of time foodstuffs should be left in a marinade depends on their size and texture and on the temperature of the marinade. In winter, large cuts of meat or game, like deer (venison) should be left in a marinade up to six days. In the summer, however, they should be marinated only 24-28 hours; only very large pieces can be left in the marinade for longer periods of time and it is important to watch the marinating product closely in hot weather because of its tendency to sour.

1. Cooked
2. Uncooked
3. Brine

COOKED MARINADE

Yield: 2 pt.

Ingredients

Carrots	3
Onions	2
Shallots	3
Black Pepper, ground	½ tsp.
Cloves	2 to 3
Juniperberries	½ tsp.
Parsley Stalks	4
Thyme	pinch
Bay Leaf	1
Water	1 to 1-1/2 qts.
White Wine	1½ pts.
Vinegar	½ pt.
Salad Oil	¼ cup

Method

Combine all ingredients and boil for 1 hour. Cool. Do not pour the marinade over the meat until the liquid is completely cold. If the meat (or game) is fresh, it will take less time for it to marinate. Large pieces will require 24 hours, smaller pieces, 4-5 hours. For game marinade add juniper and coriander.

UNCOOKED MARINADE—FOR BEEF, LAMB OR VENISON

Yield: 4 pt.

Ingredients

Red Wine	6 cups
Vinegar	1½ cups
Oil	½ cup
Bay Leaves	10
Salt	½ tbsp.
Black Pepper, ground	½ tsp.
Monosodium Glutamate	½ tsp.

Method

Combine all ingredients and pour over the meat. Marinate 2-3 days.

FOR PORK

Yield: Enough to marinate a 3-4 lb. piece of pork.

Ingredients

Salt	2 tsp.
Black Peppercorns, ground	2/3 tsp.
Thyme or Sage	large pinch
Bay Leaf	1
Allspice	large pinch
Garlic, crushed	1 clove

Method

Mix all ingredients and rub mixture into the surface of the pork. Place in a covered plastic or stainless steel bowl. Marinate 6-24 hours. It is helpful to turn the meat once in a while. Before cooking, scrape the marinade off and dry the meat well.

MARINADE FOR COOKED BEEF

Yield: Enough for 2-3 lb. of sliced beef.

Ingredients

Vinegar	4 tbsp.
Oil	14 tbsp.
Tomato Puree	4 tbsp.
Onion, chopped	2 tbsp.
Worcestershire Sauce	1 tbsp.
Salt and Pepper	to taste

Method

Carve the cooked roast into thin slices and put in a dish. Pour marinade over the sliced meat and marinate for 2-3 hours. Garnish with chopped eggs, capers and pickles.

MARINADES FOR BEEF, LAMB OR GAME

BEER MARINADE

Yield: 2 pt.

Ingredients

Ale or Dark Beer	1-3/4 pt.
White Vinegar	1/4 pt.
Sugar	7 tbsp.
Onion, medium, sliced	1
Bay Leaf	2
Cloves	5
Black Pepper, ground	1/3 tsp.
Juniperberries, crushed	2-1/2 pt.
Allspice, crushed	1/3 tsp.

Method

Mix ingredients in a crock. Put meat in it and hold it down with a weight. Meat should be well covered with liquid. Keep in a cool place.

Marinating time. . .1 week.

WINE MARINADE

Yield: 2½ pt.

Ingredients

Red Wine	1 qt.
Vinegar	1/4 pt. (5 oz.)
Oil	7 tbsp.
Salt	2 tsp.
Onion, medium sliced	1
Sugar	1 tsp.
Thyme	1 tsp.
Ginger, fresh	1 piece
Bay Leaf	1
Cloves	2
Black Peppercorns	10

Method

Mix ingredients, then put meat in marinade; set weight on top of meat to hold it down.

Marinating time. . .1-2 weeks.

MARINADE FOR SMALL CUTS OF GAME
MEDALLIONS, NOISETTES OR CUTLETS

Yield: ½ pt.

Ingredients

Vinegar	4 oz.
Red or White Wine	4 oz.
Oil	1 oz
Juniper Berries (crushed)	½ tsp.
Thyme	pinch

Method

Place the small cuts of game in a china dish. Pour the liquid over the meat and marinate 24 hours. Turn meat once or twice.

Brine—This is a solution of coarse sea salt to which sugar, saltpeter and spices are added. The purpose is to preserve foodstuffs for a longer period of time.

LIQUID BRINE FOR RAW HAMS (2 to 3)

Ingredients

Fresh Ham, medium size	2 to 3 whole hams
Salt	5 lb.
Saltpeter-dry curing mixture	1 oz.
Sugar	1 oz.
Large Crock or Wooden Barrel	
BRINE	
Salt	5 lb.
Saltpeter	1 oz.
Sugar	1 oz.
Ice Water	17½ pt.
Sachet bag made of	
Pickling Spices	2 oz.
Juniper Berries	1 oz.

Method

Rub mixture of salt, saltpeter and sugar all over the hams, then pack tightly into crock, putting more of mixture between hams as you pack them in. Put a board over the container and secure with a weight. Marinate for 14 days at about 38°-42°F. Remove hams and rotate them from bottom to top.

On returning hams to crock, put more curing mixture between layers. Mix ingredients together to make a brine. Cover the hams with brine (recipe above) and marinate two weeks longer. Ham can be served either cooked or raw.

MARINATED HAM

Ingredients

Ham, deboned	5 lb. weight
Coarse Salt	1 lb.
Saltpeter	1 oz.
Granulated Sugar	8 oz.

Method

Mix salt, sugar and saltpeter and rub boned leg with it. Special care should be taken to cover the parts without skin. Let meat remain in the mixture. The next day, repeat the procedure. Repeat for two more days. This will make a total of four periods of rubbing and curing. After this process is completed, scrape off any salt clinging to the ham and put meat into the prepared brine (recipe on next page).

BRINE FOR RAW OR COOKED HAMS (mild in flavor)
Yield: Enough for Marinated Ham recipe on preceding page (4 qt.)
Ingredients

Water	3 qts.
Coarse Salt	12 oz.
Brown Sugar	12 oz.
Saltpeter	1 tbsp.
SACHET BAG	
Juniperberries	1 tsp.
Nutmeg	a piece
Thyme Sprigs, fresh	3
Pepper, ground	1 tsp.
Cloves	4

Method
Combine all ingredients in a large pot and bring to a boil. Stir occasionally. Remove brine and strain. Add sachet bag and cool the liquid. Marinate ham in brine for 6-7 days. Remove ham and squeeze dry. Roll ham tightly in a cheesecloth, tie and hang in a dry place at 50°-60°F. for 10-15 days. If you are not sure that ham will dry properly, hang the ham for 3 days only.

Cooking Time—Cook 20-30 min. per pound. Set ham in cold water and bring to a boil. Simmer, taste liquid and change it, if it is too salty.

To Finish Ham—Leave ham in liquid to cool for 1-2 hours. Then remove and press into an oval shaped mold, holding in place with a board and weight. Hold ham in a cool place for 12 hours before serving.

To Serve Hot—The best way to serve a ham as a hot dish is to glaze it. To glaze, first peel the skin off, then coat ham with brown sugar, prepared mustard and a little brandy, and bake.

CORNED DUCK
Yield: 8-10 portions
Ingredients

Ducks	2
Lemon	½
Salt	10 oz.
Sugar	3½ oz.
Saltpeter	1 oz.
BRINE	
Salt	10½ oz.
Sugar	2½ oz.
Liquid	3 qts.

Method
Rub duck with dry ingredients. Chill 12 hours. Rinse the duck.

Bring brine to a boil and cool. Place duck in brine. Marinate for 48 hours.

For cooking, prepare court bouillon of carrots, onion, peppercorns, ½ bay leaf and parsley. Truss duck and boil for 1-1½ hours. Serve hot or cold. Duck can also be smoked. Follow method described in Chap. XI, for smoking of fish. Use 3 cups of hickory sawdust and smoke for 30-35 minutes. Chicken can also be smoked for 20-25 minutes.

XI: ESSENTIAL INGREDIENTS

Meat, poultry, game, fish and shellfish are basic ingredients of the principal dishes prepared in the garde manger. The reputation of the garde manger department depends on proper selection and handling of these basic items. The Professional Chef presents detailed information about the selection and preparation of these ingredients.

This chapter only briefly summarizes areas of importance in garde manger work. Techniques that assure proper preparation of these important ingredients are also illustrated and explained in this chapter.

An average foodservice operation spends 25% of its food dollar for meat. This investment certainly makes meat an item of importance. Preparation of all meat items should be planned for maximum effectiveness because this is where the chef can use his talents to create excellent dishes not only from the expensive prime cuts but also from the cheaper cuts. Chefs in the garde manger (or cold kitchen) department use their skills to transform these inexpensive cuts of meat into the full flavored, attractive looking food items that are most appealing to the general public.

Beef

Beef—The quality of beef varies considerably and is revealed in the marbling, smoothness and fineness in the grain of the meat and the color of the bones; they should be white. The finer the muscle fibers, the more tender the meat will be.

The following beef cuts are the most suitable for buffet and a la carte items: tenderloin, sirloin, butt, strip loin and rib. They are the primal cuts of beef and are found to be very effective when presented on buffets.

Beef cuts of lesser quality can also be used but are usually most satisfactory when cooked slowly and combined with sauces, marinated or used as salads. (See Chap. XIV for meat salads)

Beef gains flavor when larded. To lard a fillet cut fresh pork fat into narrow strips about   *2 in. long and insert into meat with larding needle. Tie fillet to hold shape while broiling.*

Veal—Veal is the flesh of milk fed calves from 10 to 12 weeks old. Veal has less fat and more moisture than beef and will dry out if cooked too long or at too high a temperature. If the veal is reddish in color, the animal has not been milk fed and is of lower quality.

Quality veal cuts are usually used in garde-manger to make forcemeats. They are also used in pates, terrines, etc. Calves' feet and bones are used to prepare aspic and enrich stocks. The cuts used most often on buffets and as a la carte items are the veal saddle, breast and rack. Calves' liver, feet and bones also find many uses in the garde manger department.

Smoked beef tongue prepared for service in the garde manger department is sliced thin, each slice rolled around a spear of marinated fresh asparagus. Cream cheese, horseradish and caviar contribute unique flavor to stuffed eggs. Tomatoes are filled with mushroom salad. Unsliced tongue is decorated with truffle circles and a cap made of mandarin orange sections and circles of tongue.

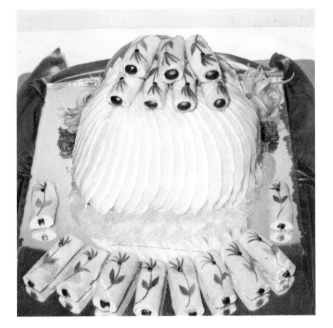

Jambon Farci (stuffed smoked ham)—Trim skin from a smoked ham. Remove bone and part of the ham and fill cavity with mousse of ham and slice ham into thin slices to cover mousse. Overlap slices all around ham as shown. Garnish with ham roulades made by rolling ham slices around ham mousse. Roulades in this picture are decorated with flowers made of bits of radish skin with leaves and stems made of leeks.

Pork—Pork is usually tender since hogs are bred solely for their meat and are marketed at an early age. The best cuts of pork have a coating of fat and the meat is white.

Many different methods of cookery are used in the preparation of pork in the garde-manger department and many lesser quality cuts are used. The fresh pork fat is used in pates, galantines, etc. Pork caul is used in special recipes. The liver goes into pates and forcemeats. The shoulder, fresh ham or loin can be smoked, cured or eaten fresh.

Smoked hams are specialties in many countries and in individual regions of the same country. A great variety of sausages are derived from pork and there are countless other recipes such as rillette (see page 90) head cheese, pate de campagne and blood sausage that are made from pork.

Ham becomes eye catching element in food display when covered with chaud froid and decorated with designs cut from aspic sheets in various colors. Thin slices of ham are placed around the ham which is then coated with clear aspic. The ham rolls on this tray are stuffed with mushroom salad. Rings of pickles fill three corners of platter with rows of ripe olives and golden kumquats placed for maximum impact.

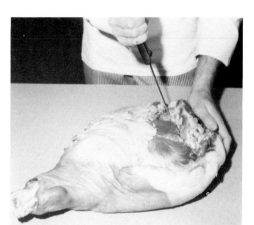

To bone a fresh ham requires these 3 steps: 1. Remove aitch bone by cutting at an angle around it as shown at left. 2. Remove skin (left below). 3. Remove center bone, cutting at angle shown in picture below.

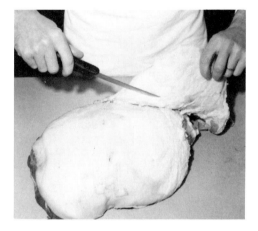

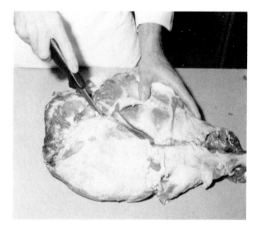

When ham is completely boned, there will be portions as shown left to right, top to bottom, shank and leg bone, skin or rind, top part of ham, bottom shank, eye section of the bottom, complete boneless bottom, silvertip pork.

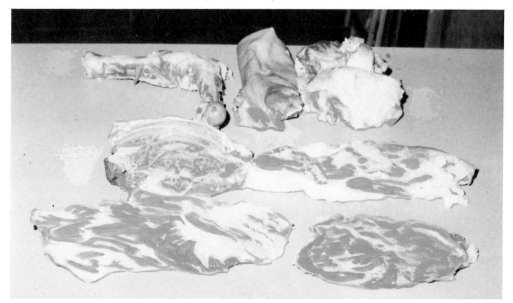

Game

During the hunting season, which is usually in late fall, fresh game is available. During the rest of the year the game that is supplied is frozen. Game meat is usually dark in color and is very lean with a strong, wild odor. Since the flesh of most game is dry and contains almost no fat, the meat is best if it is larded when it is to be used for cold entrees.

The parts of game generally used in garde-manger are the rump, saddle, fillet (for medallions), rack and, in the case of elk, the tongue. For buffet and a la carte dishes, the most suitable primal cuts of red deer are leg, saddle, rack and fillet. Hare is used whole for pate, galantines and terrines.

Feathered birds such as pheasant, quails, snipes, partridges, etc. are prepared in a variety of ways for buffet displays.

To lard Saddle of Venison use larding needle to run narrow strips of fresh pork fat about 2 in. long through saddle. Tie saddle as shown to retain shape while broiling.

Saddle of Venison a la Diane—Venison that has been butterflied is stuffed with chicken livers and truffles, then roasted. After cool- *ing, slices are carved out and brandy-flavored liver mousse is mounded over roasted saddle carcass.*

TRUSSING POULTRY
Method 1

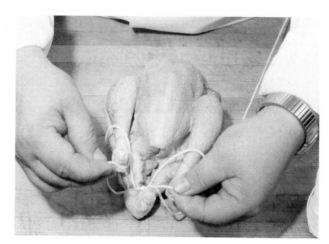

Positioning bird on its back, run butcher's twine twice a-round tail, leaving enough twine to complete trussing.

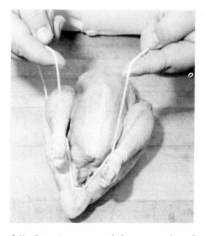

Wind twine around lower ends of thigh bones and pull them tight against side of bird.

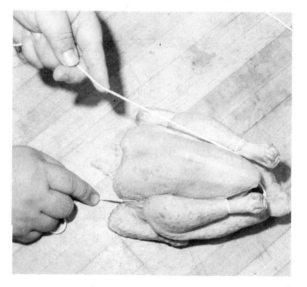

Pull twine toward you, positioning it between thighs and back of bird.

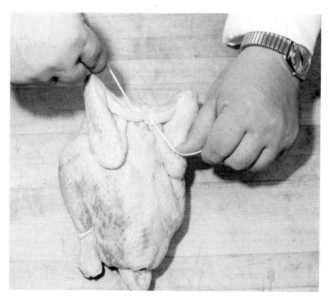

Tighten twine and wind it around birds neck; pull it tight and knot it.

TRUSSING POULTRY
Method 2

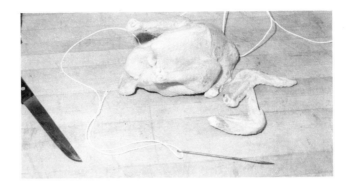

When sewing poultry, first remove wings and then put bird on its back. Have a trussing needle and thin butcher's twine at hand.

Bring thighs close to body and insert needle through both thighs to hold in place.

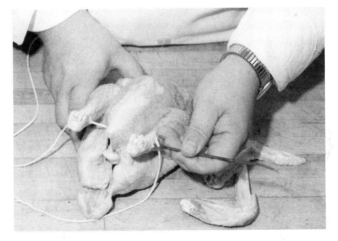

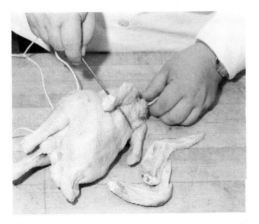

Next, insert needle through one wing, push needle on through neck skin which has been folded back and then on through other wing.

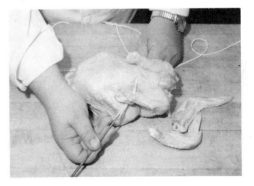

Pull needle all the way through, then pull string tight to hold wings in position. Tie string tightly to keep bird neatly trussed.

Poultry

From the culinary standpoint, poultry is divided into two groups:
1. Domestic Birds—Chicken, Fowl, Duck, Turkey, Goose, Cornish Hen, etc.
2. Game Birds—Pheasant, Grouse, Partridge, Woodcock, Mallard Duck, Wild Goose or Turkey.

Domestic Birds are sold fresh or frozen throughout the year. They are usually plucked and drawn; some are sold New York dressed, which means not eviscerated. Frozen poultry is always sold plucked and eviscerated. The giblets, (neck, liver, heart and gizzard) are wrapped separately. For commercial use, chickens are also cut into breast, legs or wings and sold separately.

Game Birds are available mostly during the fall hunting season which extends through part of winter. Fresh game birds are only available at this time. However, frozen birds are sold all year long.

Fresh-shot game birds should be aged, or, as it is usually described, hung for a period of time to insure tenderness. If water birds, like mallard ducks, are used, only young birds should be used, as old birds have a strong fishy odor.

Preparation of the Poultry—Today, with modern facilities and processing systems, poultry preparation has been considerably simplified. In some cases, no further preparation of raw poultry is required after it arrives in the kitchen. Both fresh and frozen poultry can be obtained "oven ready" or cut into portions.

Before roasting, braising or boiling, domestic or game birds should be thoroughly washed or rinsed and then tied. Domestic birds are often rubbed inside and outside with lemon juice so the meat becomes whiter and fresher in flavor.

Some lean birds, like pheasant, are barded with rashers of bacon or fresh pork fat. Another method of preparation requires trussing the bird, especially for poultry specialties produced in the garde-manger or kitchen. Poultry requires boning and cutting if it is to be used to make pates or galantines. Frozen birds should be thawed before cooking; thawing preferably should be done at room temperature.

How to Cook Poultry—Poultry is prepared in various ways. It can be roasted, grilled or boiled or, in the garde-manger department, made into forcemeats for use in aspic molds or to be coated with chaud froid. Birds which are roasted or grilled should be young and of good quality. Old fowls should be boiled or used for forcemeats, although young fowls or plump chickens, while usually roasted, are also good for boiling.

Cold domestic birds or game birds in aspic are always decorative. This specialty can be prepared in advance without any loss in flavor. The aspic (see section on aspic, p. 23), should be flavored with care, then brushed over the birds and decorated with truffles or other designs.

Another variation in poultry presentation is to coat the slices or pieces of meat from the bird or the whole bird with chaud froid, then garnish and decorate and coat with aspic.

Jellied poultry molds are usually made from boiled chicken. This is a good way to use leftovers which can be enhanced in flavor with the use of tomatoes, cucumbers, or hard cooked eggs. (See section on mousses, 104).

The Carving of Poultry—The method of cutting or carving a bird depends on its size and how it is to be served.
1. Small birds are cut in half or divided into four parts.
2. Large birds can be carved in various ways, depending on whether the slices are to be portioned on a dish or returned to the carcass.

When serving large birds with slices taken from breasts and re-arranged on the carcass, it is advisable to cut off the under part of the carcass so that the bird will be flat on the dish, making the presentation neater and more decorative. Carving is usually done in the kitchen, but can also be done on the buffet. When carving is to be done on the buffet, large birds are required.

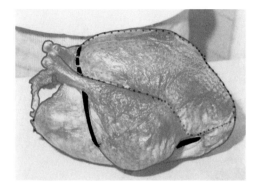

Dotted line on picture shows where turkey is to be carved. It is a good idea to know in advance where to cut.

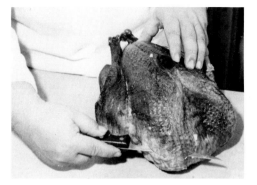

To carve a turkey to be used as a centerpiece first remove the breast by carving towards yourself, inserting knife as shown.

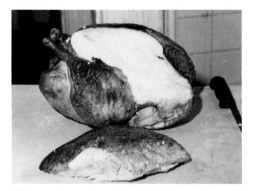

Place turkey breast on cutting board skin side up. Be sure to use sharp knife to make uniform slices.

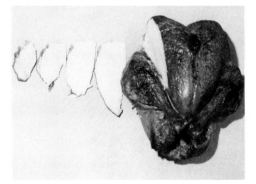

Slice breast into pieces about ¼ in. thick leaving skin on. Keep slices in order so they can be returned to carcass in order.

After breast has all been sliced, carefully put the slices back onto the turkey in arrangement shown here.

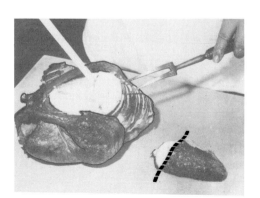

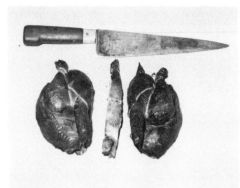

Depending on the number of portions desired, there are several ways to carve a roasted chicken for maximum eye appeal. The first step will be to cut chicken in half by removing backbone.

Then cut chicken into 4 pieces, two breasts and two legs as shown.

For smaller sections, cut breasts and legs with backbone into 12 pieces.

If smaller pieces are needed, cut as shown to provide 16 pieces.

How to carve a roast chicken for display

After whole roasted chicken has been cut into portions to meet service needs, pieces can be neatly arranged for display and service as shown here. Carrot flower makes an attractive, attention-getting decoration for the arrangement of crisp-skinned chicken portions.

How to carve a turkey for buffet service

Holding knife and fork as shown, first carve thin breast slices. To cut slices from leg, first slice horizontally, as shown left below, then vertically, positioning carving knife and fork as shown below.

To decorate a capon, first remove the breast and fill the cavity with a liver mousse. Next slice the breast and put slices back on capon, pressing them into position on top of the liver mousse. Slices of Canadian bacon inserted between slices of capon and sliced stuffed olives provide appealing color contrast.

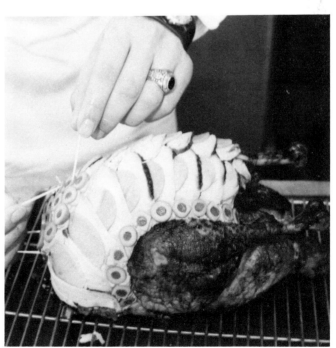

Fish and Shellfish

Many kinds of fish can be used in garde-manger work. The fish may be purchased whole or cut into steaks or in fillets. After cleaning, the fish is usually poached, unless the final preparation requires some other style of cooking. Fish for garde-manger use can also be purchased frozen, in cans, marinated or smoked.

How can you tell that fish is fresh?

When buying fresh fish, be sure to check these important points:
1. Skin should be bright in color.
2. Scales should adhere tightly.
3. Eyes should be bright and transparent.
4. Gills should be light in color.
5. Flesh should be firm and stiff.

Because of its strong penetrating odor, never store fish with other food. A separate refrigerator or a separate section of the refrigerator should be set aside for fish storage. If fish is to be stored for several days, it should be covered with crushed ice and placed in a 34°-36°F. refrigerator.

Do not expose fresh fish to the air unnecessarily, as oxidation will alter the flavor. Keep shellfish, especially clams and oysters, cold but do not pack in ice.

How should frozen fish be handled?

Do not thaw frozen fish until you are ready to use it. If it has been defrosted, do not freeze it again. There is some difference of opinion as to the best method of thawing. Formerly, the accepted method was to soak fresh fish in water. This method speeds thawing, but if the fish is eviscerated or filleted, the water leaches much of the flavor and nutrition out of the fish during the thawing period. Consequently, slow thawing in unopened packages at room temperature is more frequently recommended. Many processors advise that fish fillets be cooked without thawing as they then retain maximum flavor.

FISH MOST OFTEN USED IN GARDE MANGER

Fresh Fish

Bluefish—Available all year, but abundant from May to October.

Brook Trout or Rainbow Trout—Can be obtained all year round, although the best season is from May to October.

Dover Sole (the Genuine Sole)—Dover sole is caught all year round in the English Channel. Lemon or Gray sole may be used as a substitute for Dover sole in preparing fish forcemeats. Dover sole is a very delicate fish and is widely used in cooking.

Herring—Caught all year round. Herring can be smoked, marinated, or pickled.

Pike—Fresh water fish. Best season is June. It's a lean fish, with a firm flaky flesh and is excellent for use in fish forcemeat.

Salmon—Caught all year round. There are several varieties of salmon: Chinook, Sockeye, Cohoe, Steelhead, etc. . .The pink color and the rich flavor of some species of salmon give them great versatility for garde-manger preparations.

Turbot—Caught all year round. The turbot has a white, delicate, firm flesh and can be adapted to various cold dishes very successfully.

PREPARATION OF FRESH OR FROZEN TROUT

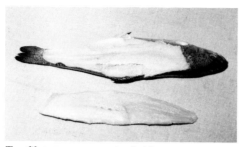

To filet trout, cut in half; remove bones.

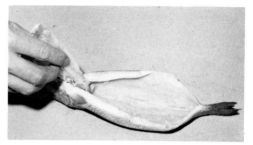

To prepare a trout for stuffing, remove center bone.

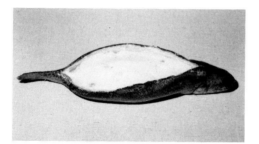

Trout is now ready to be filled with a fish forcemeat.

Trout is folded back into position around forcemeat, ready for final cooking.

To poach whole trout, pull 2 ft. piece of twine through mouth and gills.

Run other end of twine through bone above tail. Pull twine tight until the trout is shaped

as shown, then tie it in position. Poach in court bouillon 5 min. per lb.

WAYS TO PREPARE DOVER SOLE

When working with Dover Sole always use a sharp knife. First cut right behind the head through the bone, but do not cut through the

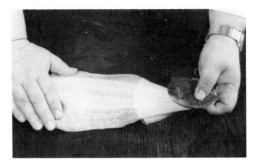

skin. Remove head and skin at the same time, pulling carefully so as not to damage the flesh of the fish.

After head and skin are removed, cut off fins to make fillet.

Tools and mise en place for preparation of Dover Sole.

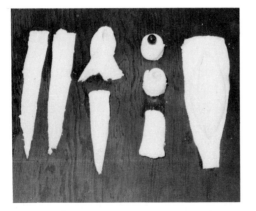

Sole fillets can be arranged in several ways for cooking. Here, from left to right: straight fillet for Menuiere; fillet folded over for poaching, roulade for medallions with domino cut below: and Colbert sole. (See picture at right for preparation of Colbert sole.)

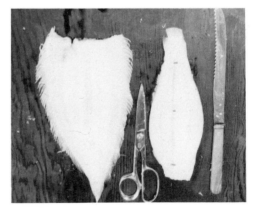

For the Colbert cut, trim off all fins, and butterfly Dover sole as shown left. Fold fillets over and cut the bone in three places using a pair of scissors. Sole is now ready to be poached or if desired, bread the fillet and deep fry it.

Canned Fish

Many kinds of canned fish are available for use in cold dishes. The most common canned fish used are:

1. *Tuna Fish*—There are four varieties:
    a. Albacore (whitemeat) This is the only one that can be so described.
    b. Yellow Fin)
    c. Blue Fin   )   These must all be labeled light meat.
    d. Skipjack)

2. *Caviar*—For more details see Chapter V, page 64.

3. *Herring*—Comes in cans, marinated or smoked. Different varieties can be found: Holland, Bismarck, Matjes etc. . .

The most popular of all herring is that packed in sour cream. As an appetizer, it is highly regarded by most patrons.

4. *Salmon*—Different grades of salmon are available canned. The best grade is the Chinook or King salmon (from the Columbia River). The second grade is the Sockeye red or Blueback; the third is the medium red silver or cohoe.

Humpback or keta, labelled pink salmon, is the lowest priced. Tall cans are filled with the tail pieces; flat cans hold center cuts. Smoked salmon is also available in cans.

More and more, fish and shellfish are canned in various ways. Sardines are packed in olive oil, tomato sauce or mustard sauce. Clams and oysters and mussels are canned in their own cooking liquor.

Lobster, crabmeat or shrimp are pasteurized in cans and generally they should be kept under refrigeration to preserve maximum flavor.

Stuffed Dover Sole with Lobster Mousse. Prepare sole as for Dover Sole Colbert. Poach in white wine, then remove bones and cool. When cold, stuff cavity with lobster mousse topped with lobster slices. Mound caviar on hard cooked egg halves at front of tray. Brilliant red of lobster shell adds height and color to display.

Marinated Fish

Herring, salmon, mackerel and other fish can be marinated. The following recipes are of Swedish origin and excellent for commercial use.

MARINATED SALMON OR GRAVE LAX

Yield: 5 lb.

Ingredients

Salmon Fillet	5 lb.
Salt	2½ oz.
Sugar	5½ oz.
Saltpeter (optional)	pinch
Fresh Dill Stems	6 to 7
Onion, thinly sliced	1
Black Pepper, ground	3 to 4 tsp.
Juniperberries, crushed	1 tsp.
Lemon	1

Method

If possible, select the middle cut. Scrape the salmon and dry it thoroughly. Do not rinse the fish.

Split salmon open along the backbone and remove the fillets. Also remove all bones.

Mix salt, sugar, and saltpeter (optional) and rub it into the salmon.

Place a layer of dill and onion in a stainless steel hotel pan and then place the fillets, skin side up, over the dill and onion layer. Sprinkle with the pepper, juniperberries, the rest of the dill and onion. Pour the juice of the lemon over the entire fish.

Put a chopping board on top of the fish with a weight over it to keep salmon in place. Marinate for 72 hours.

NOTE: Mackerel, Trout and Salmon Trout can be substituted for Salmon.

SPICED HERRING

Yield: 4 lb.

Ingredients

Herring	4 lb.
Water	3½ pt.
Vinegar	4 oz.
All Spice, crushed	4 tbsp.
Black Pepper, ground	4 tbsp.
Salt	4 oz.
Sugar	2 lb.
Bay Leaves	15

Method

Clean the herring, remove the heads and wash. Mix the vinegar and water and steep the herring in the solution for 24 hours. Take out and drain.

Mix the salt, the sugar and spices and put the herring and the mixture in alternate layers in a crock. Cover the crock and let stand in a cool place for 72 hours.

HERRING IN SHERRY PICKLE

Yield: 20 portions

Ingredients

Schmalz Herring	10
Sherry	1 pt.
Water	10 oz.
White Vinegar	10 tbsp.
Sugar	20 oz.
Allspice, crushed	1 tbsp.

Method

Clean the herring and soak in water for 12 hours. Skin and fillet the fish; wash and drain the fillets. Mix the remaining ingredients; steep herring in mixture for 24 hours. Serve with dill and sliced onions.

The Preparation of Smoked Fish

The chief reason for smoking fish is to increase its keeping qualities. However, in the process, the fish acquires aromatic flavor. Most smoked fish is sold commercially. However, fresh fish such as trout, mackerel, bluefish or sturgeon can be freshly smoked by using the method commonly used by sportsmen in the woods.

To smoke fish using this method, the following equipment is needed:

1. Large, heavy duty, double roasting pan with a cover.
2. Wire rack, the size of the pan.
3. Four metal risers.
4. Hickory sawdust.

Sprinkle 2 cups sawdust lightly over the entire surface of the pan. Set the risers into place and place roasting pan holding wire rack on top of them.

Wash fish thoroughly and season with crushed black peppercorns. Place on wire rack and cover roasting pan.

Preheat stove to highest temperature. Place roasting pan holding fish on top of the stove for 15-20 minutes, depending on the size of the fish.

Remove the pan from the fire and set aside, letting it stand for 5 minutes, uncovered, then remove fish. Fish smoked by this method can be served cold with creamed horseradish.

NOTE: To give an even better flavor, the fish can also be brined. For 24 hours marinate the whole eviscerated fish in the following mixture:

Sugar	¼ lb.
Salt	¼ lb.
Water	1½ gal.
Juniperberries	1 tsp.
Cloves	10

What kinds of shellfish are there?

Shellfish has long been regarded as a luxury, but this attitude is now rapidly disappearing. Some kinds of shellfish can certainly be economical when the supply is plentiful. Shellfish can also be obtained frozen, potted, and canned. The term shellfish includes lobster, shrimp, crabs, Maryland crabs, crawfish, oysters, clams,

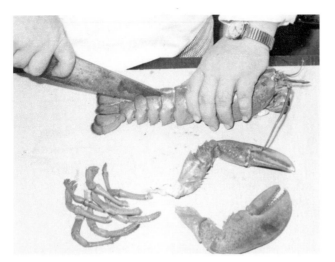

To cut a boiled lobster apart for service, first remove claws and legs. Then using a French knife, split the tail in half.

As the final step, split the body as shown. All pieces can now be easily handled.

Here, pieces of boiled lobster are arranged for service.

mussels and snails.

Clams—There are several species of clams. Soft clams are found mainly north of Cape Cod. The hard clams are suitable for eating on the half shell; they are small quahogs called cherrystones. Most clams are marketed alive in the shell, although they are also canned. The peak season is from June to September, however, fresh clams can be bought all during the year.

Crabs—There are several varieties of crabs. The most common are blue crabs, dungeness crabs, king crabs and rock crabs. Crabs can be bought alive or ready cooked. Live crabs are greyish brown, but, on boiling, turn to a brownish red. They should be well filled, heavy, firm and should not gurgle when gently shaken. The tails of live or dead (cooked) crabs should be firmly closed under the body.

Crabs are canned in Alaska, Maryland and in Norway, Russia and Japan.

Crawfish—A fresh water crustacean, the fresh water crawfish, has flesh as firm as shellfish, but it is subtly and delicately flavored. In this country, crawfish are rare in the East but are easily obtainable in the West and Midwest.

Lobsters—There are two types of lobster commonly used: one found in European waters, another in most American waters. Most of the lobsters found on the Eastern coast of North America are caught in New England. According to the

To prepare a lobster for sauteeing: 1. Remove tail and cut into equal slices as shown. 2. Split body in half. 3. Cut claws free from body. 4. Remove stomach and discard. 5. Remove coral which can be boiled for use as garnish on lobster.

Always an eyecatching presentation, Lobster Belvedere builds up the red lobster shells to provide height for the arrangement. Lemon slices and circles of lobster meat fan out from the vegetable mold.

U. S. Fish and Wildlife Dept., a five-year-old lobster measures about 10½ in. and has moulted 25 times. Lobster is marketed live, boiled, or canned. Almost all of the lobster available in the United States is sold live.

Mussels—This is an edible mollusk found in oceans all over the world but they are especially plentiful in the cold regions. The species most often used is called the Common Mussel. It has a long shell with a very slight roughness along the back. Mussels are very often used for seafood salads or cold canapes.

Oysters—A bivalve mollusk, usually eaten raw. Oysters on the Atlantic Coast are in season from September until May and are sold fresh. Oysters coming from a certain bed have come to be esteemed as most desirable and have acquired trade names such as Bluepoint, Lynnhaven, Sea Tags, etc. Pacific Coast oysters are sold all year round.

If oysters are to be used for hot appetizers, buy them in gallons, frozen.

Shrimp—Shrimps vary from the large size found off the southern coast that average one dozen to a pound, to the tiny shrimps, averaging forty to a pound. The titi shrimps are caught in Alaska and northern New England. These shrimp are less popular, but have better flavor and are excellent for salads or canapes.

Storage and Handling of Shellfish

Shellfish should be kept for as short a time as possible and should always be stored in a cool place. Shellfish, if not fresh when eaten, can be dangerous and can cause serious food poisoning. Fresh shellfish should be alive when purchased. Whether alive or canned, shellfish should have a fresh smell and a clean appearance.

Live shellfish must be rinsed with cold water before using. The shells of clams, littlenecks or oysters, should be brushed and rinsed before opening.

Cooking of Shellfish

All shellfish, with the exception of clams and oysters, must be cooked. When they are to be used for cold dishes, lobster, crabs or crawfish should be boiled in salted water with dill and a mirepoix of vegetables. Do not overcook as they will become tough and lose flavor. Shellfish should also be allowed to cool in the liquid they were cooked in.

Cooked lobsters and crabs must always be opened before serving. Mussels, however, should be cooked unopened either in a court bouillon or in their own juices. If they are to be used for cold salads, mussels should be allowed to cool in their own juice.

XII: COLD SAUCES--
BUTTER AND
CHEESE MIXTURES

The sauce should be the crowning touch for the dish it accompanies. It sometimes seems that there are as many sauces as there are menu items. However, a variety of sauces is especially important for garde manger foods.

Many of the cold sauces served as accompaniments for garde manger foods are derived from mayonnaise. Chaud froid sauce, which is covered in Chapter III, should not be confused with the sauces described in this chapter, since chaud froid is used as a coating while these sauces add a new complement of flavors to dishes they accompany.

How is basic mayonnaise prepared?

Commercially prepared mayonnaise may be purchased and this usually eliminates the need to prepare mayonnaise in the kitchen. However, knowing how to prepare mayonnaise is valuable in many instances.

BASIC MAYONNAISE RECIPE

Yield: 1½ pt.

Ingredients

Egg Yolks	4 to 5
Salt	1 tsp.
Cayenne Pepper	pinch
Prepared Mustard	2 tsp.
Oil	1½ pt.
Wine or Unflavored Vinegar or	
Lemon Juice	1 tbsp.

Preliminary Preparation

1. All ingredients should be kept at room temperature.
2. Use a whip to prepare mayonnaise in order to insure a good emulsification.
3. Pour oil slowly at the beginning to obtain a perfect emulsification from the start.

Method

1. In a stainless steel bowl, mix egg yolks, salt, cayenne pepper and mustard.
2. Slowly add oil, mixing with a whip. When thick, alternate oil and vinegar until all has been used. If sauce is too thick after all ingredients are used, add a

small amount of lukewarm water to mayonnaise.

A mayonnaise that breaks down can be restored by following this simple method which proves to be successful most of the time: in a clean, stainless steel bowl, place 1 tbsp. of cold water no matter what amount of mayonnaise is to be restored. Slowly whip a small quantity of the mayonnaise into the water in the bowl. The sauce will emulsify as it is whipped with the cold water and once emulsification starts, larger quantities of the broken mayonnaise may be added until restoration is complete.

NOTE: The use of sugar, food coloring or any other chemical ingredient in a mayonnaise should be avoided since these will improve neither the taste nor appearance.

Sauces Derived from Mayonnaise

Andalouse	Indian	Russian
Chantilly	Marchands de vins	Swedish
Devils	Mousquetaire	Tartar
Dijonnaise	Mustard	Tyrolienne
Gloucester or Piccadilly	Oriental	Vincent
	Remoulade	

Andalouse Sauce—Add to 1 cup of mayonnaise, 3 tbsp. of tomato paste and 2 tbsp. diced red pimentos, 1 tsp. lemon juice, dash of worcestershire sauce.

Chantilly Sauce—To 1 cup of mayonnaise, add ¼ cup of unsweetened, whipped cream. Season to taste.

Devil's Sauce—Reduce by two-thirds, 1 cup vinegar, 2 chopped shallots, 1 tbsp. crushed peppercorns, 1 tsp. juniperberries. Strain this reduction and add to remoulade sauce. Season with 1 tsp. English Mustard and a pinch of cayenne pepper.

Dijonnaise Sauce—A mayonnaise sauce combined with Dijon mustard, in proportions of 1 cup mayonnaise to 3 tsp. mustard.

Gloucester or Piccadilly Sauce—Add to 1 cup of mayonnaise, ½ cup sour cream. Season with 4 drops of Worcestershire sauce, 1 tsp. lemon juice and 1 tbsp. fresh chopped fennel.

Indian Sauce—Add 1 tbsp. curry powder, 1 tbsp. chives to 1 cup of mayonnaise.

Marchands de vins—Blend 3 shallots with 1/3 cup of white wine, add to 1 cup mayonnaise with finely chopped parsley.

Mousquetaire Sauce—Add to 1 cup mayonnaise, 2 tbsp. chopped shallots cooked in ¼ cup white wine and 1 tbsp. melted glace de viande.

Mustard Sauce—Add to 1 cup of mayonnaise, 2 to 3 tbsp. of prepared mustard.

Oriental Sauce—Add to 1 cup of mayonnaise, 3 tbsp. tomato paste, one pinch of saffron, 2 tbsp. diced, blanched green peppers.

REMOULADE SAUCE

Yield: 1½ pt.

Ingredients

Mayonnaise	1½ pt.
Capers	2 tbsp.
Cornichons (tiny sour gherkins)	2 tbsp.
Fillet of Anchovy, pureed	1
Shallots	1 tsp.
Tarragon	1 tsp.
Parsley	1 tbsp.
English Mustard	1 tsp.

Method

Chop all ingredients fine and combine with mayonnaise. Season with mustard and puree of anchovy.

Russian Sauce—Combine 2/3 cup of mayonnaise with 1/3 cup of caviar. Season with 1 tsp. prepared mustard and the juice of one lemon.

Swedish Sauce—Use 2 cups thick mayonnaise to 1 cup applesauce flavored with white wine. Season with 1 tsp. lemon juice, 2 tsp. grated horseradish, 1/8 tsp. sugar.

TARTAR SAUCE

Yield: 1¼ pt.

Ingredients

Mayonnaise	1 pt.
Hard Cooked Eggs	4
Chives, chopped	1 tbsp.
Shallots, chopped	1
Tarragon, chopped	1 tsp.
Chervil, chopped	1 tsp.
Parsley, chopped	1 tsp.

Method

Put eggs through food mill. Combine with remaining ingredients and add to the mayonnaise. Flavor can be adjusted with salt, pepper and lemon juice to taste.

Tyrolienne Sauce—To 1 cup mayonnaise, add 1 tbsp. chopped parsley, 1 tbsp. chopped chervil, 1/4 cup reduced, finely chopped tomatoes. Season with 1/3 tsp. black pepper, 4 drops Worcestershire sauce, 1 tsp. chili sauce.

VINCENT SAUCE

Yield: 1¾ pt.

Ingredients

Chervil, Parsley, Chives, Tarragon combined	2 oz.
Spinach	1 oz.
Watercress	1 oz.
Hard-cooked Eggs	3
Mayonnaise	2 cups
Worcestershire Sauce	5 drops

Method

Blanch all herbs. Cool, press all moisture out and blend together with eggs and 4 tbsp. mayonnaise. Add remaining mayonnaise. Season with worcestershire sauce.

Sauces Not Derived from Mayonnaise

Anchovy	Frozen Horseradish	Serbian Garlic
Apple Horseradish	Gribiche	Vinaigrette
Cranberry	Italian	Orange Horseradish
Cumberland	Plain Horseradish	Sauce Ravigotte

Anchovy Sauce—Pound 4 hard-cooked eggs and 8 anchovy fillets to a fine paste. Season with white pepper. Thin to desired thickness with oil and vinegar. Adjust seasoning.

Apple Horseradish Sauce—Peel and grate fresh apples. Mix with equal quantities of grated horseradish. Finish the sauce with a touch of oil, vinegar, salt, sugar and a small amount of beef stock.

Cranberry Sauce—Pick over 1 lb. cranberries and wash in cold water; place in pot; cover with water. Add 8 oz. sugar and juice of 1 lemon. Bring to a boil. Serve cold.

CUMBERLAND SAUCE

Yield: ¾ pt.

Ingredients

Red Currant Jelly	1 cup
Blanched Shallots, chopped	1 tbsp.
Orange and Lemon Zests, blanched	2 tbsp.
English Mustard	1 tsp.
Port Wine	1/2 cup
Orange	juice of 1
Lemon	juice of 1
Salt	1/3 tsp.
Cayenne Pepper	pinch
Ginger	pinch

Method

Melt red currant jelly, add blanched shallots julienned, orange and lemon peel (zests). Dissolve mustard in wine. Add to currant jelly. Simmer 5 to 10 minutes. Add lemon and orange juice. Season with salt, cayenne and ginger.

NOTE: **Oxford Sauce**—Add grated orange and lemon peel to this recipe.

FROZEN HORSERADISH SAUCE

Yield: 1 pt.

Ingredients

Whipped Cream	1 pt.
Horseradish, grated	2 to 3 tbsp.
Vinegar	1 tbsp.
Salt	½ tsp.
Sugar	pinch
Black Pepper, ground	½ tsp.

Method

Combine whipped cream with horseradish and vinegar. Gently mix all ingredients. Roll into greased parchment paper and freeze. At service time, cut into slices. This sauce may be served with beef, ham, corned beef and tongue.

GRIBICHE SAUCE

Yield: 1¼ pt.

Ingredients

Hard-Cooked Eggs	3
Prepared Mustard	½ tsp.
Vinegar	1½ tsp.
Oil	1 pt.
Capers, chopped	1 tbsp.
Sour Pickle, chopped	1 tsp.
Chervil, chopped	½ tsp.
Tarragon, chopped	½ tsp.
Parsley, chopped	½ tsp.
Hard-Cooked Egg Whites, julienned	2

Method

Put three hard-cooked eggs through sieve. Mix in mustard, capers, pickles and herbs. Mix in oil and vinegar. Add 2 julienned egg whites.

ITALIAN SAUCE

Yield: 1¼ pt.

Ingredients

Sweet Almonds	1/3 oz.
Pistachio Nuts	3/4 oz.
Bechamel Sauce, cold	1 oz.
Egg Yolks	3
Oil	1 pt.
Salt, Pepper, combined	1/2 tsp.
Tarragon, Chives, Parsley, Chervil, combined	1 oz.

Method

Puree pistachio nuts and almonds together with Bechamel Sauce. Mix in egg yolks and oil as in preparing mayonnaise. Season with salt and pepper and finely chopped herbs.

PLAIN HORSERADISH

Yield: 1½ pt.

Ingredients

Fresh Horseradish	2 cups
Raw Apple	1 cup
Lemon Juice	few drops
Salt	½ tsp.
Pepper	pinch

Method

Peel apples and horseradish; grate fine. Add lemon juice, salt and pepper.

SERBIAN GARLIC SAUCE

Yield: ½ pt.
Ingredients

Garlic	4 cloves
Egg Yolks	2 to 3
Oil	1 cup
Salt	½ to 1 tsp.
White Pepper	pinch
Lemon Juice	a few drops

Method

Mash the garlic with salt, add egg yolks and pepper. Mix in the oil as for mayonnaise. Finish with lemon juice.

VINAIGRETTE SAUCE

Yield: 2 pt.
Ingredients

Wine Vinegar	1 cup
Oil	3 cups
Parsley, Chives, Tarragon	2 oz.
Onion	2 oz.
Salt	1 tsp.
Pepper	pinch

Method

Combine oil and vinegar. Add finely chopped herbs and onion. Season to taste.

ORANGE HORSERADISH SAUCE

Yield: 1 pt.
Ingredients

Apples, fresh, grated	1 cup
Fresh or Prepared Horseradish	1 cup
Lemon	juice of ½
Orange, grated zest	1
Sugar	1/3 tsp.
Orange	juice of 1

Method

Mix all ingredients and marinate for two hours.

RAVIGOTTE SAUCE

Yield: About 2 cups

Ingredients

Fresh Parsley, minced	2 tsp.
Fresh Chervil, minced	4 tsp.
Fresh Tarragon, minced	2 tsp.
Fresh Chives, minced	2 tsp.
Vinaigrette Sauce (use Basic French)	2 cups
Small Onion, diced	1½
Minced Capers, well drained	2 tbsp.
Prepared Mustard	1 tsp.

Method

Combine all ingredients and blend them well.

USAGE OF COLD SAUCES

Cold sauces make good accompaniments for a large variety of dishes. The following chart can certainly be expanded but it is offered to help menu planners explore the many possibilities for cold sauces.

Asparagus, Artichokes

Chantilly
Vinaigrette
Mustard

Egg Dishes

All sauces derived from mayonnaise

Fish and Shellfish

Andalouse	Tartare	Gribiche
Italian	Remoulade	Anchovy
Russian	Vincent	Serbian Garlic

Game

Cumberland
Oxford
Cranberry

Meat

Gloucester or Piccadilly
Remoulade
Tartare
Tyrolienne

Butter and Cheese Mixtures

Butter and cheese are combined with many ingredients to make spreads that can be used to create a large variety of canapes. The spreads thus produced enhance the flavor and taste of the canapes; they also provide a flavorful base for ingredients (shrimp, olive slices, etc.) that are used to top canapes to make their presentation more appealing.

The following list of butter and cheese mixtures can be extended to include various other types of butters; in fact, there is no limit to the variations that can be created.

Anchovy Butter—Blend 12 fillets of anchovies with 4 oz. of sweet butter, then put through a fine sieve.

Caviar Butter—Blend 2 oz. of fresh caviar with 4 oz. of butter and put through a fine sieve.

Cayenne Butter—Mix ¼ oz. of cayenne with 1 lb. of butter.

Crayfish Butter—Blend 2 oz. of cooked crayfish tails with 4 oz. of butter and put through a fine sieve.

Curry Butter—To a very small onion, finely chopped and cooked in butter, add 1 tsp. of curry powder. Simmer two min., remove from stove and let cool. Add 1 cup butter; mix and put through fine sieve.

Egg Butter—Blend 12 egg yolks with 8 oz. butter and a few drops of olive oil. Put through a fine sieve and add salt and cayenne pepper.

Foie Gras Butter—Blend 4 oz. cooked foie gras with 4 oz. butter and put through sieve.

Garlic Butter—Blend 5-6 cloves of garlic with 1 lb. of butter and put through a fine sieve.

Herring Butter—Blend 2 desalted fillets of herring with ¾ lb. butter and put through a fine sieve.

Herring Roe Butter—Blend 3 oz. herring roe which has been poached in white wine with 4 oz. butter; add a pinch of mustard and put through a fine sieve.

Horseradish Butter—Mix 2 oz. of scraped horseradish with a pound of butter.

Langouste Butter—Follow procedure for lobster butter below.

Lobster Butter—Blend 4 oz. lobster coral and liver with 8 oz. of butter and put through a fine sieve.

Montpellier Butter—Green Butter—In a saucepan containing boiling water, put an equal quantity of watercress leaves, parsley, chervil, chives and tarragon (about 12 sprigs of each), two sliced shallots and twelve spinach leaves. Boil for about two minutes, then drain, let cool and press dry in a towel. Blend this with 15 anchovies, 2 tsp. capers, 6 small pickles, 1 clove of garlic and 8 hard-cooked egg yolks. Add ½ lb. butter, pepper, salt, a little nutmeg. Blend together with ½ pt. olive oil, ¼ cup tarragon vinegar. Put through a fine sieve.

Moscovite Butter—Blend 8 oz. butter with 4 oz. caviar, 6 hard-cooked egg yolks and put through a very fine sieve. Season with salt and cayenne.

Mustard Butter—Mix 1 tbsp. of English mustard with ½ lb. butter. (This can be made with prepared mustard.)

Nutmeg Butter—Blend 2 nutmegs with 1 lb. butter and put through fine sieve.

Paprika Butter—To a very small onion, chopped and cooked in butter, add 1 tbsp. paprika and simmer a minute or two. Remove from heat, let cool and add 1 cup of butter; put through fine sieve.

Perigourdine Butter—Blend 4 oz. butter with 4 hard-cooked egg yolks and 2 medium sized truffles. Put through a very fine sieve. Season with salt and cayenne pepper.

Pimento Butter—Blend 1 oz. red pimentoes with 3 oz. butter; put through a fine sieve.

Portuguese Butter—Blend 3 hard-cooked egg yolks with 5 oz. butter. Add 1 tbsp. tomato paste, salt and pepper. Put through a fine sieve and add a little red color.

Ravigote Butter—Blend in a mortar equal quantities of chervil, parsley, tarragon, chives and pimprenelle (all these herbs to be blanched) with an equal quantity of butter. Put through a fine sieve.

Smoked Salmon Butter—Blend ½ lb. smoked salmon with 1 lb. of butter and put through a fine sieve.

Sardine Butter—Blend 12 sardines, without bones, with ¾ lb. butter and put through a fine sieve.

Shrimp Butter=Blend 2 oz. grey shrimps (cooked) with 4 oz. butter and put through a very fine sieve.

Butter for Snails—Blend in a mortar 1 oz. garlic, 3 oz. shallots, 2 lb. butter; add 2 oz. chopped parsley, salt and pepper.

Tarragon Butter—Blend a handful of blanched tarragon leaves with ¾ lb. butter and put through a very fine sieve.

Tunafish Butter—Blend 1 oz. tunafish with 2½ oz. butter and put through a sieve. NOTE: Whipped cream may be substituted for butter but the mixing must be carefully done to prevent curdling.

Crab Cheese—Follow procedure for Langouste Cheese below.

Langouste Cheese—Blend the meat of 1 langouste with ½ lb. gruyere cheese and 2 oz. butter. Put through a fine sieve and finish with heavy cream and brandy.

Lobster Cheese—Follow procedure for Langouste Cheese above.

Salmon Cheese—Blend 4 oz. cooked salmon with 4 oz. gruyere cheese and 1 oz. butter. Put through a fine sieve and finish with heavy cream and a little port wine.

Truffle Cheese—Blend 4 oz. truffles with 2 oz. gruyere cheese and 2 oz. sweet butter. Add ½ glass of brandy, spices to taste and put through a fine sieve.

Tunafish Cheese—Blend 8 oz. tunafish with 8 oz. gruyere cheese. Put through a fine sieve and finish with heavy cream.

XIII: COLD FOOD PRESENTATION

The menu items created in the garde manger are largely classified as cold foods. The successful preparation and presentation of cold foods depends on the methods and rules explained here:

- Poultry to be coated with aspic or chaud froid must be thoroughly cooled, otherwise aspic or chaud froid sauce will not adhere to it.

- Before applying chaud froid sauce to food, a coat of aspic must be applied.

- The chaud froid sauce must be firm and cold before the decoration can be applied.

- All ingredients to be used as decorations must be dipped into cold, liquid aspic before they can be arranged on the main piece. The aspic will prevent the decorations from falling off the large (gross piece) piece when aspic is poured over it.

- It is essential that all decorated pieces are coated with crystal clear, light colored aspic. This will permit the full color of the decoration to shine through. The aspic should be neither too cold nor too warm when applied; the best temperature is either ice cold but not congealed or when aspic is the thickness of heavy cream.

- When working with fish, it is important to cool it thoroughly and make sure fish is dry before applying the decor and aspic.

- A whole decorated fish should never be arranged on a platter smaller than the fish. A shallow tray or a platter specially designed for fish is best. Crystal clear aspic, diced, finely chopped or in croutons, always gives a pleasing effect.

- If decorated silver skewers (see Chap. 1) are necessary, only edible food should be used to decorate them and it is important that the foods used blend with the taste of the main ingredient of the display they are presented with.

- Display foods can be served on mirrors, or on plastic, wood, china, metal, or silver platters. If the service requires the use of silver or metal trays, it is helpful to cover the surface of the tray with a coat of aspic. This will prevent discoloration of the foods, as may happen, for example, when eggs are placed on silver trays. When metal trays are used, the coat of aspic will prevent the development of undesirable metal flavor.

- The proportion of the garnish should be balanced in relation to the food item it is used with. The garnish should not be larger than the main piece. The garnish is designed to call the diner's attention to the food it is used on, not just to the garnish.

• It is important to plan and sketch the decoration and arrangements of the main food trays carefully. Planning ahead keeps the work cleaner as there are fewer errors made. It is also easier and faster to arrange food and decoration according to a plan. It is important to remember that if foods are handled too often they may be damaged. Too much handling can also contaminate foods. *Once the food has touched the tray, it should not be removed until it is served.*

NOTE: According to chefs and gourmets, amateur and professional alike, chaud froid dishes are not as popular today as they were many years ago. This decline in popularity can be traced to a shortage of skilled labor as well as to the time required to make the dishes. This book suggests a method of chaud froid preparation that makes it possible to create these dishes faster and more economically in the hope that one day, they will again become as popular as they once were.

While the short cuts suggested may seem obvious, if they are followed by the kitchen staff, producing artistic and beautiful food trays for the buffet table can be justified both from the time and cost standpoint.

To carve a capon for chaud froid (cold set-up): Remove breast and fill cavity with a mousse of liver (Chap. XI). Slice breast into thin slices; place slices in sequence on a tray *so they can be replaced in order on the chicken. Put slices of capon back into the breast cavity, starting at the top of the capon, overlapping slices.*

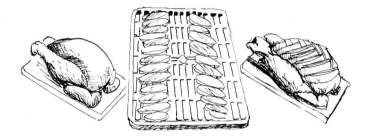

To carve a chicken for chaud froid:
Slice breast of chicken into even slices. Stuff cavity of bird with a chicken mousse *(Chap. XI) and place breast slices back on the chicken in sequence as shown below; coat with clear aspic.*

Breast with slices in place ready for coat of clear aspic.

Stuffed leek salad (recipe, p.44) is highlighted with asparagus spray holding radish flower.

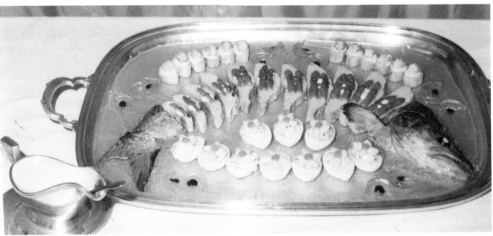

Salmon Froid a la Belvidere—The impact of cold poached salmon is heightened by colorful decorations and garnishes. Spears of asparagus centered with golden egg yolk, then criss crossed with pimento are placed on the salmon filets. A circle of slices of cucumber stuffed with a deviled egg mixture fills out top of tray. Stuffed eggs in the foreground hold a mixture of mayonnaise, horseradish, caviar and cream cheese, are topped with an egg yolk flower with a red dot of tomato in the center.

Cauliflower salad (recipe, p. 158) is used as centerpiece from which barquettes of ham fan out to fill tray. Wedges of gelatin filled oranges provide border.

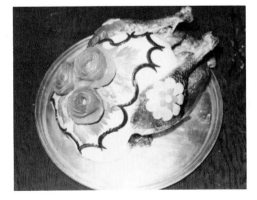

Roast capon chaud froid—Celery leaves provide the background for the tomato skin roses. Half moon shapes cut from aspic truffle sheets border the main design. The tear drop flowers are cut from egg and pimento aspic sheets. (See drawing, p. 28.)

Elaborate decorations made from figures cut from sheets of aspic are limited only by the imagination. White chaud froid provides an excellent background to set off these designs. If desired, display designs like these may be prepared in advance and stored in freezer.

Roast Spring Chicken (with watercress chaud froid). Roast chicken; cool. When cold, remove breast of chicken and fill cavity with a Russian Salad; then coat with watercress chaud froid. Decorate chicken with leeks and stuffed tomatoes. Small medallions of breast meat are coated with chaud froid and decorated with asparagus and pimento, then arranged in circle around chicken Stuffed cherry tomatoes complete the display.

The roast beef and vegetable display uses carrot triangles and whole green beans to accent the onions and cauliflower surrounding the thin slices of beef. A larger piece of roast beef has design made of half moon truffle sheets and gets added height from three tomato roses.

XIV: SALADS

The only limit to the number of salads that can be created is the imagination of the chef. However, before experimenting with untested combinations, the chef-salad maker should perfect his presentation of the established salad favorites. A large variety of salads, attractively displayed on a buffet, will be a drawing card for most patrons.

Salads are usually served with appropriate dressings, although sometimes, instead of having a dressing added, the salad ingredients are marinated for a period of time in oil, vinegar, lemon juice or other liquids. Marinated salads can be preserved for several days. Selecting the right dressing is an important element of salad preparation.

Marinades and Dressings

BASIC FRENCH DRESSING (called vinaigrette in French)

Yield: 4 tbsp.

Ingredients

Salt	1/3 tsp.
Wine Vinegar	1 tbsp.
Olive Oil	3 tbsp.
Pepper, freshly ground	2 grinds

Method
Dissolve salt in vinegar, then add oil and pepper. Mix all ingredients well.

Variations of Basic French Dressing—Listed here are several popular ways to vary Basic French Dressing:

1. After mixing salt with vinegar, add 1 tbsp. of prepared mustard, mix well, then combine with oil and freshly ground pepper.

2. Mix one raw egg yolk with 1 tbsp. prepared mustard, season with salt and pepper. Add 3 tbsp. of oil and 1 tbsp. vinegar. Mix well.

3. Put one hard cooked egg through a sieve, add 3 tbsp. oil and 1 tbsp. lemon juice, season to taste with salt and pepper. Beat until the sauce reaches a creamy consistency.

4. Blend 2 tbsp. of blue cheese with Basic French Dressing.

5. Coarsely chop one hard cooked egg. Mix with Basic French Dressing, add chopped parsley and chopped tarragon and one chopped shallot.

6. Combine 1 tbsp. chopped onion, 1 tbsp. chopped, crisp bacon, 1 tbsp. chopped pimentoes and mix with Basic French Dressing.

Russian Dressing—Mix one cup of mayonnaise with ½ cup of red chili sauce, add 2 tbsp. of red peppers, one chopped hard cooked egg, one dash of Worcestershire sauce, and one dash of hot sauce. Mix all ingredients thoroughly.

EMULSIFIED FRENCH DRESSING
(This type of dressing is very popular in the U. S. A., although it is practically unknown to Europeans.)
Yield: 2¾ pt.
Ingredients

Salad Oil	1 qt.
Cider Vinegar	1 cup
Eggs	2
Salt	1 tsp.
Fresh Garlic, crushed and chopped	1 clove
White Pepper	¼ tsp.
Dry Mustard	1 tsp.
Paprika	2 tbsp.
Worcestershire Sauce	1 tbsp.
Lemon Juice	¼ cup

Method
Beat eggs with dry ingredients. Add oil slowly; when mixture has thickened, add a little vinegar. Alternately add oil and vinegar until it all has been used. Add Worcestershire sauce; finish with lemon juice.

GREEN GODDESS DRESSING
Yield: 2¾ pt.
Ingredients

Garlic	6 cloves
Anchovies, drained	1 can
Chives	1/4 cup
Parsley, chopped	1 cup
Salt	2 tsp.
Black Pepper	1/2 tsp.
Lemon Juice	1/3 cup
Tarragon Vinegar	1/4 cup
Mayonnaise	1 qt.
Sour Cream	2 cups

Method
Chop parsley, strain and save liquid to add as coloring.
Blend liquid ingredients first, then add remaining ingredients

Thousand Island Dressing—Combine equal parts of chili sauce and mayonnaise with heavy cream. Blend till mixture is thick.

Vegetable Salads

TOMATO SALAD

Yield: 4 portions
Ingredients

Tomatoes, fresh firm	2
Oil	3 tbsp.
Wine Vinegar	1 tbsp.
Onions, chopped	1 tbsp.
Chives, chopped	1 tbsp.
Salt	1/3 tsp.
Pepper	2 to 3 grinds
Oregano	a pinch

Method
Blanch and peel tomatoes. Slice 1/8 in. thick.

Prepare as Basic French Dressing: combine oil and vinegar, add onions, chives, salt, pepper and oregano. Arrange tomatoes in ravier and cover with dressing. Allow to stand 30 min. Serve chilled.

CELERY SALAD NO. 1

Yield: 2 lb. or 10 portions
Ingredients

Celery	4 roots
Lemon	juice of 1
Basic French Dressing	½ cup
Thin Mayonnaise	½ cup
Parsley, chopped	to garnish

Method
Peel and cook celery with water and juice of 1 lemon. Cool and cut julienne; marinate in French dressing. Remove from marinade and mix with mayonnaise, Before serving, cover with mayonnaise, sprinkle with chopped parsley.

CELERY SALAD NO.2

Yield: 4 portions
Ingredients

Celery	1 heart
English Mustard	1 tsp.
Heavy Cream	1/2 cup
Lemon	juice of 1
Mayonnaise	4 tbsp.
Salt	1/3 tsp.
Pepper, freshly ground	2 grinds

Method
Clean and peel celery stalks. Cut into julienne. Combine heavy cream, lemon juice, English mustard, and mayonnaise, seasonings and mix all ingredients well. Mix in the julienne of celery and marinate for 30 min.

CELERY SALAD NO.3

Yield: 8-10 portions

Ingredients

Celery	2 hearts
Apples, medium, peeled	3
French Mustard	1 tbsp.
Heavy Cream	½ cup
Lemon	juice of 1
Salt	½ tsp.
Pepper, freshly ground	2 grinds

Method

Clean and peel celery, cut into small julienne. Peel and dice apples and combine with celery.

Mix heavy cream, French mustard and lemon juice. Combine all ingredients and marinate a few minutes before serving.

ASPARAGUS SALAD

Yield: 4 portions

Ingredients

Asparagus Stalks	16
French Dressing	1 cup
Prepared Mustard	2 tbsp.
Parsley, chopped	1 tbsp.
Chives	1 tbsp.
Tarragon	1 tsp.
Salt	1/3 to 1/2 tsp.
Pepper, freshly ground	4 grinds

Method

Peel and cook asparagus, cut into pieces 2 to 3 in. in length. Marinate in French dressing made with mustard, parsley, chives, tarragon and salt and pepper.

MUSHROOM SALAD NO.1

Yield: 3-4 portions

Ingredients

Mushroom Caps	1 lb.
Oil	2 tsp.
Onion, medium, diced	1
Vinegar	1/4 cup
Oil	3/4 cup
Salt	1/2 to 1 tsp.
Pepper	1/3 tsp.
Tarragon Leaves, fresh, frozen, chopped	1/2 tsp.

Method

Wash and slice mushrooms. In a saute pan, heat oil and cook onions and mushrooms; season.

Prepare Basic French Dressing, adding chopped tarragon.

Marinate mushrooms in dressing for 1 hour.

MUSHROOM SALAD NO.2

Yield: 4-5 portions
Ingredients

White Mushroom Caps	1 lb.
Lemons	juice of 3
Salt	1/2 to 1 tsp.
Pepper	1/3 tsp.
Soy Sauce	3 tsp.

Method
Wash and slice mushrooms very thin; marinate for 1 or 2 hours in lemon juice, salt, pepper and soy sauce.

RED CABBAGE SALAD NO.1

Yield: 8-10 portions (1 lb. 11 oz.)
Ingredients

Red Cabbage, medium	1
White Vinegar	1/3 cup
Onion, medium, diced	1
Salt	1/2 tsp.

Method
Shred cabbage. Mix onion and vinegar; add salt to taste. Marinate cabbage in mixture for 24 hours or more.

RED CABBAGE SALAD NO. 2

Yield: 8-10 portions (1 lb. 13 oz.)
Ingredients

Red Cabbage, medium	1
Red Currant Jelly	1/4 cup
Oil	1 cup
Vinegar	1/3 cup
Salt	1/2 to 1 tsp.
Pepper	1/3 tsp.

Method
Shred the cabbage fine and blanch for 3-4 min. in vinegar flavored water.

Mix vinegar, salt, pepper, oil and currant jelly and pour over cabbage. Marinate for 2-3 hours.

LEEK SALAD

Yield: 12-15 oz.
Ingredients

Leeks	1 bunch
White Stock	1 pt.
Basic French Dressing made with	
1 tbsp. prepared mustard	1 cup
Hard Cooked Eggs, chopped	3

Method
Wash leeks and remove outside leaves. Cut leeks lengthwise, leaving 1 in. above the root uncut.

Tie leeks in a bundle and braise in white stock until cooked; drain carefully. Cut leeks into 2-3 in. pieces and combine with remaining ingredients. Serve sprinkled with egg.

MACARONI SALAD

Yield: 2 lb. 11 oz.

Ingredients

Macaroni	8 oz.
Tomatoes, seedless, peeled and diced	2
Vinegar	2 tsp.
Mayonnaise	1 cup
Green Peppers, diced	1 oz.
Red Peppers, diced	1 oz.
Salt	1/2 tsp.
Pepper	1/3 tsp.

Method

Cook macaroni in boiling, salted water for 10-15 min. Mix mayonnaise with remaining ingredients and combine with macaroni.

GREEN PEPPER SALAD

Yield: 17 oz.

Ingredients

Green Peppers	1 lb.
White Vinegar	1/2 cup
Oil	1 cup
Sugar	1 tsp.
Tarragon, chopped	1 tbsp.
Chives	1 tbsp.
Salt	1/2-1 tsp.
Pepper	1/2 tsp.

Method

Wash peppers and cut in half. Remove seeds and cut into fine julienne.

Mix all remaining ingredients together and add to the peppers.

BEET SALAD NO.1

Yield: 15 oz.

Ingredients

Beets	1 lb
Heavy Cream	1/2 cup
English Mustard	1 tsp
Lemons	juice of 2
Sugar	1 tsp.
Salt	1 to 1-1/2 tsp.
Pepper	1/3 to 1/2 tsp.

Method

Wash beets and cook in boiling water till tender. Cool and slice.

Blend heavy cream, mustard, lemon juice, sugar, salt and pepper and combine with beets.

BEET SALAD NO. 2

Yield: 1 lb.

Ingredients

Beets	1 lb.
French Dressing	1 cup
Onion, medium, diced	1
Salt	1/2 to 1 tsp.
Pepper	1/3 tsp.
Worcestershire Sauce	1/2 tsp.
Parsley, chopped	1 tsp.

Method

Wash beets and cook in boiling water until tender. Cool and cut in medium julienne.

Mix remaining ingredients and combine with beets. Before serving, sprinkle with chopped parsley.

BASIC POTATO SALAD
(See picture above)

Yield: 2 lb. 12 oz.

Ingredients

Potatoes (not mealy)	2 lbs.
Oil	1/4 cup
Vinegar	1/4 cup
Hot Chicken Stock	1/4 cup
Onion, medium diced	1/2 cup
Salt	1 tsp.
Pepper	1/2 tsp.
Sugar	1/3 tsp.
Parsley, chopped	1 tbsp.

Method

Wash and cook potatoes in jackets. When done, cool potatoes and peel while still warm. Dice or slice.

Mix oil, vinegar, stock, onion, salt, pepper, sugar and parsley. Marinate potatoes in this mixture for 1 to 2 hrs. before serving.

GERMAN POTATO SALAD

Follow procedure on facing page but add 1 diced peeled apple and 1 tbsp. chopped chives.

DUTCH POTATO SALAD

Follow Basic Potato Salad Recipe but add 2 tbsp. diced bacon and 1 diced herring, smoked.

FRENCH POTATO SALAD

Yield: 2 lb. 6 oz.
Ingredients

Potatoes (not mealy)	2 lb.
Shallots, chopped	4
Wine Vinegar	¼ cup
Oil	¼ cup
Salt	½ to 1 tsp.
Pepper	½ tsp.
Parsley, chopped	1 tsp.

Method

Scrub potatoes, cook in boiling water until tender. Cool potatoes, peel and slice thin.

Mix sliced potatoes with chopped shallots, oil, vinegar, salt, pepper and chopped parsley.

NOTE: All of the above types of potato salad can be mixed with mayonnaise.

CARROT SALAD NO. 1

Yield: 15 oz.
Ingredients

Carrots, fresh	1 lb.
OR	
Belgium Carrots, (14 oz. can)	1
French Mustard	2 tbsp.
Garlic, finely chopped	1 clove
Oil	1/2 cup
Vinegar	1/4 cup
Salt	1/2 to 1 tsp.
Pepper	1/3 tsp.
Chives, chopped	2 tsp.

Method

Peel fresh carrots; cook until tender; slice. If using canned carrots, drain before using.

Combine all remaining ingredients and hold for 30 minutes before serving.

CARROT SALAD NO. 2

Yield: 1 lb.
Ingredients

Carrots	1 lb.
Basic French Dressing	1/3 cup
Prepared Mustard	1 tbsp.
Lemon	juice of 1

Method
Peel carrots and grate.   Mix Basic French Dressing, lemon juice and mustard; add carrots and allow to stand in dressing for a few minutes before service.

BASIC CUCUMBER SALAD

Yield: 20-22 oz.
Ingredients

Cucumbers (10-11 oz.)	2
Basic French Dressing	½ cup
Parsley, chopped, or dill	1 tbsp.

Method
Peel cucumbers and slice thin. Marinate in dressing for a few minutes. Sprinkle with chopped parsley or dill.

ENGLISH CUCUMBER SALAD

Yield: 20-23 oz.
Ingredients

Cucumbers (10-11 oz.)	2
Celery stalks, cut julienne	2
Heavy Cream	½ cup
Lemons	juice of 2
Salt	to taste
Pepper	to taste

Method
Peel cucumbers and slice thin. Peel celery and cut into julienne.

Combine cucumbers and celery and add other ingredients; mix thoroughly and allow to stand for 1/2 hour before serving.

FRENCH CUCUMBER SALAD

Yield: 20-22 oz.
Ingredients

Cucumbers (10-11 oz.)	2
Salt	1 tsp.
Basic French Dressing	½ cup
Parsley, chopped	1 tsp.
Onion, medium, sliced thin	½

Method
Peel cucumbers, cut lengthwise. Remove seeds, slice thin and add salt. Place in bowl for ½ hour.

Place cucumbers in a clean towel. Squeeze all water out.

Mix cucumbers with dressing and onions and sprinkle with chopped parsley

RUSSIAN CUCUMBER SALAD

Yield: 24-26 oz.

Ingredients

Cucumbers (10-11 oz.)	2
Mayonnaise	1/4 cup
Sour Cream	1/4 cup
Dill, chopped	1 tbsp.
Lemon	juice of 1
Salt	1/3 to 1/2 tsp.
Pepper, freshly ground	2 grinds
Onion, medium, sliced thin	½

Method

Peel and slice cucumbers.

Combine mayonnaise, sour cream, lemon juice, dill, onion, salt and pepper. Add cucumber to mixture.

HUNGARIAN CUCUMBER SALAD

Prepare Russian Cucumber Salad as above, then add 1 tbsp. chopped chives, ¼ cup thin julienne slices of green pepper and ¼ cup thin julienne slices of pimento.

GREEN BEAN SALAD

Yield: 1 lb. 16 oz.

Ingredients

Green Beans, fresh or frozen	1 lb.
Basic French Dressing	1/2 cup
Pimento, diced	1/2 cup
Garlic Powder	1/3 tsp.
Salt	1/2 to 1 tsp.
Pepper	1/2 tsp.
Bacon, diced, cooked crisp	4 oz.

Method

If using fresh beans, cut tips from both ends and cut in 2-in. pieces. Cook beans in boiling salted water til done. Drain thoroughly and cool. If using frozen beans, cook according to directions. Combine pimento, bacon and seasonings with dressing. Add cooked beans to dressing. Mix well.

BEAN SPROUT SALAD

Yield: 1 lb. 4 oz.

Ingredients

Bean Sprouts	2 cups
Soy Sauce	2 tbsp.
Seasame Seeds, ground	2 tbsp.
Pimento, diced	¼ cup
Scallions, chopped	¼ cup
Vinegar	2 tsp.
Garlic, chopped	1 clove

Method

Combine all ingredients and mix with bean sprouts. Refrigerate for 1 hr. before serving.

ARTICHOKE PROVENCALE SALAD
(See picture above)

Yield: 6 portions
Ingredients

Artichoke Bottoms	12
Tomatoes, medium	3
Anchovy Fillets, canned	1 small can
Lemon	juice of 1
Pepper	½ tsp.
Salt	½ tsp.
Chives	1 tsp.
Ripe Olives	6
Green Olives	6

Method
Quarter the cooked artichoke bottoms and deep fry a few seconds.
Quarter tomatoes and dice half of anchovies.
Combine artichokes, tomatoes, anchovies, lemon juice, salt, pepper and chives. Arrange on dish and decorate with remaining anchovy fillets and ripe and green olives.

CAULIFLOWER SALAD

Yield: 20-25 oz.
Ingredients

Cauliflower, medium (16-20 oz.)	1
Basic French Dressing	1 cup
Prepared Mustard	1 tbsp.
Lemon	juice of 1
Garlic, chopped	1 clove
Hard Cooked Egg Yolks, chopped	3

Method
Wash cauliflower and cook in boiling water until done. Cool and cut into small pieces.
Combine remaining ingredients and mix with cauliflower buds. Marinate for 1 hr. in refrigerator.

CABBAGE SLAW—FARMERS STYLE

Yield: 1 lb. 15 oz. (10-12 portions)

Ingredients

White Cabbage	1
Basic French Dressing	2 cups
Caraway Seeds	1 tsp.

Method

Shred cabbage and blanch for two min.

Drain cabbage, then mix with dressing and caraway seeds. Refrigerate 1 hr. before service.

INDIAN RICE SALAD

Yield: 2 lb. 6 oz.

Ingredients

Rice	1 cup
Smoked Fish	2 oz.
Tomatoes, blanched and peeled	2
Green Pepper	1
Basic French Dressing	1 cup
Salt	1/3 tsp.
Pepper, freshly ground	2 to 3 grinds
Worcestershire Sauce	1/2 tsp.

Method

Boil rice in 2½ cups of salted water for approx. 20 min. When cooked, drain and cool.

Dice fish, tomato and green pepper and combine with rice. Add salt, pepper, dressing and Worcestershire sauce to mixture.

ITALIAN SALAD

Yield: 12 oz.

Ingredients

Celery Stalks	2 oz.
Tomatoes, blanched and peeled	2 oz.
Artichoke Bottoms	2 oz.
Apples	2 oz.
Olive Oil	1/2 cup
Lemons	juice of 3
Salt	1/3 tsp.
Pepper, freshly ground	2 to 3 grinds
Romaine Lettuce	1 leaf
Fennel, julienned	2 oz.

Method

Dice celery, tomatoes, artichokes and apples.

Mix oil, lemon juice, salt and pepper and blend with diced celery, tomatoes, artichokes and apples.

Arrange on a leaf of Romaine lettuce and top with julienned fennel.

To prepare Roast Duck with Waldorf Salad, remove and slice breasts of duck. Mound Waldorf Salad in cavity and place a row of sliced breast meat down one side of bird as shown. Arrange a row of mandarin orange slices and cherries along side. In this arrangement, halved unpeeled bananas hold additional servings of Waldorf Salad.

WALDORF SALAD

Yield: 1 lb. 14 oz.

Ingredients

Apples	1 lb.
Celery	4 oz.
Walnuts	2 oz.
Mayonnaise	1/4 cup
Sour Cream	1/4 cup
Lemon	juice of 1
Salt, optional	1/3 tsp.

Method

Dice apples, celery and walnuts. Mix mayonnaise, sour cream and lemon juice. Blend apples, celery and walnuts into mayonnaise mixture.

SAUERKRAUT WITH APPLES AND PINEAPPLE

Yield: 1 lb.

Ingredients

Sauerkraut, fresh	8 oz.
Apples, fresh	2
Pineapple, sweet, fresh	6 oz.

Method

Wash and drain sauerkraut and chop into coarse pieces.
    Peel and cut apple into small dice; cut pineapple into small dice.
    Combine all ingredients and serve on a bed of lettuce.

SALAD RACHEL

Yield: 24 oz.

Ingredients

Artichoke Bottoms	4 oz.
Celery	4 oz.
Asparagus Tips	8
Mayonnaise	1 cup
Boston Lettuce	1

Method

Cut artichokes and celery into julienne and mix with mayonnaise.
    Place mixture on a bed of Boston lettuce and arrange asparagus tips on top.

STOCKHOLM SALAD

Yield: 17 oz.
Ingredients

Celery, cooked, julienned	4 oz.
Beets, cooked, julienned	4 oz.
Dill, chopped	2 tbsp.
Vinegar	1/4 cup
Salt	1/3 tsp.
Pepper, freshly ground	2 to 3 grinds
Chantilly Sauce	1 cup

Method
Combine celery and beets with dill, vinegar, salt and pepper and marinate for 24 hours.

Drain liquid from vegetables and mix them with Chantilly Sauce.

HUNGARIAN SALAD NO. 1

Yield: 2 lb. 8 oz.
Ingredients

Ox Tongue, cooked	24 oz.
Pickled Cucumber	1
Red Pimento	2 oz.
Belgian Endive	2
Truffle	1 head
French Dressing	1 cup
Paprika	1 tsp.

Method
Cut ox tongue, pickled cucumber, red pimento, endive and truffle into julienne strips.

Combine all ingredients with dressing and paprika and mix.

RUSSIAN SALAD

Yield: 1 lb. 7 oz.
Ingredients

Beets, cooked, drained, diced	2 oz.
Potato, cooked, diced	2 oz.
Carrots, cooked, diced	2 oz.
Peas, cooked	2 oz.
Beans, cooked, diced	2 oz.
Mayonnaise, well seasoned	½ cup
Asparagus, cooked	5 oz.

Method
Combine all vegetables except asparagus tips with mayonnaise. Arrange salad on plate and top with asparagus.
NOTE: To give additional flavor, grated onions can be added to salad.

HUNGARIAN SALAD NO. 2

Yield: 8 oz.
Ingredients

Green Peppers	2 oz.
Red Peppers	2 oz.
Apples	2 oz.
Basic French Dressing	1 cup
Salt	1/3 tsp.
Boston Lettuce	

Method

Cut red and green peppers into fine julienne strips. Peel apples and cut into julienne strips.

Mix all ingredients except lettuce with dressing; add salt.

Place mixture on a bed of Boston lettuce before serving.

POLISH SALAD

Yield: 4-6 portions
Ingredients

Hard Cooked Eggs	4
Herring Fillets	2
Potatoes, cooked	2 oz.
Gherkins	2 oz.
Beets	2 oz.
Carrots	2 oz.
Parsley, chopped	3 tbsp.
Tarragon	2 tbsp.
Mayonnaise	½ cup
Salt	1 tsp.
Pepper	½ tsp.

Method

Mix each ingredient separately with parsley, tarragon, salt and pepper. Arrange each mound of ingredients seperately on a silver platter, like a Bouquetiere.

Serve mayonnaise separately.

SALAD NICOISE

Yield: 10 oz.
Ingredients

String Beans, cooked	2 oz.
Potatoes, diced	2 oz.
Tomato Wedges, peeled	2 oz.
Basic French Dressing	1/2 cup
Salt	1/3 tsp.
Pepper	1/3 tsp.
Anchovies	2 oz.
Capers	1 tsp.
Ripe Olives	1 oz.

Method

Combine stringbeans, tomatoes and potatoes with dressing. Add salt and pepper.

Arrange mixture on platter and garnish with anchovies, capers, and olives.

SALAD MIGNON

Yield: 14 oz.
Ingredients

Shrimp, cooked	4 oz.
Artichoke Bottoms	2 oz.
Mayonnaise	½ cup
Heavy Cream	1 tbsp.
Cayenne Pepper	1/16 tsp.
Chicory Lettuce	1 head
Truffle	1 (optional)

Method
Dice shrimp and artichoke bottoms.

Mix mayonnaise with heavy cream and cayenne pepper.

Mix all ingredients except truffle together and serve on bed of chicory lettuce. Julienne truffle and place on top.

SALAD MIMOSA

Yield: 8 portions
Ingredients

Boston Lettuce	2 hearts
Watercress	1 bunch
Basic French Dressing	½ cup
Hard-Cooked Eggs, grated	3

Method
Wash and drain lettuce hearts and cut into quarters. Arrange on platter surrounded by watercress.

Pour dressing over greens and sprinkle half with grated hard-cooked egg yolks and the other half with grated hard-cooked egg whites.

SALAD MARIE-LOUISE

Yield: 2 portions
Ingredients

Banana	1
Celery	1 pc.
Apple	1
Truffle	1
Mayonnaise	½ cup

Method
Peel and slice banana; peel and quarter apple; peel and dice celery.

Combine all ingredients with mayonnaise and arrange on platter with a slice of truffle on top.

SALAD LORETTE

Yield: 9 oz.
Ingredients

Beets, cooked	4 oz.
Celery	4 oz.
Basic French Dressing	¾ cup
Boston Lettuce	1 leaf

Method
Cut beets and celery in julienne strips. Combine with dressing; mix thoroughly.
    Place on leaf of Boston lettuce.

OXFORD SALAD

Yield: 1 lb. 14 oz.
Ingredients

Chicken, cooked, diced	1 cup
Sour Gherkins, sliced	2 oz.
Tomatoes, cut into wedges	2 oz.
Hard Cooked Eggs, sliced	3
Basic French Dressing	½ cup
Boston Lettuce	1 head
Tarragon, chopped	2 tbsp.
Truffle, diced fine	1 oz.

Method
Combine chicken, gherkins, tomatoes and dressing and mix well. Place mixture on
a bed of Boston Lettuce and sprinkle truffles and tarragon over salad. Decorate
with slices of hard cooked egg around the salad.

ITALIAN VEGETABLE SALAD

Yield: 15 oz.
Ingredients

Carrots, cooked, diced	1 oz.
Green Beans, cooked, diced	1 oz.
Green Peas, cooked, diced	1 oz.
Tomatoes, peeled, diced	1 oz.
Salami, diced	1 oz.
Stuffed Green Olives, sliced	1 oz.
Anchovy Fillets, small can	1
Mayonnaise	½ cup
Parsley, chopped	1 tsp.

Method
Blend all ingredients except parsley thoroughly and mix with mayonnaise. Sprinkle
with fresh chopped parsley.

Fish Salads

Fish to be used for fish salad is usually cooked.

Fish salads are seasoned with a variety of dressings, although mayonnaise is most frequently used.

The following recipes can be made using any leftover fish:

TUNAFISH SALAD NO. 1

Yield: 23 oz.

Ingredients

White Tuna, 14 oz. can	1
Mayonnaise	1/2 cup
Onion, chopped	1 oz.
Salt	1/3 tsp.
Pepper, freshly ground	2 to 3 grinds
Lemon	juice of 1
Worcestershire Sauce	1/2 tsp.
Parsley, chopped	1 tbsp.

Method

Flake tunafish.

Combine mayonnaise and onions; season with salt, pepper, lemon juice and Worcestershire sauce. Blend tunafish with mayonnaise mixture.

Arrange mixture in a dish and sprinkle chopped parsley over the top. There are many garnishes that can be used to enhance the presentation of the fish.

TUNAFISH SALAD NO. 2

Yield: 24 oz.

Ingredients

Olive Oil	4 tbsp.
Onion, chopped	1 oz.
Garlic, crushed, chopped	2 cloves
Tunafish, 14 oz. can	1
Sweet Corn	4 oz.
Green Peppers, cut julienne	1 oz.
Red Peppers, cut julienne	1 oz.
White Wine	1/4 cup
Lemon	juice of 1
Salt	1/2 to 1 tsp.
Pepper	1/3 tsp.

Method

Heat oil in saute pan.

Add onions and garlic; when lightly colored, add tunafish, corn, red and green pepper. Cook for 5 min., then add white wine and lemon juice. Season with salt and pepper.

Cook on low fire until vegetables are done.

Cool and serve with marinated tomatoes.

Radish slices are overlapped to create scales for this mold of fish salad. Four ripe olives are centered on spine. Ripe olive slices outline head which has stuffed olives for eyes. Truffle strips add note of realism to tail. Garnishes alongside fish are cucumber slices topped with salad and decorated stuffed eggs. See recipe for fish salad, p. 168.

HERRING SALAD

Yield: 18 oz.
Ingredients

Bismark Herring	8 oz.
Apples	2 oz.
Beets	2 oz.
Potatoes, cooked	2 oz.
Basic French Dressing	1/2 cup
Salt	1/3 tsp.
Pepper	2 to 3 grinds

Method
Soak herring in water. Dice apples, beets and potatoes. Drain herring and dice.
    Combine all ingredients. Add dressing, salt and pepper. Refrigerate for one hour.

SALMON SALAD

Yield: 15 oz.
Ingredients

Salmon, cooked	8 oz.
Cucumbers	2 oz.
Tomatoes	2 oz.
Basic French Dressing	¼ cup
Salt	1/2 tsp.
Pepper, freshly ground	2 to 3 grinds
Mayonnaise	½ cup

Method
Season salmon with dressing, salt and pepper.
    Arrange salmon mixture on a platter. Surround with tomato wedges and sliced cucumbers.
    Serve with mayonnaise.

Bowl of Lobster salad is circled with button mushrooms. Asparagus spears provide color contrast for pale salad. Meat removed whole from lobster claws holds asparagus spears and provides rosy identification for contents of bowl.

LOBSTER SALAD

Yield: 21 oz.
Ingredients

Lobster Meat	8 oz.
Hard-Cooked Eggs	2
Lemon	juice of 1
Mustard	1 tbsp.
Salt	1/3 tsp.
Pepper	2 to 3 grinds
Mayonnaise	1/2 cup
Lettuce	
Parsley, chopped	1 tsp.
Lobster coral	1 tsp.

Method

Dice lobster meat; combine with chopped egg.

Blend mayonnaise with lemon juice, mustard, salt and pepper and combine with lobster and egg.

Place salad on lettuce leaf. Sprinkle with chopped parsley and coral.

KING CRAB SALAD

Use same procedure and amounts of ingredients as for Lobster Salad, above, except substitute crabmeat for lobster.

SALAD OF LEFTOVER FISH

Yield: 23 oz.
Ingredients

Shallots, chopped	1 tbsp.
Olive Oil	¼ cup
Capers	2 tsp.
Green Olives, sliced	2 oz.
Cepes (wild mushrooms)	4 oz.
Garlic Cloves, chopped	2
White Wine	½ cup
Pickles, diced	2 oz.
Tarragon	1 tbsp.
Chili Sauce	¼ cup
Salt	1 tsp.
Pepper	½ tsp.
Lemon	juice of 2
Fish, leftover, flaked	8 oz.

Method

Saute chopped shallots in oil, add capers, green olives, cepes and garlic. Cook until transparent. Deglaze pan with white wine.

Add pickles, tarragon, chili sauce, salt, pepper and juice from lemons. Cook for 5 minutes.

Pour sauce over fish, mix and cool for 2 hours.

MUSSEL SALAD

Yield: 9 oz.
Ingredients

Mussels, cooked, cleaned	4 oz.
Asparagus tips	1 oz.
Green Beans, french cut, cooked	1 oz.
Tomato, peeled, diced	1 oz.
Onions, chopped	1 tbsp.
Horseradish, grated	1 tsp.
Basic French Dressing	1/2 cup
Salt	1/3 tsp.
Pepper	1/3 tsp.

Method

Combine all ingredients, blend with dressing. Refrigerate for one hour before serving.

Meat and Poultry Salads

CALVES' BRAINS SALAD

Yield: 11 oz.
Ingredients

Calves' Brains	4 oz.
Vinegar	1 tbsp.
Bay Leaf	1
Onions, sliced	1 oz.
Pepper	1 tsp.
Tarragon Leaves	1 tsp.
Parsley, chopped	1 tsp.
Chives	1 tsp.
Dill	1 tsp.
Mayonnaise, with 1 tbsp. mustard	½ cup
OR	
Ravigotte Sauce	½ cup

Method

Blanch calves' brains in salted water for 5 min. Water should contain vinegar, bay leaf, onions, pepper and 1 tsp. tarragon leaves.

Cool and drain calves' brains. Slice brains. Sprinkle remaining herbs over brains and blend in mayonnaise with mustard or ravigotte sauce.

CHICKEN SALAD

Yield: 17 oz.
Ingredients

Chicken Meat	8 oz.
Celery, diced	4 oz.
Onions, chopped	1 oz.
Mayonnaise	¼ cup
Salt	½ tsp.
Pepper	2 to 3 grinds
Worcestershire Sauce	½ tsp.
Leaf Lettuce	

Method

Dice chicken meat. Combine all ingredients and mix well.

GAME SALAD

Yield: 17 oz.
Ingredients

Leftover Game Meat, (venison, pheasant, hare, etc.)	8 oz.
Mayonnaise	¼ cup
English Mustard	1 tsp.
Orange, julienned	1 tbsp.
Red Currant Jelly	¼ cup
Walnuts, chopped	2 tbsp.

Method

Cut game into julienne strips. Mix mayonnaise with mustard, red currant jelly, and orange zest (grated outer layer, no white).

Combine all ingredients, and sprinkle with walnuts.

AMERICAN SALAD
(See picture above)

Yield: 24 oz. (5-6 portions)
Ingredients

Frankfurters	8 oz.
Swiss Cheese	8 oz.
Egg Yolks	2
French Mustard	1 tbsp.
Olive Oil	1 cup
Vinegar	¼ cup
Shallots, chopped	1 tbsp.
Salt	1 tsp.
Pepper	½ tsp.
Chives, chopped	2 tbsp.

Method

Boil frankfurters and slice in ½-in. pieces.

Cut cheese into julienne strips. Mix egg yolks with mustard; incorporate oil, as for mayonnaise. Add sauteed shallots, salt, pepper and vinegar to the sauce.

Combine frankfurters, cheese and sauce.

Mix all ingredients with chives.

ITALIAN MEAT SALAD

Yield: 24 oz.
Ingredients

Salami, Veal or Bologna	8 oz.
Pickles	2 oz.
Apples	1 oz.
Mayonnaise	½ cup
Worcestershire Sauce	½ tsp.
Anchovies, chopped	½ oz.
Eggs, chopped	2
Pickles, chopped	1 tbsp.

Method

Cut salami, veal or bologna in fine julienne strips. Cut pickles and apples into julienne. Combine above ingredients with mayonnaise, blend well.

Add Worcestershire sauce and chopped anchovies.

Mix all ingredients well; decorate salad with chopped egg and chopped pickle.

BEEF SALAD NO. 1

Yield: 19 oz.
Ingredients

Beef, boiled or roasted	8 oz.
Onions, chopped	2 oz.
Basic French Dressing	¼ cup
Salt	1/3 tsp.
Pepper, freshly ground	2 to 3 grinds
Hard-Cooked Eggs, sliced	2
Tomato, sliced	1

Method

Cut beef into julienne strips or dice. Combine with onions and dressing. Add salt and pepper.

Marinate salad for 24 hours, then arrange in bowl. Decorate by alternating slices of egg and tomato.

BEEF SALAD NO. 2

Yield: 1 lb.
Ingredients

Beef, cooked	8 oz.
Pickles	1 oz.
Tomatoes	1 oz.
Celery	1 oz.
Basic French Dressing	1/4 cup
Salt	1/3 tsp.
Pepper	1/2 tsp.
Garlic Powder	1/3 tsp.
Prepared Mustard	1 tbsp.
Parsley, chopped	1 tsp.
Tarragon, chopped	1 tsp.
Chives, chopped	1 tsp.
Green Olives	1 tbsp.
Hard-Cooked Eggs, sliced	1

Method

Cut beef, pickles, tomato and celery into julienne. Marinate in dressing containing salt, pepper, garlic powder, prepared mustard, parsley, tarragon, and chives.

Before serving, decorate dish with sliced egg and sliced olives.

SWISS SALAD

Yield: 24 oz. (5-6 portions)
Ingredients

Shallots, chopped	2 tbsp.
White Wine	1 cup
Basic French Dressing	1/2 cup
Hard Cooked Egg Yolks, chopped fine	1 oz.
Heavy Cream	1/4 cup
Ham, julienned	8 oz.
Swiss Cheese, julienned	4 oz.
Celery, julienned	2 oz.
Hard Cooked Egg Whites, julienned	2 oz.
Tomato, diced small	1 oz.
Salt	1/2 to 1 tsp.
Pepper	1/3 tsp.
Parsley	1 tsp.
Chives	1 tsp.

Method
Reduce shallots and white wine to 2/3 of original amount; cool and combine with dressing and finely chopped egg yolk. Add heavy cream.

Combine ham, cheese, celery, egg whites and tomato.

Mix all ingredients together, season to taste

Sprinkle each portion of salad with chopped tarragon, chives and parsley.

LANGOSTINO SALAD

*This salad is a combination of langostinos,
diced apples and celery blended with mayonnaise, catsup and finely-chopped fresh dill.
Salad is decorated with langostinos, hearts of
artichokes, sliced radishes and chopped eggs.
Marinated green beans are used as a border.*

Fruit Salads

SALAD ALICE

Yield: 4 portions
Ingredients

Lemon	juice of 1
Apples, medium	4 apples
Almonds, sliced, toasted	3 tbsp.
Red Currant Jelly	6 tbsp.
Heavy Cream, whipped	1/4 cup
Salt	1/3 tsp.
Sugar	1/3 tsp.
Lettuce	4 leaves

Method

Cut tops, leaving stems attached, from the apples and set aside; remove all pulp from inside using a parisian scoop. Remove all seeds from apple and squeeze juice of one lemon over pulp.

Dice apple pulp and mix with toasted almonds, red currant jelly and whipped cream; season with salt and sugar.

Fill hollowed apples and put the tops over them.

Serve whole, topped apple with stem on a bed of lettuce.

SALAD MONTE CARLO

Yield: 5 portions
Ingredients

Oranges, medium	5
Pineapple, small	1
Maraschino Cherries	1/2 cup
Heavy Cream, whipped	1/2 cup
Lemon	juice of 1
Salt	1/3 tsp.

Method

Wash oranges and cut tops off. Scoop out fruit from inside of oranges. Reserve shells. Peel pineapple and dice fruit. Combine fruit from ½ orange with ½ pineapple.

Add maraschino cherries and whipped heavy cream; season with lemon juice and salt.

Fill empty orange shells and replace tops. Serve on crushed ice.

SOUTH AMERICAN SALAD

Yield: 6 portions
Ingredients

Bananas, large	3
Apple, medium	1
Celery	1 pc.
Seedless Green Grapes	4 oz.
Mayonnaise, flavored with lemon juice	¼ cup
Pistachio Nuts	1 oz.

Method

Cut bananas in two the long way; peel and save skins. Peel apples; remove any strings from celery.

Slice bananas, celery and apples in 1/3 in. pieces. Combine grapes with fruit

Blend mayonnaise into above mixture.

Fill half a banana skin with the mixture and sprinkle peeled pistachio nuts over it.

MACEDOINE OF FRUITS

Yield: 60-65 oz.
Ingredients

Apples	2
Pears	2
Peaches	2
Pineapple, medium	1
Bananas	2
Oranges	2
Sugar	as needed
Walnuts	1 oz.
Pistachio Nuts	1 oz.

Method
Peel fruit and cut into slices or dice.

Combine all fruit and mix well; add sugar if necessary.

Serve chilled in crystal bowl or in individual portions in champagne glasses. Top servings with chopped walnuts and pistachio nuts. Maraschino brandy can be added.

Fruits Stuffed with Salads

STUFFED CANTALOUPE

Yield: 4 portions
Ingredients

Cantaloupe	2
Peach Halves	4
Langostino Tails	8 oz.
Salt	1/3 tsp.
Lemon	juice of 1
Madeira Wine	1 oz.
Chantilly Sauce	1/2 cup

Method
Cut cantaloupe into halves, scoop melon from shells and slice lengthwise in thin slices.

Slice peaches and cut langostinos in half.

Mix melon, peaches and langostinos and marinate with salt, lemon juice and madeira wine. Blend Chantilly Sauce into mixture.

Fill melon shells with mixture and serve well-chilled.

CANTALOUPE STUFFED WITH CHICKEN, LOBSTER OR CRABMEAT

Yield: 4 portions

Ingredients

Cantaloupe	2
Chicken, lobster or crabmeat	8 oz.
Pickles, diced	4 oz.
Mayonnaise	½ cup
Lemon Juice	1 tsp.
Tarragon, chopped	1 tsp.

Method

Cut cantaloupe in half, remove melon from shells.

Dice melon and combine with chicken, lobster or crab and pickles.

Combine mayonnaise, lemon juice and chopped tarragon and blend into above mixture.

Fill melon halves with salad, chill and serve on crushed ice.

STUFFED PEACHES

Yield: 8 portions

Ingredients

Peach Halves	4
Lobster Meat	4 oz.
Pears	4 oz.
Salt	¼ tsp.
Pepper, freshly ground	4 grinds
Orange Juice	¼ cup

Method

Dice lobster meat and pears. Season with salt, pepper. Mix above ingredients, adding orange juice.

Stuff peach halves with mixture and chill. Serve with mayonnaise and lemon juice.

STUFFED TOMATOES
VARIATION I

Yield: 6 portions

Ingredients

Tomatoes, medium-sized, cut in half and scooped out	6
Chicken Meat	4 oz.
Pineapple	2 oz.
Chutney, chopped	1 oz.
Chili Sauce	1 oz.
Oil	2 tbsp.
Lemon	juice of 1
Salt	1/3 tsp.
Pepper	1/3 tsp.

Method

Dice chicken and pineapple, then combine with remaining ingredients.

Stuff tomatoes with mixture and serve cold.

STUFFED TOMATOES (cont.)

VARIATION II

Yield: 6 portions
Ingredients

Tomatoes, medium-sized, cut in half and scooped out	6
King Crabmeat	12 oz.
Mushrooms, cooked	6 oz.
Oil	1/4 cup
Lemon	juice of 2
Chili Sauce	2 oz.
Salt	1/3 tsp.

Method
Dice crabmeat and mushrooms. Season with oil, lemon juice, chili sauce and salt. Stuff tomato halves and serve cold.

VARIATION III

Yield: 8 portions
Ingredients

Tomatoes, medium-sized, cut in half and scooped out	4
Artichoke Bottoms	4
Green Beans	8 oz.
Basic French Dressing	¼ cup
Parsley, chopped	1 tbsp.
Tarragon, chopped	1 tsp.

Method
Cut artichokes into julienne strips. Combine with beans and season with dressing. Stuff tomato halves and sprinkle with tarragon and parsley.

VARIATION IV

Yield: 12 wedges
Ingredients

Tomatoes, firm, red, ripe, small	3
Egg Yolks	5
Butter	4 oz.
Prepared Mustard	1 tsp.
Paprika	½ tsp.
Worcestershire Sauce	½ tsp.

Method
Cut tops off tomatoes and remove all seeds. Set aside.

Mix egg yolks with butter and season with mustard, paprika and Worcestershire sauce.

Fill tomatoes with egg yolk mixture. Allow to cool for 1 hour.

Slice filled tomatoes or cut into wedges.

VARIATION V

Follow directions for Variation IV except to the egg yolk mixture add: 1 tbsp. fresh chives, ½ oz. parsley, ½ oz. spinach that have been pureed together.

XV: CHEESES

Knowing what various kinds of cheeses taste like and how they are made is essential for two reasons:

1. To blend each kind of cheese successfully with other ingredients in cooking.

2. To select the proper cheese as the finishing touch for a successful dinner.

Cheese is made from the curds of milk from various domestic animals—cows, sheep, goats. The curds are separated from the whey by the action of the rennet and of certain bacterias or mold spores. After the curds are separated, the whey is molded into different shapes and sizes which are ripened into cheese, according to the tradition of the region where it is produced.

What is whey? the rennet? the curd?

Whey is the fluid that separates from the curds when milk coagulates.

Rennet is an extract taken from the fourth stomach of newly born calves.

The curd is the main factor in cheese making. It is formed during the coagulation of the casein (one of many proteins) which occurs when rennet is added to separate the water from the milk.

Why are bacteria used?

Bacteria or mold spores are added to the rennet to give the cheese its individual characteristics. When using these bacteria, or, in trade language, starter cultures, the utmost care is required:

Molds work in different ways:

The blue mold develops inside the cheese and forms blue or sometimes green veins. (See blue cheese or Roquefort cheese).

The white mold makes a layer on the surface of the cheese (like brie or Camembert).

The most frequently used bacteria are the lactic acids. These are the bacteria which develop as milk sours. These bacteria influence the texture and consistency of the cheese and it is the source of the enzymes which break down the proteins in the cheese. The greater the breakdown of protein, the better the flavor and aroma of the cheese. Cheese is classified according to its fat content.

Cheeses are made to preserve the most valuable constituents of the milk, and to add special aromas and flavors to foods to which they are added.

Among the many cheeses that may be used in the garde manger department are: 1. Cantal (French Cheddar); 2. Bleu de Bresse; 3. Comte; 4. Emmenthaler; 5. Beaumont; 6. Fromage au Marc de Raisin; 7. Port Salute; 8. Chabichou; 9. Reblechon; 10. Roquefort; 11. Brie de Meaux; 12. Valencay (Pyramid Goatcheese); 13. Selle sur Cher; 14. Baron de Provence; 15. Baguette d'Avenes; 16. Colommiers;

17. Poivre Deux; 18. Triple Creme (Boursin); 19. Livarot; 20. Ascot; 21. Saint Maure; 22. Camenbert; 23. Petit Swiss; 24. Montrcal; 25. Belletoile Triplecreme; 26. Chaource; 27. Brillat-Savarin; 28. Munster; 29. Fromage de Cure; 30. Guerbigny; 31. Angelot; 32. Gervaise; 33. Edam; 34. Tomme de Savoie; 35. Reblechon.

Courtesy Foods of France.

Every country and, as a matter of fact, in many countries every district, has its own unique cheese. Many local cheeses have become famous as menu items and are considered "kings" in their own right. Among the "kings" of cheesedom: the Cheddar, an English cheese which was first made in a village named Somerset; the Emmenthaler cheese named after a Swiss valley, the Emmenthal Valley in the Canton of Bern; or the Roquefort, a cheese from France, named after a town in the Sain Affrigne district.

As time has passed, however, many of these cheeses, although originally only made in a specific place, are being made elsewhere. For example, today, there are American cheddars and bries from Wisconsin and blue cheese from Denmark. These cheeses are known as variants of the originals and sold as such.

What are the varieties of cheeses?

1. Fresh cheese (unfermented, made from raw curds)
2. Fermented cheeses, usually divided into two types:
    a. Soft cheese (Brie)
    b. Hard cheese (Cheddar)
3. There are also cheeses made from scalded curds: Emmentaler or Parmesan. These cheeses are also called Rennet Cheeses.
4. Semi-soft cheese (Bel Paese, Munster.)
5. Blue mold cheese (Roquefort, Stilton)
6. White mold cheese (Camembert)
7. Sour milk cheeses.
    a. fresh sour milk cheese (cream cheese)
    b. stored sour milk cheese (basket cheese)

The following is a list of the kinds of cheese most often used:

Bel Paese (semi-soft Italian cheese)
Blue Cheese (made in Denmark)
Brie (called the King of cheese)
Camembert (perfected in 1790 by Mme Marie Harel)
Cheddar (an English cheese)
Cream Cheese (an American cheese)
Edam (famous Holland cheese)
Emmentaler (named after a Swiss valley)
Gruyere (Swiss cheese)
Liederkranz (the only original cheese made in America)
Roquefort Cheese (famous for its flavor)
Stilton (an English cheese)

Bel Paese—This fine Italian cheese is semi-soft in consistency and of mild flavor.

Brie—It is a French, white mold cheese, with a soft consistency and a fine mild aroma. The cheese is round and flat, about 1 to 1½ in. thick and sold on a straw matting. Brie remains in perfect condition for only a short time during which the rind is firm and thin and the inside mellow and soft in texture.

Camembert—It is a white mold cheese from Normandy; however, a similar cheese is produced and sold under the same label in this country. This cheese reaches maturity after one month. The consistency is waxy and semi-soft. The crust is white. As the cheese continues to ripen the skin becomes brownish red.

Cheddar—This cheese is generally available in large cylinders, weighing 50-100 lbs. It is wrapped in cheesecloth and stored at a low temperature for 6-12 months.

A good cheddar should be uniformly colored, free of holes and there should be no cracks in the rind.

Cheddar—This cheese is generally available in large cylinders, weighing 50-100 lbs. It is wrapped in cheesecloth and stored at a low temperature for 6-12 months. A good cheddar should be uniformly colored, free of holes and there should be no cracks in the rind.

Danish Blue Cheese—It is made from cow's milk and looks somewhat like roquefort but the taste is sharper and the consistency, smoother. Danish Blue Cheese ripens very quickly. It must always be listed as Blue Cheese.

Edam—All of these Dutch cheeses have a characteristic appearance. They are spherical in shape with an outer covering of red wax and weigh 2-4 lbs. A smaller variety, weighing 1 lb., is known as Baby Gouda. It is slightly flattened in shape and wrapped in red cellophane. Edam cheese is light golden in color. The taste is mildly sour and rather salty. Storage time 2-4 months.

Emmenthaler—It originated in Switzerland but is now produced all over the world and also in the U. S. A. Emmentaler cheese takes between 7-12 months to ripen. When ripe it has a firm, dry texture with large tunnels or holes that contain a clear liquid. Cheese is made in the shape of wheels that measure about a yard in diameter and weigh up to 200 lbs.

Gruyere—It closely resembles Emmentaler cheese, but is made in smaller sizes. It is stored in cellars having high humidity and as a result a putty-like layer is formed on the outer surface, giving the cheese a strong flavor and aroma. The period of aging is 8-12 months.

Parmesan—A cheese that belongs to the group of Italian Grand Cheeses and is only used for grating. The storage period is 2-5 years, the texture is hard and brittle. The flavor is mild but pronounced. The surface is black since it is smeared with oil containing lamb fat.

Roquefort—This French, blue-veined cheese is made from sheep's milk. A salty cheese, it is stored in caves near the town of Roquefort under special conditioning of temperature and humidity. The cheese is cylindrical in shape and wrapped in tin foil.

Stilton—It is a blue mold cheese of high fat content with a brown wrinkled surface and a whitish-yellow inside. The flavor is strong, aromatic and salty.

Storing Cheese—All cheeses require cool storage, because if the room is too warm and moist, cheeses ripen too fast; if it is too dry, they become hard. Small pieces of cheese may be stored under cheese covers or rolled aluminum foil or a damp cloth. Larger pieces of cheese, should be folded in cheese cloth that has been soaked in a strong brine

Soft cheeses, like Brie or Camembert, are difficult to store. These types of cheeses should be bought when just ripe and should be used as soon as possible. Leftover pieces, which have become hard, can be grated, ground or dried and stored in a screwtop jar in the refrigerator and used in salads or other dishes.

How should cheese be served?

Men invented cheese by accident, but ever since it has served faithfully as a nutritious food as well as a food that refreshes the palate. Today, cheese is still in demand on most buffets and in ala carte setups.

If cheese has been stored in the refrigerator, it must be taken out at least one-half hour before serving to give it a chance to breathe. The cheese is always served before the dessert. Cheeses should follow the main course or be served with the salad. Cheese is served on separate plates, if served individually, or for variety or more dramatic presentation it can be served on a cheese board.

Butter can be served with the cheese, however, connoisseurs will reject it. Among the breads that are excellent as accompaniments for cheese are Russian pumpernickel, Knaeke-Brot, various crackers, rye bread, toast, croutons, French or Italian Bread. For extra color and flavor, radishes and celery can be added to cheese servings. Sticks of celery, tomato wedges, olives or bulb fennel also make very good accompaniments for cheese as do all kinds of fruit except citrus fruits.

What wines should be served with cheese?

Cheeses, especially strong ones, can be served with all wines, except sparkling wines. Strong cheeses demand red wine; lighter cheeses demand light wines.

Cheese Recipes

ROQUEFORT CHEESE STUFFING FOR CELERY
Yield: 16 oz.
Ingredients

Roquefort	½ lb.
Butter	½ lb.
Paprika	to garnish

Method
Mix together into a fine paste. Pipe to fill pieces of cleaned and peeled celery. To add color, sprinkle some paprika over filling. Chill before serving. Serve on folded napkin.
NOTE: Grated Cheddar cheese may be substituted for Roquefort cheese.

DEEP FRIED CHEESE
This dish can be made from Swiss cheese or Camembert. Let's take the Swiss cheese version first; medium-thin slices of Swiss cheese are dipped into beaten eggs and then are breaded with white bread crumbs and baked in butter.
OR
Camembert wedges are cut in half, dipped in beaten eggs and breaded with white bread crumbs and deep fried. Serve on doily-covered plate with deep fried parsley.

BELGIAN ENDIVE WITH BLUE CHEESE
Yield: 14 oz.
Ingredients

Belgian Endive, washed and trimmed	2
Hard Cooked Eggs	4
Blue Cheese	3½ oz.
Butter	3½ oz.

Method
Put egg yolks through sieve; add cheese and butter; beat together until creamy.
Stuff endive leaves with the mixture. Garnish with grapes and rings of green peppers.

XVI: NON EDIBLE DISPLAYS

Although food holds the spotlight in all buffet presentation—and the objective of buffet planning must be to achieve visual beauty both in the artistic presentation of each item of edible food, as well as in the arrangement of the many dishes on the buffet table, nothing heightens the beauty of the buffet more than an outstanding centerpiece, made of ice, tallow or other non-edible material.

The guest should be able to identify the theme of the buffet at a glance, just by observing the non-edible decorations that provide an eye-catching background for the presentation.

A non-edible decorative display piece should be a work of art, always in good taste, whether the figure is made of ice, sugar, tallow, or any other material.

The garde manger staff can use various methods and materials to enhance the presentation of a buffet. Their list of possibilities would include:

    1. Ice carvings

    2. Tallow displays

    3. Decorative touches created with miscellaneous items which may be either made or assembled (flowers; styrofoam figures; boats made of bread, fruits and vegetables; candles; wine bottles; flags made of wax leaves and similar items.) China, posters, items from antique shops, can also be rented to achieve the objective of a buffet.

Ice Carving

The ice sculpture is the highlight of any buffet, the artistic touch, the focal point. Ice can be carved in any shape, size or figure that fits the theme or occasion; as an example, for Christmas, there could be a Santa Claus; for an anniversary, a heart; or for an Easter Buffet, a bunny.

Before starting an ice carving, the following items should be assembled:

a. A 100- to 300-lb. block of ice, 40-in. high by 20-in. wide by 10-in. thick. Blocks like this can be purchased.

b. A pair of ice tongs—for moving and handling the ice.

c. An ice shaver with 3 to 6 prongs; this is used to carve out the details and do the small cutting on the block of ice.

d. An ice pick, used to split the block into smaller pieces.

Telling Touches for Showcase Presentation

Non-edible items are used very effectively in both of these eye-catching food presentations. The Roast Duck has a background of shiny leaves and a top knot frill of foil. Sawtooth cut tomato halves around whole duck hold yellow filling topped with a bit of truf- *fle. Outer rows of medallion of duck filled with pistachio chaud froid have V-shaped garniture of asparagus and pimento. Paper frills in pink and blue sharpen the appeal of golden poultry. Radish roses and pimento strips add another welcome note of color.*

e. A hand saw—used to remove large cuts of ice or to make rough outlines.

f. Wood chisels—ranging in size from 1/2 to 2 in.

g. A compass—for drawing circles.

h. An electric chain saw; when working with this type of saw, it is important to have the saw grounded to prevent accidents.

i. A template made on graph paper of the shape of the ice carving that is to be made.

The best temperature for ice carving is 28°F. or less. An ice block will melt at the rate of 1/2- to 1-in. per hour under normal conditions (room temperature).

NOTE I: Each ice carving must have a base that is at least 4-5 in. high; in other words, when planning the carving, deduct 5-in. from the total height for the base. Be sure to draw the template accordingly.

NOTE II: If a piece of ice breaks off, dip each broken piece into salt and press pieces back together for a few minutes; the length of time will depend on the size and weight of the broken pieces. With the salt added, the broken pieces will freeze together and hold.

How to Display the Ice Carving on a Buffet

1. The table used for the carving must be sturdy and strong enough to support the weight of the ice.

2. The carved ice block should be placed in a specially constructed metal pan, wider than the base of the carving; wooden blocks should first be placed in the bottom of the pan and the carving should rest securely on top of the blocks.

3. Colored rotating lights can produce a dramatic effect as they play over an ice display; this is especially effective when the lights themselves cannot be seen.

4. The pan under the ice sculpture should be covered with a linen cloth, flowers, ferns, or other decorative material.

(For additional assistance in planning and producing ice carvings, refer to the book *"Ice Carving Made Easy"* by Joseph Amendola.)

Before starting work on an ice carving, draw the figure to scale on a piece of graph paper. This pattern is called a template.

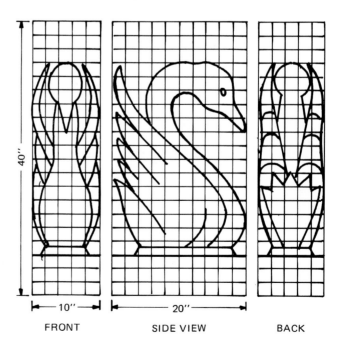

40"

10"   20"

FRONT   SIDE VIEW   BACK

An ice carving provides an elegant centerpiece to heighten the beauty and set the theme for a buffet. Proper lighting can enhance the effectiveness of a carving. Here is the swan produced from the template on the facing page.

Two tools essential to producing a professional ice carving are the 6 prong shaver and the 1/2-in. chisel. The correct techniques for their use are pictured at left and at left below.

To prepare a large piece of ice for a carving, a handsaw is recommended as used below.

Tallow Displays

When deciding on the selection of a pattern for a tallow display piece, it is essential that the display piece chosen match the theme of the buffet; however, it is even more desirable to select a pattern that may also, later on, fit into the decor theme of several other buffets. Creating an eye-catching tallow piece is always time-consuming and should be planned well in advance.

A French restaurant serving a French buffet would add effectiveness to the presentation by displaying a bust of Napoleon, Escoffier or the Eiffel Tower. Such displays can be used over and over, but they should be covered with transparent wrap when not in use as dust tends to stick to them.

Pictured in these pages are several tallow displays executed by the authors, with the assistance of students. All have been made at the Culinary Institute of American and were displayed on buffets, at exhibitions and at private parties.

To be successful in the execution of a tallow display, it is essential that certain rules be followed:

The person making the tallow display should have a photograph or model of the piece to be made. This is especially helpful in creating busts as it helps to keep the proportions right. (See illustrations: mermaid, Napoleon, Buddha, etc.)

Architectural blue prints and photographs have been used by the authors to reproduce accurately in tallow the proportions of the Eiffel Tower, the Leaning Tower of Pisa and the U. S. Capitol Building.

This 3-dimensional tallow piece reproduces a wide variety of cheeses. Chef/Author Nicolas stands beside his striking tallow display.

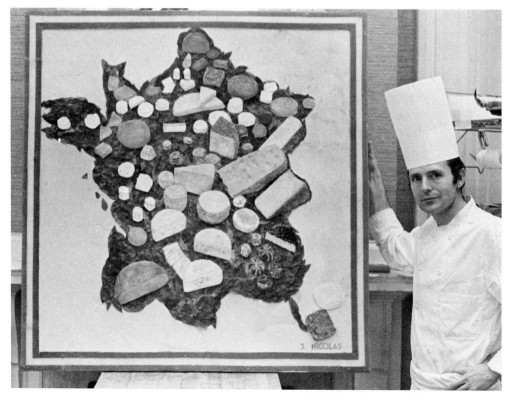

The composition of the material used in making a tallow display depends upon the piece to be made. In general, a formula made up in the following proportions works well in tallow displays, except for tall pieces like the Eiffel Tower, a Chinese Pagoda or the Leaning Tower of Pisa:

1/3 beeswax
1/3 paraffin
1/3 beef fat

These ingredients should be melted together in a pot. The beef fat can be freshly diced fat, cooking fat, or other fat that solidifies when cold. The quantity of fat can be increased if a more pliable and workable mixture is needed, especially if the working area is cool, i.e. below 65°F. Most of the tallow illustrations in this book have been made with the above formula and can stand temperatures up to 90°F.

Preparing the Tallow

In a large pot, melt:

5 lbs. of beeswax
5 lbs. of paraffin
5 lbs. of beef fat

The preferred method of melting the mixture is in a water bath although that is not absolutely necessary; it is, however, dangerous to melt paraffin over a flame. When the wax and fat are melted, pour mixture into empty milk cartons or other containers that can be opened. Allow to cool at room temperature, not under refrigeration. When tallow is completely cold, figures can be carved from the solid block. Great care should be exercised while carving as the tallow is brittle and may break.

The tallow can also be grated as it can then be molded like clay. When grating large amounts, use the coarse plate of the meat grinder.

A solid structure and base for the tallow piece must be created, especially if the finished piece has to be transported. A wooden base with dowels and a rough structure made of styrofoam have both been used in the following illustrations:

Presiding over a Hawaiian buffet, this seated Buddha was placed on a mirror-topped riser. The formula was prepared in proportions of 1/3 paraffin, 1/3 bee's wax and 1/3 beef fat.

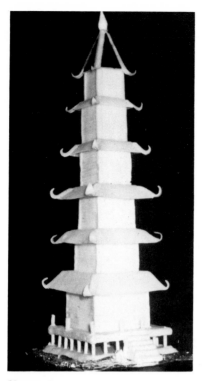

The base of these Greek columns is made of styrofoam covered with tallow. Easy to produce, piece provides effective background for a Mediterranean buffet.

Unusually tall pieces like this pagoda are made of tallow that is half paraffin and half beeswax. Mixture is melted, poured on trays and figure shaped while tallow is still hot.

Tallow animals amuse young and old diners.

Donkey playing violin adds light-hearted note to buffet presentation.

Additional Decorative Touches

These illustrated directions show how aluminum foil frills can be made for roasts and chops to be displayed as part of a buffet presentation. Ways to fold napkins into interesting shapes are also pictured.

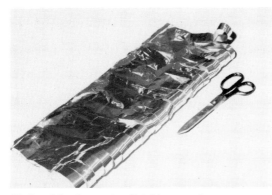

Frills add a decorative finishing touch to many cuts of meat such as ham, chops and crown roast. To make a frill fold the aluminum foil in half, shiny side inside, and cut strips with scissors.

After cutting strips, reverse foil so shiny side is outside. Roll foil around bone as shown to crown decorated ham.

To fold napkin into decorative shape, first lay flat and then fold each of the four corners into the center.

Fold each of newly made corners into center again and turn napkin over so smooth square is available for next step.

Fold corners into center again. Next pull out tabs from other side of napkin. (Note picture for position.) Arrange tabs in petals.

Now open corners from other side of napkin to make square as shown to serve as background for napkin flower.

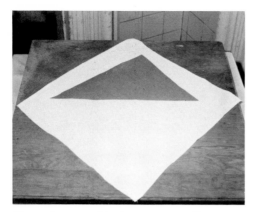

To make a napkin into a swan, first cut a piece of aluminum foil or brown paper into a triangle. Place triangle in center of napkin.

Fold napkin into triangle around foil or paper. Determine center of triangle, fold left corner to center, making sure edges are patted down

Fold right corner to center.

Fold newly-made corners into center.

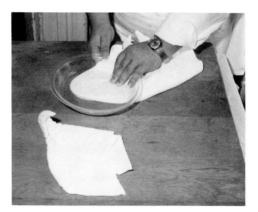

Wrap folded napkin in another cloth with open side towards you.

Set a weight on cloth, pull weight toward you firmly to form Swan's head; crease napkin.

XVII: BUFFET PRESENTATION

In a period of changing foodservice requirements, the buffet has proven to be a device for pleasing the public that can be used 24 hours a day. It can be styled as a formal presentation of elaborate food displays or it can offer a choice of favorite foods in casual array for the speedy service of roadside travelers or the weekly luncheons scheduled to meet the minimum time requirements of service club members.

Whatever the level of presentation, it is important that buffet foods be planned and necessary preparations completed well in advance so that the presentation for final service can be done speedily and without difficulty.

To plan a buffet effectively the following information should be received well in advance:

1. Number of covers (persons to be served)
2. Price per cover
3. Time of serving
4. Location where the buffet tables are to be displayed
5. Menu and zoning arrangement
6. Number of serving lines (based on the number of covers and zones)
7. Number, sizes, and shapes of sectional tables available
8. Type of cloth (and color) desired
9. Non-edible pieces (ice carving, tallow, etc.) that will be needed based on the theme, or as requested by the guests.
10. Other artifacts that might be needed to enhance the theme, or atmosphere, or as requested by the guests.

A buffet table in the desired size and shape can be constructed by assembling collapsible sectional tables that have been specially designed for this use. These sectional tables come in 6 basic shapes:

-Oblong (6-ft. x 30-in.; 6-ft. x 36-in.; or 8-ft. x 30-in.; 8-ft. x 36-in.)
-Round (60-in. in diam. or 72-in. in diam.)
-Half-round
-Quarter-round
-Serpentine (built to fit with the above dimensions)
-Trapezoid (built to fit with the above dimensions)

What kinds of tops can be used in assembling buffet tables?
Tops come in six basic shapes:

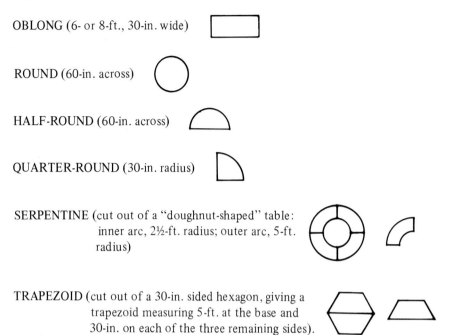

OBLONG (6- or 8-ft., 30-in. wide)

ROUND (60-in. across)

HALF-ROUND (60-in. across)

QUARTER-ROUND (30-in. radius)

SERPENTINE (cut out of a "doughnut-shaped" table: inner arc, 2½-ft. radius; outer arc, 5-ft. radius)

TRAPEZOID (cut out of a 30-in. sided hexagon, giving a trapezoid measuring 5-ft. at the base and 30-in. on each of the three remaining sides).

The most popular shapes for buffet tables are the first four mentioned above. The other two types are sometimes necessary in setting up buffets that are to be presented on tables in special shapes.

The size of a buffet table should be calculated first, its shape second. To calculate the size, allow 1 linear foot of table per piece or arrangement of food (bowl or platter) to be displayed. Thus, a buffet menu having 36 pieces on display would require a table that measured at least 36 ft. for the full presentation.

When counting the number of pieces to be included in the display, do not forget to include the number of pieces that are not edible, i. e. centerpieces, stacks of plates, pepper mills, floral arrangement, and similar items.

The shape of the buffet table will be determined by one or more of the following factors:
1. Number of serving lines
2. Size and shape of the room
3. Seating arrangement
4. Occasion
5. Preferences of the guests

Before the tables are to be assembled, a sketch should be made by the chef indicating the number of zones and courses. Each zone, or table area, contains a complete selection of the buffet items being offered. The number of times the selection is repeated depends on the number of persons to be served. This must be determined before the number, size and shape of the buffet tables can be settled. In the illustration below only two zones were needed.

The zoning must be correlated with the number of serving lines, and the number of serving lines will depend on the number of covers to be served. If there is more than one serving line, the guests will be served more efficiently and quickly.

Each zone would be divided into course areas; these will be duplicated in each zone. For example, the type of food displayed in Course Area No. 4 in Zone I should be identical to that displayed in Course Area No. 4 in Zone II.

In an a la carte dining room (as differentiated from banquet rooms), the buffet table should preferably be placed in the center of the dining room; this is often done in restaurants that feature a Smorgasbord. Such a centrally-located table will discourage guests from forming a line, and the operation will benefit from increased turnover. When a centrally located buffet table is not possible, the table can be built against a wall in a zig-zag fashion (like teeth on a saw). This will generate a "scrambled" serving line that will speed and insure the proper turnover.

ZONING AND COURSE AREA FOR 48 PCS. (6 x 8')

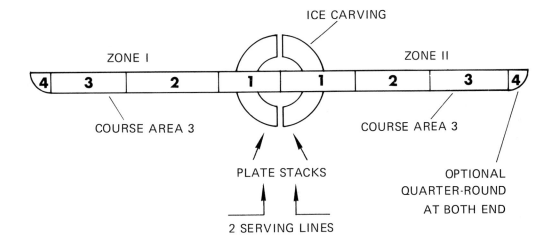

BUFFET FOR 50 COVERS (See diagram, facing page)

A. Ice Carving
1. Roast Beef Platter, Texas style. (Rib of Beef as centerpiece and Roast Beef Roulades)
2. Roast Capon with Canadian Bacon and Asparagus
3. Poached Salmon cut into slices with stuffed eggs and cucumbers
4. Stuffed Eggs Spring Style
5. Pate d' Foie Volaille (Garnish: poached apple rings and chopped pineapple). Flavored with Kirschwasjer
6. Medaillons of Veal with liver pate and black cherries.
7. Roulades of Beef tongue with creamed horseradish (Garnish of artichoke bottoms stuffed with Ham Mousse)
B. German Potato Salad
C. String Bean Salad
D. Vegetable salad
E. Italian Salad
F. Fish Salad
8. Prosciutio Ham and Melon
9. Prosciutio Ham and Pears
I. Creamed Horseradish Sauce
II. Sauce Verte
III. Sauce Chantilly
IV. Sauce Cumberland
NOTE: Hot foods and desserts should be on separate tables.

BUFFET FOR 100-150 COVERS (See diagram, facing page)

1. Prawn Salad or Langostino Salad (See Hors d'oeuvre).
2. Smoked Salmon, Smoked Eel and Brisling Sardines.
3. Tea Sandwiches and Canapes
4. Stuffed Eggs and watercress plus stuffed tomatoes.
5. Rooster baked in a crust (See Pate).
6. Boiled ham with bone in and ham roulades.
7. Roast Sirloin roulade (slice Roast Beef and spread sweet relish mixed with mayonnaise over slices, then roll slice around a piece of celery).
8. Stuffed Roast Chicken in madeira. Gelee.
9. Saddle of Venison stuffed with liver pate and decorated with grapes.
A. Tomato salad
B. Swiss Salad.(See Recipes)
C. Asparagus Vinaigrette
D. Cucumber sald, English style.
I. Sauce Cumberland
II. Creamed Horseradish Sauce
For this buffet extra platters of food should be ready to make speedy replacements.
NOTE: Hot food should be set on separate tables.

BUFFET FOR 200 COVERS (See diagram, facing page)

1. Roast Turkey with Pineapples and Truffles
2. Westphaelian Ham and Canned Ham with Pickled Vegetables
3. Pate of Pheasant with Orange Salad in Port Wine
4. Smoked Fresh Trout with Frozen Horseradish
5. Roast Duck with Bananas
6. Roast Veal with Tunafish Sauce
7. Stuffed Dover Sole with Lobster Mousse and Stuffed Eggs
A. Sauce Cumberland
B. Sauce Raiford- (Horseradish)
C. String Bean Salad - Beet Salad Coleslaw - Waldorf Salad - Salad Niscoise
   Mousse of Salmon garnished with cucumbers
   Parfait of Chicken Liver in Port Aspic
NOTE: Hot foods and desserts should be on separate tables.

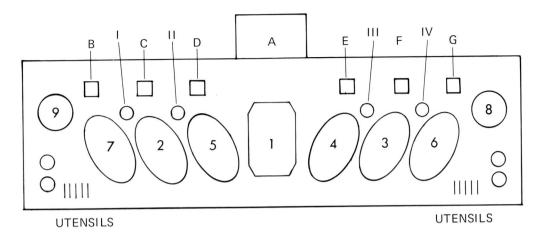

UTENSILS   UTENSILS

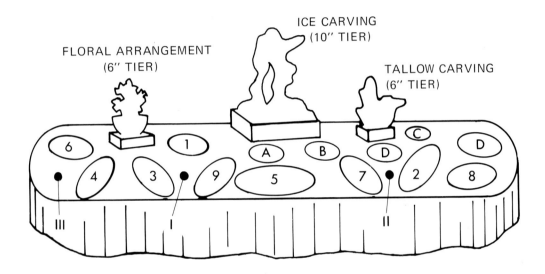

FLORAL ARRANGEMENT
(6" TIER)

ICE CARVING
(10" TIER)

TALLOW CARVING
(6" TIER)

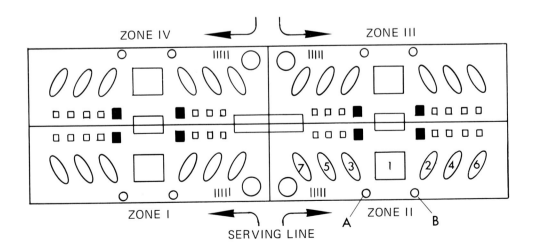

ZONE IV   ZONE III

ZONE I   ZONE II

A   B

SERVING LINE

Low Calorie Buffets

Because of the increasing demand for low calorie meals by today's diet-conscious public, some foodservice operations have successfully featured low calorie menu items. A logical out-growth of low calorie menu items is the low calorie buffet.

It is not suggested that foodservice operations plan low-calorie menus *unless they have qualified dietitians on their staff.*

The field of dietetics is actually an important part of medicine since it complements therapies prescribed by doctors for the cure of various illnesses or of conditions leading to ill-health.

Because of the background information needed, the therapeutic values of foods cannot safely be recommended by men or women who have been trained solely in the preparation of food intended exclusively for the pleasure of the palate.

However, it is the belief of the writers, that all cooks should have a basic knowledge of calories so that they may prepare better balanced menus from which normal individuals can select their daily diets.

Cooks should be aware that the average healthy person requires approximately 2000 to 3000 calories per day. One calorie is the amount of heat required to raise 1 gr. (.03502) of water to 1^O Centigrade between 15° and 16° Centigrade.

The calories eaten each day should provide the human body with the energy required to perform its many functions.

Food, no matter how varied, is composed of the following nutritive ingredients: proteins, fats, sugars, mineral salts, water and vitamins. Quantities of these elements are found in food in various combinations.

Proteins are the block builders of the body; they help to assure that body and bone cells are constantly renewed.

Fats are the major heat generators and are found mostly in oils and solid animal fats.

Sugars are energy producers. They are found 1) in sugar itself, known chemically as "saccharose" (Saccarin), which produce instant energy, and 2) in starches (flour, rice, and pastas) which the body must first digest before converting them into sugar.

These three elements—proteins, fats, and sugars provide calories at the rate of

> 4 calories for 1 gr. of protein
> 9 calories for 1 gr. of fat
> 4 calories for 1 gr. of sugar

A balanced daily food ration must apportion calories as follows:

> 15% from protein
> 30% from fat
> 55% from sugar

With this information, chefs can evaluate *approximately* the number of calories in each portion of the items they prepare.

To estimate the percentage of protein, fat and sugar contained in the total weight of a portion, the protein, fat and sugar can first be weighed separately, then the weights of each can be converted to grams, using the following formula— .02 ÷ .035 or $\frac{.02 \times 100}{3.5}$ Finally, each weight in grams should be multiplied by its respective number of calories: 4, 9, and 4.

Thus, if a 16-oz. pound cake is estimated to contain 10% protein, 30% fat and

60% sugar, each of the elements would weigh:

Protein	1.6 oz.	or	45.7 gr.
Fat	4.8 oz.	or	137.1 gr.
Sugar	9.6 oz.	or	274.2 gr.
	16 oz.		457 gr.

The total number of calories for this 16-oz. cake would be as follows:

Protein	45.7 x 4 =	182.8 calories
Fat	137.1 x 9 =	1,233.9 calories
Sugar	274.2 x 4 =	1,096.8 calories
		2,513.5 calories

When the cake is cut into 8 portions, each 2 oz. portion would contain 314 calories (2,513.5 ÷ 8).

Calorie charts are available to help in determining the number of calories in food portions although some of them may seem contradictory at first. Confusion occurs because portion sizes are often measured in units other than weight units (i.e. 1 slice, 1 tsp., 1 tbsp., 1 cup, etc.)

Individuals interested in their daily consumption of calories should be aware that another factor to consider, in addition to calorie consumption, is their eating habits. The sources of calories must also be understood and their effect on the utilization of foods by the body.

Since interest in keeping calorie consumption at the proper level is shared by many patrons, the promotion value of a low calorie buffet is clear. A small display card listing the calories in each item would help patrons in making their choices among the items displayed.

Typical of possible low calorie buffet offerings are the foods featured on the trays pictured in the buffet presentation on pp. 198 and 199. Each tray contains enough items for 3 patrons and the calories are listed for the 3 servings. The total would be divided by 3 to indicate the calories to be consumed by one person.

Listed below are the calories for the foods included in Buffet Selection No. 1:

1.	Yogurt cocktails with cantaloupe slices	160 calories
2.	4-6 Belgian endive leaves	3-4 calories
3.	3 half slices of fresh pineapple	66 calories
4.	2 oz. of diced tomatoes (concassee)	12 calories
5.	3 oz. yogurt with chopped red pepper	45 calories
6.	3 apple rings with 3 oz. of fresh grated carrots and 3 walnuts	48 calories
7.	3 oz. of green grapes (36 cal.); stuffed with 2 oz. uncreamed cottage cheese (22 cal.)	58 calories

Food on tray contains 413 calories providing 138 calories for each serving.

Foods in Buffet Selection No. 2 (portions for 2)

1.	2 pear halves with slices from 3 radishes marinated and garnished with 2 sprigs of dill and a little lemon juice	108 calories
2.	2 oz. sliced cucumber; 2 oz. red cabbage and apple	33 calories
3.	2 oz. julienne of beets (7 cal.); ½ oz. apple (4 cal.); 1/3 oz. fresh Horseradish (3 cal.)	14 calories
4.	Grated carrot in orange shell, topped with orange section and 1/3 tsp. chopped red pepper	28 calories

Food on tray contains 183 calories providing 82 calories for each serving.

This buffet offers many items that calorie counters can enjoy. Unexpected twists in flavor and color keep patron ratings for these low calorie combinations at the same level that richer foods enjoy. On tray at left front: *Grated Carrot in Orange Shell,* topped with orange sections and chopped red pepper; *Julienne of Beets and Apples,* zipped up with fresh horseradish; *Sliced Cucumber, Red Cabbage and Apple; Pear Halves* topped with rad- ish slices that have been marinated in dill- flavored lemon juice. Tunafish mold in cen- ter is flanked by lobster timbales. Tray at right holds apple slices, topped with a mound of grated carrot and a walnut half. Endive leaves are combined with mound of green grapes filled with low calorie cottage cheese. Fresh pineapple slices, diced tomato and yo- gurt sparked with diced red pepper is an- other unusual combination. *Yogurt cock-*

tails are garnished with thin wedges of canta-loupe. Trays on center level present: Chicken Galantine with cherry tomatoes stuffed with cottage cheese, framed by cherry topped orange slices; Poached Salmon, Galantine of Veal with tuna sauce in cantaloupe shell decorated with melon balls held in place by skewers. Top row: Roast Capon with medallions of capon filled with liver and yogurt; Roast Chicken with fruit and asparagus;

Sliced Proscuitto Ham with melon wedges and gelatin-filled orange shells; Saddle of Veal with Vegetable and Yogurt Salad; Slices of Roast Turkey with fresh orange slices and gelatin filled orange shells. While the number of calories was kept to the minimum, a maximum amount of imagination was used in planning and presenting this collection of low calorie foods. For other low calorie ideas, see p. 200.

MORE LOW CALORIE SUGGESTIONS

Other dishes low in calories and also in salt that could be featured in a Buffet for Dieters are listed below.

Artichokes: Fresh artichokes cleaned and cooked in water and lemon juice and served cold with 2 oz. of cottage cheese per artichoke.

Asparagus: 4 oz. fresh asparagus, peeled and boiled, then marinated with ½ tsp. of lemon juice and served with 2 oz. cottage cheese.

Bananas and Radishes: Cut 2 bananas in half; save the skin; cut banana meat into thin slices; slice an equal amount of radishes. Mix juice of a half orange with 1 tsp. lemon juice. (A mixture of 1 part each crushed strawberries, sliced bananas and sliced fresh radishes can also be used.)

Beet, Apple, and Horseradish: 4 oz. peeled, fresh beets cut into julienne strips, 1 oz. of fresh apples cut into julienne strips, ½ oz. fresh horseradish cut into very fine julienne; mix with ½ tsp. lemon juice and ½ tsp. honey; serve on lettuce leaf. 3-4 sliced toasted almonds can be added.

Belgian Endive with Ginger: 2 oz. diced endive, 1/2 oz. diced tomatoes,1/2 oz. diced fresh pineapple, 1 oz. fresh orange sections. Mix all ingredients with 1-2 oz. cottage cheese and 1-2 tsp. of lemon juice. Sprinkle 1/3 tsp. of powdered ginger over the dish. Serve on lettuce leaf.

Carrot and Apple: peel 6 new carrots and grate; mix with 1 tsp. honey and 2/3 tsp. lemon juice; add one grated medium apple; toss together and serve in a glass dish on a lettuce leaf to provide contrasting background.

Celery: Take the center (sometimes called the heart of celery) and peel it, removing all leaves. Wash carefully and braise for 15-20 min. in some lemon juice and a little beef stock. Season with Seasalt. Serve cold with cottage cheese.

Celery and Fresh Pineapple: 4 oz. diced celery, 2 oz. diced apples, 1 oz. diced pineapple, 1 oz. fresh mandarin oranges. Mix with 2 oz. plain yogurt and 2 tsp. of orange juice; decorate with celery leaves.

Cucumber: 4 oz. of cucumber, peeled and sliced thin, mixed with ½–1 tsp. lemon juice; season with 2 grinds of pepper, 1/3 tsp. chopped dill and 1/3 tsp. salt; serve on lettuce (salt can be omitted).

Melon: Mix 2 oz. of cantaloupe cut into julienne with 2 oz. of red peppers cut into julienne; add ½-1 tsp. of lemon juice.

Mushroom and Spinach: 2 oz. of spinach, cut into julienne, 1½ oz. sliced mushrooms, 1 oz. diced apple. Mix with 2-oz. uncreamed cottage cheese and season with 3 tsp. of orange juice and ½ tsp. honey.

Mushroom and Tomato: 2 oz. sliced raw mushrooms, 2 oz. diced tomatoes, 2 oz. diced apples, 2 oz. of diced melon. Mix with 4 oz. cottage cheese, 2 tsp. orange juice and 1 tsp. lemon juice; garnish with watercress.

Radishes: 2 oz. of fresh radishes sliced and mixed with ½ tsp. of lemon juice; serve on a lettuce leaf sprinkled with chopped parsley.

Red Cabbage: 4 oz. red cabbage cut into fine julienne and 1 oz. apple cut into julienne mixed together with 2 tsp. lemon juice and ½ tsp. honey.

Sauerkraut: Mix ½ part sauerkraut (fresh) with ¼ part grated apple and ¼ part diced fresh pineapple; serve on lettuce.

Spinach: Wash carefully and cut into julienne. Mix ½ part julienne cut spinach with ½ part julienne cut apple and a little honey and lemon juice.

Watercress: 2 oz. of watercress, 1 oz. grated apple mixed together with ½– 1 tsp. lemon juice added. A little sugar can also be added.

This Danish Buffet was prepared by Chefs S. Arnoldi, E. Kristensen, E. Eliason and students of the Culinary Institute of America. Ship with figurehead, swan and shields of tallow establish the theme for the buffet. Cold foods arranged on the upper level include: herring, head cheese, smoked turkey, lobster and asparagus salad, Danish lobster tail with dill mousse. Displayed foods on the lower level were flanked by two chafing dishes, one filled with Swedish Meatballs in Dill Sauce, the other with Veal Roulades in Brown Sauce. Tray in forefront holds Smoked Tenderloin of Pork with Ham Mousse, garnished with artichokes holding cones of pureed peas. Other dishes: Pork Liver Pate in Aspic, varieties of imported herring on stand, assorted cheeses, Galantine of Eel.

*The Sphinx, sculptured in tal-
low, reigns over the Middle
East buffet prepared by Chefs
P. Van Erp, C. Cristodlous and
students of the Culinary Institute of America. Display on
native cloths presents: top
level—Syrian bread; white bean
salad; olives; feta cheese; meat-
filled pastry triangles; baklava
and Beirut bread. Lower level
—Hot dishes, stuffed grape
leaves; shrimp marinated on a
skewer; Cous Cous Marga and
toppings; marinated lamb and
sweetbreads on skewers; cold
dishes, eggplant appetizer;
Arab bread; kibby; spinach-
filled pastry triangles; stuffed
eggplant, assorted olives, yogurt topped with fresh mint.*

The grand finale for any buffet is a dessert display. Prepared by Pastry Chefs W. Schreyer and A. Kumin and CIA students, display has as focal point a pastillage replica of CIA's main building done in a mixture of confectioner's sugar, egg white and gelatin. Beneath it, shadow boxes frame, at left, a pulled sugar basket filled with sugar flowers and, at right, a nougat basket holding marzipan fruits. Cakes on either side are framed in marzipan and decorated with cocoa painting. Boxes made of chocolate hold pralines. The lower level displays on either end pulled sugar baskets surrounded by petit fours decorated with assorted fruits; next to basket from left— Cream Cheese Torte; Hudson Valley Apple Torte; Marzipan Roulades arranged with sugar basket filled with chocolate truffles and marzipan fruits; torte of fresh California fruits, blueberry cheese cake.

INDEX

Alaska King Crabmeat Hors d'oeuvre 41
Aluminum foil frills 189
American Salad 170
Appetizers, see Hor d'oeuvre
Apple Bird 17
Artichoke Hearts a la Greque 38
Artichoke Provencale Salad 158
Asparagus Salad 151
Aspic
  Clarification 24
  Coating for pate en croute 34
  Color sheets 25-26, 28
  Croutons 26
  Designs on chaud froid 147
  Food decoration 28
  Game 24
  Golden 24
  Meat Jelly 25
  Medallion, coated 27
  Molds 34
  Poultry 24
  Preparation 23
  Sheets 26
Avocado
  Mousse 106
  Salad, Mexican Style 40
Baked goods
  Food decoration 22
Barquettes
  Bagration 54
  Beauharnois 54
  Cancalaise 54
  Decorations for 54
  Definition 54
  Fillings 54
  Marivant 54
  Normande 54
Bean Sprout Salad 157
Beef
  Cold food
    Roast beef platter 147
  Cuts for buffet 115
  Fillet, larding 116
  Larding 116
  Marinades 112
  Salad No. 1 and No. 2 171
  Tongue, platter 116
Beet Salad No. 1 153
       No. 2 154
Beets, pickles 47
Beluga 65
Boar's Head Centerpiece 44
Brine
  Ham, liquid 113-14
  Poultry, liquid 114
Buffets
  Dessert 203
  Tables
    For 50 94-95
    For 100-150 94-95
    For 200 94-95
  Theme
    Austrian-German viii
    Danish 201
    Mid-Eastern 202
  See also Low Calorie Buffet
Butter
  Anchovy 142
  Caviar 142
  Cayenne 142

Crayfish 142
Curry 142
Egg 142
Foie gras 142
For Snails 143
Garlic 142
Green 142
Herring 142
Herring roe 142
Horseradish 142
Langouste 142
Lobster 142
Montpellier 142
Moscovite 142
Mustard 142
Nutmeg 142
Paprika 143
Perigourdine 143
Pimento 143
Portuguese 143
Ravigote 143
Salmon, smoked 143
Sardine 143
Shrimp 143
Tarragon 143
Tunafish 143
Cabbage Slaw—Farmer's Style 159
Calves' Brain Salad 169
Canape
  Assortment 37, 40
  Boar's Head centerpiece 44
  Cold 38
  Hot 36
  Varieties 38-49
    Anchovy 48
    Brioche of Foie Gras 49
    Cancalaise 48
    Caviar 48
      Cigarettes 48
    D'Arkangel 49
    Danoise 48
    Domino 48
    Eggs a la Greque 48
    Fish 48
    Game 48
    Goujons a la Russe 48
    Ham 48
    Langostinos 48
    Lobster 48
      Eggs 48
    Paulette 49
    Profiterolles 49
    Rejane 48
    Rigoletto 48
    Salmon, smoked 48
    Sardine 48
    Shrimp 48
    Sole a la Brasset 49
    Tongue 48
    Vie Ville 49
Capon
  Decorating 125
Capon Roti 72
Careme, Marie-Antoine 13
Carrot
  Flowers 16
  Salad No. 1 155
       No. 2 156
Cauliflower Salad 146, 158

Caviar
  Accompaniments 67
  Definition 65
  Ice carving base 67
  Lump fish 66
  Malosol 65-66
  Paiusnaya 66
  Processing 66
  Quality 65-66
  Sources 65-66
  Storing 66
  Sturgeon producing 65
    Beluga 65
    Ocictrova or osetra 65
    Sevruga 65
Celery Salad No. 1 and No. 2 150
       No. 3 151
Center piece
  Boar's head 44
  Pastry shell 21
Chaud Froid
  Applying 31-32
  Background for decoration 28
  Capon, carving 145
  Chicken, carving 145
  Coating ham 32
  Decoration 28, 147
  Definition 29
  Melting 32
  Recipes 29-31
  Roast capon 146
  Types
    Brown 31
    Classical 29
    Cream Sauce 31
    Green 30
    Mayonnaise 31
    Red-Tomato 30
  Use 31, 33
  Watercress 147
Cheese
  Bacteria, use of 177
  Kinds 177-80
  Recipes
    Belgian endive with
      blue cheese 181
    Deep fried 181
    Roquefort cheese stuffing
      for celery 181
  Selection 177
  Serving 181-82
  Storing 180
  Varieties, most used 179-80
    Bel Paese 179-80
    Blue 179-80
    Brie 179
    Camembert 179
    Cheddar 179-80
    Cream cheese 179
    Edam 179-80
    Emmenthaler 179
    Gruyere 179-80
    Liederkranz 179
    Roquefort 179-80
    Stilton 180
Cheese Butters
  Crab 143
  Langouste 143
  Lobster 143
  Salmon 143

Truffle	143
Tunafish	143
Chicken	
Breast of Chicken Bombay	49
Carving	124
Carving for chaud froid	145
Galantine a la Rosenthal	103
Roast Spring	147
Salad	169
Salad cocktail	43
Chicken Livers	
Mousse	106
Parfait	90
Pate	76, 80
Clams	133
Cold bain-marie, see Refrigeration	
Cold Foods	
Aspic, use of	144
Chaud froid, use of	144
Decoration	
Arrangement	144
Aspic	144
Chaud froid	144
Garnish	144-45
Handling	145
Platters and trays	144-45
Presentation	144
Skewers	144
Color	
Aspic sheets	21
Coronets of ham	52
Crabs	133
Crawfish	133
Cream cheese	
Mushrooms	22
Roses	22
Cucumber	
Danish style appetizer	42
Salads	
Basic	156
English	156
French	156
Hungarian	157
Russian	157
Stuffed, appetizer	43
Curd	177
Dairy products	
Food decoration	22
Decoration, see Food decoration	
Displays	
Non-edible	
Aluminum foil frills	189
For poultry	183
Ice carving	183-85
Tallow	183, 186
With roast duck	183
Domino Hors d'oeuvre	48, 52
Dough	
Pate	75
Dover Sole	
Paupiette of	64
Preparation	128
Stuffed with lobster mousse	129
Duck	
Corned	114
Decorating	125
Galantine	97
Medallion	182
Roast	182
With Waldorf Salad	160

Egg dishes for hors d'oeuvre	
Boiled	
Danish	55
Moskow	55
Frog	57
Hard-cooked	
Norwegian	56
Pikant	56
Russian	55
Spanish	55
Stuffed with Pheasant	55
Stuffed with Seafood	55
Vegetable Salad	56
Penguins	57
Pickled	58
Poached	
Gourmet	56
Sicilian	56
Washington	56
Soft	
Boiled, Farmer's style	56
In tomatoes	56
On croutons	56
Nicoise	56
Eggs	
Food decorating use	21
Pickled	58
Eggs in Cocottes	
Asparagus tips	58
German	58
Hungarian	57
Margaret	58
Preparation of	57
Spatini	58
Tea	58
Escoffier, Auguste	13
Farce, see Forcemeat	
Fish	
Aspic jelly	27
Canned	
Caviar	129
Herring	129
Salmon	129
Tuna	129
Defrosting	126
Fresh	126
Handling	126
Marinades	130
Mousse	107
Pate	86
Popular kinds	126, 131-33
Preparation	
Colbert	128
Dover Sole	128
Trout	127
Purchasing	126
Quenelles	69, 86
Salad, left over	168-69
Storage	126
Varieties	126
Fish and Shellfish (for hors d'oeuvre)	
Anchovies, Moscovite	50
Barquettes of fillets of	
Dover Sole Caprice	51
Boutarque, mullet eggs	50
Codfish a l'Indienne (salted)	50
Crayfish a la Moscovite	50
Frog legs a la Bearnaise	50
Goujons a la Russe	50
Herring a la Dieppoise	50

Herring a la Livonienne	50
Herring a la Lucas	50
Herring a la Russe	50
Langostino a l'Admiral	50
Lobster a la Boulognaise	50
Mackerel a la Suedoise	
(marinated)	51
Mackerel in Marinade	51
Mullets a l'Orientale	51
Mullets au Saffron	51
Mussels	51
Mussels a l'Antiboise	51
Mussels a l'Indienne	51
Oysters	51
Paupiettes, Dover Sole fillets	51
Pickerel a la Georgianne (slices)	51
Pickled oysters	51
Salmon, Canadian style	51
Salmon horns, a la Imperiale	51
Shrimp	52
Shrimp with Saffron a l'Orientale	52
Smelts a la Caucasienne	51
Smelts, Marinated	52
Sturgeon a la Bariatinski	52
Trout a la Champagne	50
Trout a la Saint Menehould	50
Tuna a l'Antiboise	52
Foie-Gras	
Ancient times	59
Canned	60
Definition	59
Earthenware jars	60
French	59-60
Fresh	60
Hors d'oeuvre	60
Pate de foie	60
Preparation	59-60
Processing	61
Strasbourg	59-60
Tureens	60
Varieties	60
Food decoration	
Apple bird	17
Aspic	20-21
Baked goods	22
Carrot flowers	16
Color	12, 21
Aspic	21
Blue	12
Fish roe	21
Cream cheese	22
Mushrooms	22
Roses	22
Creating	12-14
Dairy products	22
Eggs	21
Fish roe	21
Fruits	13, 15, 20
Herbs, fresh	20
Ingredients	14
Leek flowers	18
Suckling pigs	92
Theme	12
Tomato rose	20
Variations	
Classical	12
Commercial	13
Vegetables	13, 15, 19-20
Forcemeat	
Definition	68

Garde manger	69
Ingredients	74
Liver dumpling	72
Mousseline	72
Panada	68-69
Preparation	68-69
Seasoning	74
Use	68
Variations	
Croutons or barquettes	71
Game	71
Gratin	70-71
Freezers	5
Frog eggs	57
Frozen Foods	
Defrosting	11
Storing	11
Thawing	11
Fruits	
Food decoration use	20
Salads	
Alice	173
Macedoine	174
Monte Carlo	173
South American	173-74
Stuffed Salads	
Cantaloupe	174
Chicken, lobster or crabmeat	175
Peaches	175
Tomatoes	175-76
Galantine	
Basic recipe	91
Capon Royale	101
Chicken	93
Chicken a la Rosenthal	103
Defined	91
De Volaille	94
Display pieces	92
Duck	97
Eel	92
Ham, fresh	92
Pheasant roast with galantine	95
Pig, suckling	92, 96
Pork	92
Preparation	93
Recipes	
Basic	91
Varieties	94-103
Salmon	100
Snapper, red	92
Stock ingredients	102
Veal	
Breast	96, 119
In aspic	98-99
Game	
Aspic jelly	24
Characteristics	119
Gratin Forcemeat	71
Larding	119
Parts used in garde manger	119
Pate	83, 85
Salad	169
Garde Manger department	
Equipment	4
Layout planning	2-4
Relationship to foodservice operation	
Combined pick-up and distribution	5
Distribution basis	1

Pick-up basis	1
Tasks performed	1
Tools	4
Gelee	
Definition	23
Goose liver	
Use	73
Gratin Forcemeat	
No. 1	70-71
No. 2, Barquettes	71
No. 3	83
Liver dumplings	72
Mousseline	72
Green Bean Salad	157
Ham	
And veal pate	81
Boning	118
Decorated	117
Mousse, Strasbourg	105-6
Pate	81
Stuffed (jambon farci)	117
Herbs	
Food decoration	20
Herring	
Salad	166
Sherry Pickle	131
Spiced	130
Hors d'oeuvre	
Assortment	36, 52
Barquettes	54
Eggs	55-58
Luncheon	35
Recipes	38-47
Salads	53-54
Types	
Canape	35
Cold	35, 38
a la Francaise	35
Before a meal	35
Freshly prepared	35
Hot	36
Luncheon	35
Provencal	35, 46
Ready to serve	35
Zakuski	35, 48-49
Vegetables	53-54
When served	35
Hungarian Salad No. 1	161
No. 2	162
Ice carving	
Swan	184-85
Temperature	184
Template	184
Tools	183-85
Indian Rice Salad	159
Italian Meat Salad	170
Italian Salad	159
Italian Vegetable Salad	164
Jambon Farci	117
Keta	66
King Crab Salad	167
Layout, planning	1-5
Leek	
Flowers	18
Salad	152
Stuffed	44, 146
Liver	
Dumpling forcemeat	72
Preparation	73

Lobster	
Belvedere	133
Cutting boiled	132
Preparation for sauteing	133
Salad	167
with grapefruit	40
Low Calorie Buffets	
Calorie requirements	196
Fats	196
Figuring calories	197
Menu	198-99
Proteins	196
Specialties	197-200
Sugars	196
Macaroni Salad	153
Macedoine of Fruits	174
Marinades	
Defined	110
Marinating time	110
Recipes	110-14
Mayonnaise	
Basic recipe	135-36
Not derived from	138-41
Preparation	135
Restoration after break-down	136
Sauces derived from	136-37
Meat Jelly (commercial)	25
Medallion of veal	
Preparation	27
Service	27
"Mise en place"	1, 4
Molds	
Aspic	34
Barquette	34
Mousse	104
Timbale	34
Mousse	
Chicken	108
Liver	106
Cornucopia of fruits	109
Definition	104
Fish	107
Molds	104
Preparation	105
Recipes	
Avocado	106
Fish	107
Ham	105
Roquefort	105
Salmon	107, 109
Mousse of Tuna in Lemon shell	47
Mousseline Forcemeat (farce)	72
Mushroom a la Greque	39
Mushroom Salad No. 1	151
No. 2	152
Mushrooms, raw, carved	18
Mussel	
Bombay, a la	39
Described	134
In mustard sauce	39
Salad	168
Tomato Stuffed with Mussels	38
Napkins	
Decorative shape	189-90
Orange aspic sheets	26
Oxford Salad	164
Oysters	134
Panada	
Bread	68
Flour	68

Potato	69
Pate	
Aspic coating	34
Decoration	85
Definition	73
Dough	75
En croute	
Baking method	75
Decoration	75
Preparation	75, 77-78
Slicing	79
Facon du chef	63
Fillet of Sole	87
Fish No. 1 and No. 2	86
Game	83
Garnish	75
Gibier, simple	84
Gratin, forcemeat	83
Ham	81
Ham and veal	81
Hare	84
Ingredients	73
Pheasant	64, 85
Quenelle forcemeat	69
No. 1 and No. 2	86
Recipes	76-87
Chicken	80
Chicken liver	76
Rooster a la Gabriela Kriens	82
Saddle of Reindeer	85
Saddle of Venison	85
Salmon No. 1 and No. 2	87
Seasonings for forcemeat	74
Turkey liver	76, 85
Penguin eggs	57
Pick-up basis	
Meaning	1
Combined with distribution	5
Pickle garnishes	19
Pickled eggs	58
Polish Salad	162
Pork	
Cuts for garde manger	117
Potato	
Panada	69
Rose, deep fried	19
Poultry	
Aspic jelly	24
Boning	122
Carving	122-25
Cooking	122
Preparation	122
Quenelle	70
Sewing	121
Thawing	122
Trussing	120, 122
Types	
Domestic	122
Game	122
Quenelle Forcemeat for fish	69, 86
Quenelles	
Fish	69, 86
Poultry	70
Veal	70
Refrigeration	
Basic principles	5
Cold bain marie	5
Counters	5
Cycle	6
Equipment, primary	5

Heat entry causes	5
Methods	
Conduction	5
Convection	5
Radiation	5
Qualities, essential	7-8
Temperature	7
Refrigerators	
Design	
Pass-throughs	10
Pull-outs	10
Reach-ins	9-10
Roll-ins	9
Walk-ins	8
Storage	
Bakery products	7
Pans	7
Varied foods	7
Rennet	177
Rice, Turban of (in jelly)	46
Rillettes	90
Rooster a la Gabriela Kriens	82
Roquefort, mousse of	105
Russian Salad	161
Salads	
Fish	
Herring	166
King Crab	167
Langostino	172
Left over	168
Lobster	167
Mussel	168
Salmon	166
Tuna No. 1 and No. 2	165
Fruit	
Alice	173
Macedoine	174
Marie-Louise	163
Monte Carlo	173
South American	173-74
Stuffed	
Cantaloupe	174
Chicken, lobster or	
crabmeat	174
Peach	175
Tomatoes	175-76
Waldorf	160
Meat	
American	170
Beef No. 1 and No. 2	171
Calves' Brain	169
Chicken	169
Game	169
Italian	170
Swiss	172
Vegetables	
Artichoke Provencale	158
Asparagus	151
Bean Sprout	157
Beet No. 1	153
No. 2	154
Cabbage, Red No. 1 and	
No. 2	152
Slaw, Farmer's Style	159
Carrot No. 1	155
No. 2	156
Cauliflower	158
Celery No. 1 and No. 2	150
No. 3	151

Cucumber	
Basic	156
English	156
French	156
Hungarian	157
Russian	157
Green Bean	157
Green Pepper	153
Hungarian No. 1	160
No. 2	162
Italian	159, 164
Leek	152
Lorette	164
Mignon	163
Mimosa	163
Mushroom No. 1	151
No. 2	152
Nicoise	162
Oxford	164
Polish	162
Potato	
Basic	154
Dutch	155
French	155
German	155
Rachel	160
Rice, Indian	159
Russian	161
Sauerkraut with apples	
and pineapple	160
Stockholm	161
Tomato	150
Stuffed No. 1	175
No. 2	176
No. 3	176
No. 4	176
No. 5	176
Dressing	
Basic French	148
Variations	148-49
French, emulsified	149
Green Goddess	149
Russian	149
Thousand Island	149
Salmon	
Belvedere	146
Marinated	130
Salad	166
Sauces	
Anchovy	138
Andalouse	136
Apple horseradish	138
Asparagus, artichokes	140
Chantilly	136
Chart	140
Cold	140
Cranberry	138
Cumberland	138
Devil's	136
Dijonnaise	136
Egg	140
Fish and Shellfish	140
Game	140
Gloucester or Piccadilly	136
Gribiche	139
Horseradish	138-39
Indian	136
Italian	139
Marchandes di vins	136
Meat	140

Mousquetaire 136
Orange Horseradish 140
Perigueux 64
Ravigotte 141
Remoulade 137
Russian 137
Serbian Garlic 140
Swedish 137
Tartar 137
Tyrolienne 137
Vinaigrette 140
Vincent 137
Sauerkraut with apples
  and pineapple 160
Seafood cocktail 43
Seasoning
  Forcemeat 74
Shellfish
  Cooking 134
  Kinds 131, 133
  Storage and handling 134
  See also fish and shellfish
    hors d'oeuvre
Shrimp 133
  a l'Indienne 45
  Salad 41
South American Salad 173-74
Stockholm Salad 161
Storage
  Frozen foods 11
Swiss Salad 172
Tallow
  Animals 188
  Buddha 187
  Cheese in 186
  Displays 186-88
  Formula 187
  Greek columns 188

Pagoda 188
Preparing 187
Selection of pattern 186
Tartelettes a la Walterspiel 42
Terrines
  Chicken Liver Parfait 90
  Dishes 90
  Family style 89
  Ingredients 88
  Preparation 88-89
  Rillettes 90
Thawing 11
Theme buffet, see Buffets
Tomato
  Cocktail 46
  Rose 20
  Salad 150
  Stuffed
    Variations 175-76
    With mussels 38
Tools 4
Trout
  Marinated 45
  Preparation 127
Truffles
  Appearance 62
  Areas of growth 62, 64
  Composition 64
  Described 62
  Development 62, 64
  Flavor 62
  Fresh 63
  Italian studies 62
  Kinds
    Black and white 64
    Italian 64
  Preparation 73

Processing 63
Sauce Perigueux 64
U. S. consumption 64
Tunafish Salad No. 1 and No. 2 165
Turkey
  Carving, centerpiece 123
  For buffet 125
  Liver pate 76
Veal
  Medallion 27
  Quenelle forcemeat 70
  Used in garde manger 116
Vegetables
  Bouquet arrangement 20
  Decoration 14-15
  Raw 14-15
Vegetables (for hors d'oeuvre)
  Artichokes a la Egyptienne 53
  Artichoke a la Parisienne 53
  Artichoke bottoms 53
  Cordons a l'Italienne 53
  Carrots, marinated 53
  Celery a la Greque 53
  Celery Knob a la Viennoise 53
  Celery Knob Ravigotte 53
  Cucumber a la Danoise 53
  Cucumber a la Savoyarde,
    fillet 53
  Tomato antiboise 53
Venison
  a la Diane 119
  Larding, saddle 119
Waldorf Salad 160
Whey 177
White aspic jelly 24
Veal quenelle 70
Zakouski 35, 48-49